JEWRY IN FRANCE

JEWRY IN FRANCE

Or, The Original Mr. Jacobs

by
Telemachus Timayenis

Edited by
Thomas Dalton, PhD

Clemens & Blair, LLC
— 2026 —

CLEMENS & BLAIR, LLC

Clemens & Blair, LLC, is a non-profit educational publisher.
www.clemensandblair.com

Library of Congress Cataloging-in-Publication Data

Timayenis, Telemachus Thomas (1853-1918)
Jewry in France: Or, The Original Mr. Jacobs

Original edition published as *The Original Mr. Jacobs* (1888).

p. cm.
Includes bibliographical references

ISBN 978-1963-1436-21
(pbk.: alk. paper)

1. Jews and Judaism
2. History, Jews
3. History, France

Printing number: 9 8 7 6 5 4 3 2 1

Printed in the United States of America on acid-free paper.

CONTENTS

INTRODUCTION
THOMAS DALTON

The reader will be excused if he does not recognize the name of the author of the present book—so little has his name or works been discussed in the West. Telemachus Timayenis acquired a fair amount of fame and notoriety in late 1800s America for having the audacity to write and publish three anti-Jewish books: *The Original Mr. Jacobs* (1888), *The American Jew* (1888), and *Judas Iscariot* (1889). For this achievement, he has been called "the father of anti-Semitic publishing in America." Alas, he thereby earned the dislike of the American Jewish community, who promptly proceeded to isolate, censor, and ban his books wherever possible. Soon, he and his works had fallen into obscurity. For a few years, however, Timayenis found a ready audience for his books and he sold many thousand copies during the final decade of the 19th century. His books were of signal importance, marking a new phase of American writing on the subject, and demonstrating the relevance and timeliness of the topic at hand: the adverse role of Jews in Western societies.

But first things first. Timayenis was born in 1853 in Smyrna, then Greece but today part of Turkey. Given that his father was a university professor, the young Timayenis likewise developed a love of learning, of history, and of the study of languages. The family immigrated to America (Boston) in 1871 when Timayenis was 18 years old. Within a few years, he obtained a teaching position at a local preparatory school, earning the title 'professor,' by which he became commonly known. In 1881, he published a two-volume book, *History of Greece*. His teaching career also brought him into contact with some wealthy upper-class families of the East Coast, including those of Gould, Scribner, and most famously, Rockefeller; Timayenis came to know John D. quite well and engaged in some small business projects with him, though they later had a falling out.

Marrying in 1886 at the age of 33, Timayenis moved to New York and expanded his writing *oeuvre*, working now on plays, novels, and other theater works. His knowledge of Greek, Latin, and French gave him a wide range of material to consider, including new translations in English.

As it happens, in that same year, a French journalist and writer named Edouard Drumont published a book in France which addressed in detail the growing 'Jewish problem' there; the work was titled *La France Juive* ("Jewish France"). A massive book, comprising two volumes and some 1,200 pages in total, it caused a great sensation in Europe; rarely had anyone challenged so directly and so explicitly the role of Jewish power in one nation. Notably, the book focused not on religious issues, such as Jews as the killers of Jesus, but rather on social, political, and racial matters; this marked a real turn in anti-Jewish writing, which until then was heavily oriented toward religious conflict and, occasionally, the problem of usury. As such, it quickly became a bestseller in Paris, earning Drumont a high degree of notoriety, not to mention a considerable sum of money.

Timayenis apparently became aware of the book and its success by early 1887 and, impressed with the detailed research and courage of the author, decided that he would introduce similar ideas into the USA. (To this day, the book remains untranslated into English.[1]) Thus Timayenis conceived of a new book that would highlight the nature of the "original Jacob," that is, the original Jew in himself—Jacob (aka "Israel") being the biblical progenitor of the infamous "12 tribes" of the Jews; see Genesis 35 for details. Hence the book assumed a rather cryptic title, *The Original Mr. Jacobs*.

Acknowledging his heavy reliance on Drumont, Timayenis quotes from *La France Juive* frequently, and also paraphrases or summarizes numerous other insights from the French original. As such, Timayenis' book is strongly focused on the nation of France—its history with the Jews, its centuries of conflict and strife, and its present-day struggles with the Hebrew tribe. Consequently, I, as editor, have elected to re-title this work; not quite "Jewish France" but neither is it really the story of "the original Jacobs," I have opted for *Jewry in France*—with the subtitle, *Or, The Original Mr. Jacobs*. This, indeed, captures perhaps 90% of the content of the book, while acknowledging that many of the Jewish characteristics cited there, and the many lessons learned, apply universally to any nation with a significant Jewish population. And this was precisely Timayenis' point: that everything

---

[1] Significant portions of chapter one, however, appear in translation in *Classic Essays on the Jewish Question*, Volume One (T. Dalton, ed.; 2022).

Drumont had exposed about the Jews of France applied as well to the then-burgeoning Jewish population of the United States.[2]

Due to the controversial nature of the topic, Timayenis was compelled to publish his book anonymously, and further to create his own small publishing firm, Minerva Publishing, to produce the book. Consequently, the book is a bit rough in spots and very much reads as if it would have benefitted from some judicious editing. This service I have provided here; while the vast majority of the text is unchanged, I have taken small liberties at points to adjust grammar, sentence structure, and emphasis. A handful of obscure wordings have been altered to reflect modern meanings. I have added a few selected footnotes to clarify the text at certain points (all notes are mine). Further, I have deleted a few paragraphs and short passages that were either largely incoherent or did not add anything to the argument being presented; I suspect that most of these passages were erroneous or incomplete translations from Drumont's French original. Timayenis' book was also oddly structured: one short "Chapter One" (although unmarked as such), followed by a very long "Chapter Two" (again unmarked)—and nothing more. To remedy this, I have restructured the book into five coherent chapters, each with a relatively focused subject matter. I also included section headers throughout the chapters, some original and some new. In any case, I think this new edition is far more readable and enjoyable than Timayenis' original, all while retaining the force and insight of his writing.

Timayenis understood that his book was primarily about the Jews of France, and thus he quickly undertook to write a second book on the topic, now focusing on America. It too was issued in 1888: *The American Jew*. Smaller than his first book, this second work targets American Jews in a variety of settings: the ghetto, the summer hotel, the oil business, the legal profession, and so on. Each chapter is an elaboration on a central theme: the Jew is a parasite on productive society, and therefore he must be sent away. "The Jew must go!" says Timayenis, with emphasis.

By mid-1889, he was ready to release his third and final work in the series: *Judas Iscariot*. Somewhat more authoritative and academic than his first two works, Timayenis strives here to bolster his case with better documentation and more authoritative sources. Once again, the book is in need of

---

[2] This new title also pairs well with the classic 1930's work of Jewish-critical writing: *Jewry in England*, by Fritz Krueger; I have recently edited the first English translation of this important book.

professional editing, but even so, it is effective in its relentless attack. Clearly, by this time, he had become quite a scholar of criticism of the Jews, and his confidence shows throughout. Timayenis was more convinced than ever: the Jew must go.

But this was to be his final effort in Jew-criticism. Initial discussion of yet another book on the theme, and even a dedicated periodical, came to nothing. In 1898, at the age of 45, he moved back to Boston, got into the cigarette business, and wrote syndicated articles on various topics of the day. When his wife died in 1909 (apparent suicide), he created a new journal aimed at Greek-Americans, *The Eastern and Western Review*. His health began failing in 1917, and he died in 1918, aged 65.

From 1900 onward, Timayenis' books seem to have fallen out of favor, failing to collect much attention—though surely a Jewish-led blockade was partly to blame. And indeed, anti-Jewish writings seemed to have generally subsided around the world during the first two decades of the 20th century. But then along came World War One and, especially, the Bolshevik revolution in Russia, which put several Jewish Marxists, including Trotsky and Lenin (a quarter-Jew), in control of a major nation. Now, suddenly, the issue of Jewish power and Jewish malevolence again became of central importance, at least for Europe. At the same time in America, Jewish immigration had been accelerating since around 1880. By 1920, there were about 3.5 million Jews in the US, comprising about 3.5% of the total population. This vast number, in itself, created a growing awareness of a Jewish problem in America. Thus, between WWI and the booming number of American Jews, much of the Western world became interested once again in the Jewish Question.

Uncoincidentally, it was just around this time (1920) that the "Protocols of the Elders of Zion" came to prominence, first in the UK and then in the US and Europe. That same year, American industrialist Henry Ford chose to begin his infamous two-year string of weekly newspaper articles attacking Jewish power, in what came to be known as the "International Jew" series.[3] Hence, the Bolshevik Revolution, the Protocols, and Henry Ford all brought a renewed and harsh light on global Jewry. These events largely superseded

---

[3] I have edited new editions of both the Protocols and the full 80-piece set of Ford's essays (now in two volumes); see *Protocols of the Elders of Zion: The Definitive English Edition* (2023) and *The International Jew* (2024). Both works are published by Clemens and Blair.

older anti-Jewish writings, and thus Timayenis' works did not really benefit from a resurgence in the topic.

Still, his books never really disappeared from the scene. Reprints began to appear in the 1960s, and they received renewed attention from right-wing groups through the 70s and 80s. With the coming of the Internet in the 1990s, online versions of Timayenis' books appeared, reaching more people than ever. And all along, through the present day, Jewish power continued to expand in the US and Europe—making Jew-critical literature and discourse more important than at any time in the past.

Telemachus Timayenis earned the right to be known as the first 'anti-Semitic' author in America; if for no other reason than this, he deserves to be read and re-read today.

JEWRY IN FRANCE

CHAPTER 1
THE LIFE, CUSTOMS, AND HABITS OF THE JEWS

It must not be supposed that the Jews as a class are an intelligent race. Confidence is often mistaken for intelligence. I admit that there have been eminent men among the Jews, as, for instance, their renowned lawgiver and leader in ancient times, Moses. But a careful examination of this anomaly (it is not an exception) will show that the great men among the Jews have drunk copious draughts of Aryan civilization, and have quickly either renounced Judaism or adopted a nominal, sometimes a real, Christianity. Thus their famous men—Heinrich Heine, Ludwig Borne, Edward Gans, Moses Mendelssohn, Disraeli, and Johann Neander—cannot be fairly called Jews; for either they became rank infidels, or they carefully tried to conceal their origin by a change of name, a practice followed to the present day.

What a difference between the Aryan and the Jew! The one is the child of light, the other of darkness. See how the Aryan raises his head and looks toward the sky; while the Jew constantly looks on the ground, always thinking, always meditating, always contriving, always plotting, plotting, plotting. By the term 'Aryan' we designate the superior family of the White race. The word is akin to a Greek word meaning best or noblest, which enters into the formation of many English words, as, for instance, 'aristocrat,' etc.[1]

"No one," says Emile Littre, "can deny to the Romans their Aryan character." Modern erudition recognizes the common parentage of the Latin and the Greek with the Persian and the Sanskrit, and has drawn together all these scattered brothers into one and the same fold. There is, therefore, a brotherhood existing among all the superior White nations. A misfortune to the one, like an electric shock, reaches the heart of all. These different nations of Aryan origin fraternize easily with one another, amalgamate, and in time become one, and to such an extent that it is difficult when so amalgamated to separate or to distinguish them. The Jew alone, ever since his first

---

[1] 'Aristocrat,' like 'Aryan,' derives from the Greek words *aristos* and *aria* (best, noblest). They are related to the Sanskrit *arya-*.

appearance upon the Earth, has remained separate and distinct, and will to the end remain an alien in the great family of nations.

No race of men excepting, perhaps the negroes, have a physiognomy so characteristic; no race has preserved more faithfully the original type. "It is our own ideas," says Edward Drumont, "which obstruct our thorough understanding of the Jew, and our clearly depiction of him—ideas due mainly to the atmosphere in which we live, an atmosphere absolutely distinct from that breathed by the Jew."

"The Jew is a coward" is a common expression. Eighteen centuries of persecution supported with incredible endurance testify that if the Jew lacks combativeness, he has that other form of courage called persistence. Can we seriously treat as cowards people who have suffered everything rather than renounce their faith?

"The Jew is a worshiper of money." This affirmation is rather a declamatory phrase than a thoughtful or serious utterance.

How often do we see men and women with time-honored names offer their greetings to a Seligman, an Oppenheimer, or a Rothschild, every one of whom regards Christ, whom the Christians adore, as the greatest of impostors. What prompts them to do this? Has the Jew who attracts them superior intelligence? Is he an incomparable entertainer? Has he rendered service to the government? By no means. He is an alien, a German or a Pole, a Jew in faith, little given to conversation, a vain fellow, who often repays the hospitality that he gives to his guest with vulgarities; a hospitality that he extends only through vanity and ostentation. What motive brings together these eminent men? The love of money. Why do they go there? To kneel before the golden calf.

"Would you know what the voice of the blood is?" a French duke said to one of his friends, who, despite the tears of his mother, had married a Rothschild of Frankfurt. He called his little boy, took out a gold coin from his pocket, and showed it to him. The eyes of the child almost started from their sockets. It was the Semitic instinct manifesting itself.

It has already been stated that nearly all Christian nations are linked together by the closest ties by reason of their common descent from the Aryan race, which has given to the world its greatest civilizations. Sidon, Carthage, and Tyre no doubt attained, in times gone by, a high degree of commercial prosperity. Tradition has it that the Hebrews had connections with certain of the old, half-Arab inhabitants of the Sinai Peninsula, and the Arabian Empire in ancient times attained a passing splendor. But this ephemeral prosperity in no way resembled the fertile and enduring civilization of Greece or Rome, or even the Christian society of the Middle Ages.

The Aryan alone possesses the idea of justice, the sentiment of liberty, the conception of the beautiful.

Eugene Gellion-Danglar, in his admirable work, *Les Semites et le Semitisme* (1882), says: "The Semitic civilizations, however brilliant they may appear, are only vain images, more or less vulgar parodies, paper edifices, which certain people have the complacency to display as enduring works made of marble and bronze. The bizarre, the monstrous, hold in it the place of the beautiful; while profusion and ostentation have banished from art both taste and decency."

From the earliest times, we find the Aryan in conflict with the Jew. Alexandria Troas was a city peopled by Jews, and the conflict between the two races explains the peculiar vibration emanating from the Trojan War. Louis Benloew says "[the mythological prince] Paris was one of those ambulatory Jews who wandered about the coast of Greece. Not content with carrying off the beautiful Helen, which an Aryan might have done in the blindness of passion, he also carried away the treasures of his host. Herodotus the historian describes him as having been forced by a tempest to land in Egypt, and, being denounced to Pharaoh not only for having dishonored the host who had welcomed him, but also for having stolen his treasures, he was ordered by the Egyptian king immediately to depart from his dominion; Pharaoh was unwilling to violate the laws of hospitality which Paris had disrespected".[2]

From the earliest dawn of history, the dream of the Semite, in fact his fixed thought and purpose, has been to reduce the Aryan to servitude, to put him to the severest straits. He sought to reach that point by war. Hannibal, who pitched his camp under the walls of Rome, nearly succeeded. But the ruins of Carthage and the bleaching bones of the Saracens record the lesson given to these presumptuous devils.

Judaism, however, is still confident of success. But it is no longer the Carthaginian or the Saracen who conducts the movement. It is the Jew of today who has replaced violence with treachery and fraud. Silent, progressive, serpent-like, slow encroachment has succeeded the boisterous invasion of old. No more armed hordes announce their arrival with cries, but separate

---

[2] *Histories*, Book II.112-120.

companies wind their way slowly, group by group, and take silent possession of all places, of all functions of a country, from the lowest to the highest.

In the environs of Vilnius, that hot-bed of Judaism, has been organized many an exodus which has brought misfortune to Germany, France, and England, and now threatens to do likewise in the United States. Previously to the year 1825, there were hardly any Jews in America. Today the Jewish societies in New York city alone own real estate valued at nearly $30 million. There are now more than 900,000 Israelites in the United States. Let the reader stroll down Broadway, or down any of the leading streets of New York City, and he will find Jewish names plenty as the locusts of Egypt. By far the greater number of these Jews come from Vilnius, and these Jews during the Franco-Russian War [circa 1812] assassinated the wounded French soldiers lying upon the battlefield. Adolphe Thiers relates this episode in his *Histoire du Consulat et de L'Empire.* "Horrible thing to be told" he says; "the miserable Polish Jews, as soon as they saw the enemy in retreat, began to throw our wounded soldiers out of the windows, and sometimes even to strangle them, thus getting rid of them, after having despoiled them of everything. A sad homage offered to the Russians, the partisans of whom they were."

The Jew is a born trafficker, a born liar, full of cunning and intrigue. The Aryan is enthusiastic, heroic, chivalrous, frank, and confident. The Jew sees nothing beyond the present. The Aryan is the child of Heaven, constantly preoccupied with superior aspirations. The one lives in the real, the other in the ideal.

The Jew is mercenary by instinct. He has the bent for everything pertaining to business, for everything that gives him the opportunity to cheat his fellow men. The Aryan is agriculturist, poet, and, above all, a soldier. War is his element. He goes merrily to face danger, and he despises death.

The Jew has no creative faculty. On the other hand, the Aryan invents. Not one invention ever was made by a Jew. There is not a word of truth in the stereotyped phrase that the Jews invented the letter of credit [loans]. The letter of credit, the check, was in use in Athens four centuries before the Christian era. In Isocrates, this fact is plainly told. The Aryan organizes, creates, while the Jew derives all the resulting advantages, which he naturally keeps for himself. The Aryan undertakes voyages of adventure and discovers unknown regions. The Jew waits until all has been explored, until the country has been opened, to enrich himself at the expense of others. In a word—everything pertaining to daring deeds, everything tending to enlarge the terrestrial domain is absolutely beyond the Jew. He can exist only in the midst of a civilization he has not created. The Aryan is hail, fellow, well-met. He is happy, provided one relates to him one of those legends for which his imagination longs, being wholly enwrapped in the marvelous. What pleases him is not one of those Semitic adventures contained in the *Thousand and One Nights*, in which singers discover untold treasures, and fishermen cast their nets in the sea and draw them out full of diamonds. To move the Aryan, there should be heroic deeds full of devotion, a hero who scorns danger, like Gilbert de Roussilon, for instance, who, after having refused to wed the daughter of a Sultan, pierced 5,000 miscreants with a single blow of his unerring lance.

However perspicacious the intelligence of the Jew may appear, it is in reality limited. He has neither the faculty to foresee events, nor of looking beyond his hooked nose; nor the gift of understanding delicate shades of thought and character, for which the Aryan exposes his life without regret.

Ernest Renan has thus described many of these points:

> The Semitic race is recognized in a unique manner by negative characters. It has neither mythology nor epic poetry, neither science nor philosophy, neither fiction, plastic arts nor civil life; in a word, absence of complexity of shade—exclusive sentiment of unity—is its characteristic.
>
> Morality itself has always been understood by that race in a manner different from ours. The Jew recognizes duties peculiar to himself. To carry out his vengeance, avenge that which he believes to be his right, is, with him, a sort of obligation. On the other hand, to ask him to keep his word, render justice in a disinterested manner, is to ask him to do the impossible. There is nothing that takes the place in these passionate souls of the indomitable sentiment of 'me'. Besides, religion is, with the Jew, a sort of special duty which has but a distant tie with everyday morality.

Elsewhere he adds: "The spirit of the Jew lacks breadth and delicacy. Interest is never banished from his morality. The ideal woman, depicted in the Book of Proverbs, is an economical housekeeper, profitable to her husband, but, withal, of a very limited morality. Jewish poetry offers scarcely a page embellished with the charm of sentimentality. Love enters into it only in the form of a lascivious and burning voluptuousness."

Gustave Tridon, in his book *Le Molochisme Juif*, calls the Jew, "The stain in the picture of civilization, the evil genius of the Earth. His gifts are pests. To fight the Semitic ideas is the duty of the Aryan race."

Renan wrote the above before the unheard-of successes of Judaism during recent years. Nothing is more curious than to study the manner with which Renan, so wonderfully endowed in a scholarly point of view, yet so low in respect to character, kneels before his victors. Renan, after having asserted that the supposed services rendered to civilization by the Jews amount to nothing, suddenly declares, in a lecture delivered before the Society for the Promotion of Jewish Studies, that the Jews are our benefactors. But Alphonse de Rothschild presided over the society—a fact which explains the lies uttered by Renan. The Jew banker smiled upon the orator prostrated before him, with a smile at once patronizing and scornful. "What a servant!" he seems to say; "What a miserable fellow." For our part, we would say, how much he is to be pitied. You, both great and small; you, who defend as well as you can the victim of Calvary [Jesus], the God whom your fathers have prayed to, do you not feel a thousand times happier than this apostate, who kisses the hand of the executioner of Christ [i.e. the Jew] for a handful of gold thrown at him with disgust? Do you not believe that the poor missionary, who offers his prayer before a piece of bread, has a more tranquil soul than this rich academician of princely income, and friend of the Rothschilds?

The Jews yearn for whatever flatters their vanity. With grotesque eagerness, they seek military titles, titles of baron and count, which look as nice on those money-manipulators as a woman's hat upon a monkey, "There is no trickster," says Edward Drumont, "no matter of how low degree, no dealer in cast-off clothing, no special partner in a pawn-shop, who is not a member of the Legion of Honor."

The right of the Jew to oppress others is a part of his religion. It is for him an article of faith. It is repeated in every line of the Bible and the Talmud: "Thou shalt break them with a rod of iron. Thou shalt dash them in pieces like a potter's vessel" (Psalm 2:9). All means are good, provided they are directed against the Christian—the Goy (singular Goy, plural Goyim):

- "One can and must kill the best of the Goyim".[3]
- "The money of the Goyim belongs to the Jews. Hence it is permitted to rob and deceive them".[4]

The social evolution itself of the Jew is absolutely different from ours. The type of the Aryan family in the state of civilization is that of the Roman *gens*, which gave rise to the feudal family. During many generations, the vital force and the genius are, so to speak, limited, but at once, and unexpectedly, there appears an illustrious representative who has the sum total of the qualities of his manly race. This predestined being often takes a century to make his appearance, but from the lowest extraction there sometimes rises one of those complete figures, at once charming and valorous, heroic and lettered, just and great, such as are to be met with so often in the pages of history.

In the Semitic race, things occur differently. In the East, a camel-driver, a water-carrier, a barber, is often raised to the highest honors by a whim of the sovereign. He suddenly becomes a pasha, a vizier, a confidant of the prince, like Mustapha-ben-Ismael, who introduced himself to the bardo by selling small cakes, and who, according to the suggestive expression of M. Dauphin, "rendered to his master services both day and night."

The same case applies to the Jew. Beyond the sacerdotal families, which constitute a veritable nobility, distinction of rank does not exist. There are no illustrious families among the Jews. Glory is never left as a legacy. In less than 20 years, if circumstances are favorable, the Jew attains his full development. He is born in the bosom of a *Judengasse* [a 'Jew-street'], earns a little money in a successful operation, gravitates into a great city, buys the title of baron, and assumes the manners of one who has always been reared in velvet. The transition is instantaneous. He experiences no astonishment; he ignores all the delicacies of modesty.

---

[3] Soferim 15,10: "R. Simeon b. Yohai taught: Kill the best of the heathens; crush the brains of the best of serpents." Midrash Tanchuma, Beschalach 8,1: "The best among the Egyptians—kill him." Jerusalem Talmud Kiddushin 4:11: "Rebbi Simeon ben Yohai stated: Kill the best of Gentiles."

[4] *Shulchan Aruch*, Choshen Mishpat 156,5: "the belongings of non-Jews are like unclaimed property, and everyone who comes to them first is entitled to them." Bava Kamma 113b,9: "It is permitted to financially benefit from a business error of a Gentile." Bava Batra 54b,5: "Anyone who takes possession of [a Gentile's property] has acquired it." Sanhedrin 57a,17: "It is permitted for a Jew to rob a Gentile."

Take a Russian Jew, as he is in his native place: clad in dirty garments that beggar description, wearing earrings long as a corkscrew, and after a month of baths, he installs himself in a box at the opera with the aplomb of a Seligman or a Wormser.

We know, here in the United States, of two Jew brothers, who in Germany were itinerant venders of notions, and who, from village to village, their pack on their shoulders, sold cheap wares. They made a little money, came to New York, engaged a gentleman to write a book in German for them. The elder put his name on it as the author, opened a school, gave to himself the title of professor, engaged two or three teachers of foreign languages, had them write as many books in their native tongue, repeated the same effrontery as in the case of the German work, except that now he appeared as co-author. And today, the ignorant suspender-dealers of Germany enrich themselves by selling at a high price their assurance to the easily-gulled Americans.

On the other hand, an honest Gentile of the middle, or even of the lowest class, who has enriched himself in an honorable way, will always have an embarrassed air and will avoid the elegant centers of society. His son, reared in the midst of better conditions, will, with greater ease of manner, enter the refined circles of the world. The grandchild will, in the course of time, if the family continue to live in easy circumstances, live honestly, and in the true Christian spirit, represent the picture of the true gentleman so common in our American society. He will be endowed with a delicacy of thought and a refinement of sentiment that the Jew never possesses.

If the Jew suddenly reaches the extreme of assurance, he never attains distinction. Excepting in the case of a few Portuguese Jews who in youth have beautiful and expressive eyes, and in old age a certain Oriental majesty, one can never find among the Jews that indescribable calm, courtesy, and dignity which distinguish the American, the Englishman, the Frenchman, or any other Christian gentleman, though clothed in threadbare garments.

The Jew is insolent, never proud. He never gets beyond what is termed 'cheeky.' The Rothschilds, and others of the same class, notwithstanding their millions, appear little better than dealers in cast-off clothing. Their women with all their diamonds always look like venders of toiletry, clothed in gaudy garments. Equality, the first condition of social intercourse, is lacking among the Jews. The Jew—let this remark be well kept in mind—will never be the equal of the Gentile. He either cringes before you or seeks to crush you. He is either above you or below you, never your equal.

Let the reader only refresh his memory, and he will acknowledge that even in a few minutes' conversation, this phenomenon clearly manifests itself. As soon as you enter into a friendly conversation with a Jew, he will seek to overwhelm you. It is necessary to continually remind him who you are and what he is.

The monotony of type is the striking peculiarity of the Jewish race. The Jew lacks that refined culture, that sparkling cleverness, which is the very salt of conversation. One rarely meets with those piquant observations and witty remarks which many a conversationalist sows by hazard in the intimacy of the social circle. Were the Jew equipped with these advantages, he would turn them to his own pecuniary profit. The Jew is a monochord, and the longest conversation offers no surprise to him.

It is necessary to become acquainted with the native, the Oriental Jew, in order to understand fully the Jew of civilization. The Slovakian Jew, particularly, gives an idea of the intermediate state between the sordid Jew of Galicia [Poland] and the opulent Jew of the capitals.

Picture to yourself a road that creeps up dry, dusty, almost whitish. To the right and left are small, dingy little shops, or small houses like those in the Orient, furnished with bars not unlike those in the Middle Ages. In the public highway exists pell-mell—in the midst of dirt of all kinds, bits of iron, broken pieces of odds and ends, heaps of garbage—a population of seven to eight thousand Jews. Yonder swelter the old men, remarkable for their ugly features, and by their side lie young girls of wondrous beauty, clothed in tatters. The long coat dominates among men, who mark the present by the greasy tall hat they wear, and recall the past with their dirty feet, which are always bare, and with their never-combed hair. One seems everywhere to recognize faces of familiar acquaintances, and this corner of the Ghetto has the air of a little Paris or New York. Those two dirty Jews yonder, revolting in their general aspect, do they not resemble Dreyfus, Lockroy, or better still, are they not the striking picture of many well-known Jews here in New York? Notice this young bony girl who walks barefooted, dressed in a dirty camisole and a skirt that reaches to her knees. Is she not the very type of Sarah Bernhardt when a child? In fine, put on diamonds, new garments, on all these people, on all these dealers in second-hand articles, receivers of stolen goods, keepers of pawnshops, moneylenders on wages, and you will have the upper class of the New York Jews.

These Jews, however, are not in the least dissatisfied with their condition, for they wait patiently for the time of full tide which will carry them into a city, and shortly afterward to fortune.

At the end of the hill, one finds himself before the castle of Schlossberg, the four walls of which alone remain standing, but where once were crowned the kings of Hungary. This castle stands like a motionless giant with a strange relief looking at space. At its feet slowly flows the Danube, sleepy and morose, and seeming to oppose itself with a dogged resistance to the steamboats that with difficulty ply their way up the stream. To the left lies the island of Au, with its small country seats. At your feet stretch banks of sand, and in the far distance are to be seen large islands called "The Garden of Gold." This spot, once the seat of royalty, has today a profoundly melancholy aspect. The feudal world, with, all its glories, its heroic recollections, its triumphant pomp, is in ruins, like yonder deserted castle. The new world moves and agitates itself a few steps distant in yonder Jewish colony, from which will rise, until the hour of Christian regeneration strikes, the Jew millionaires, worshiped by a servile society, the Jew traders who delight in glaring advertisements—in fact, all those who, with Jewish effrontery, pose before an imbecile and easily-gulled public.

One must not judge of the artistic or literary ability of the Jews by what they publish today. The Jew is incapable of rising above a very limited height. They have no men of genius to compare with Dante, Shakespeare, Bossuet, Victor Hugo, Emerson, Longfellow, Newton. The man of genius is a superior being, ready to sacrifice himself for the good of humanity. It is the nature of the Jew to sacrifice nothing at all. Their Shakespeare is Adolph D'Ennery, and their Raphael is Jules Worms. What more striking example of the utter lack of creative power among the Semitic races could we have than in Carthage, which, though she was for a time mistress of the world, has not left behind a single work of art? The excavations made there have brought to light only a few insignificant objects, while the humblest town of Greece daily yields new treasures. There was more art in the homeliest water-pot made by an artisan of Tanagra or of Boeotia than in the whole of Carthage. In Perrot's and Chipiez's *History of the Art of Antiquity*, we are told: "The Phoenicians knew how, by cunning or force, to snatch away everything not sold to them. They were slave-traders, and used every means that enabled them to rob or to carry off beautiful girls or young boys. No one was able to cope with them, and all feared and detested them."

In art, the Jews have created nothing original, powerful, or touching. They produce only low, vulgar works. They busy themselves with what enables them to make money; with what flatters the vulgar appetites of the multitude; with what satisfies their Jewish venom and hatred. They often accomplish this by ridiculing the pious recollection, heroic deeds, august traditions of the Christians, at whose expense they live.

Drumont writes:

> Note well the manner in which the Jew carries out his work. If called upon to ridicule the army at a time when a terrible war is about to break forth, the Jew, Ludovic Halevy, produces the disgraceful composition known as the "General Bourn." If heroism, honest love, or any immortal masterpiece is to be ridiculed, the Jew, Offenbach, is at hand. Is it necessary to hold up to scorn the works of Shakespeare, of Racine, or of Molière? The Jew, Busnach, is ready to perform the task. In a word, the Jew corrupts everything that exists. The innocent and mirth-provoking old French dance, the *bonne enfant*, is turned by the Jew into the ignoble can-can. From the light, airy, joyous songs of old he constructs those obscene, rude, and lascivious airs that disgrace the stage. The quick, aggressive, and, at times, cutting journalism of old he has converted into blackmail.
>
> From the attractive and occasionally *décolletée* photographs of the eighteenth century, he develops the most obscene pictures to be thought of. From the innocent and amusing caricatures of Daumier, he makes the infamous, impure pictures of Strauss, a worthy parent of the musician of the same name.
>
> The dancing halls, where the youth of by-gone days amused themselves in an honest way, have degenerated into a place of prostitution, thanks to the Jew Markowski, and the androgynous Wolff. Thus while these low creatures commit these infamous acts in France and elsewhere, they have the effrontery to cover themselves by declaring, "Behold how low France has fallen! Behold her literature! Behold what she is producing!"

When have the ancestors of these men prayed with our own? In what corner of the village or of the city are their family tombs? In what parish registry does one find the names of these newcomers, who, less than a century ago, had not the right to live upon the earth from which they now seek to drive us away? By what tie do they attach themselves to the traditions of our race?

The Jew acquires easily the slang of a language, but never its purity and finish. In order to speak a language, one must first of all *think* in the language. There is, between the expression and the thought, the closest connection. One must not expect a Jew to naturalize his style as he does his person. One must have sucked, at one's own birth, of the native beverage, have truly arisen from the native soil. Then one can defend, like Henry Clay or Daniel Webster; write like Hawthorne or Shakespeare, who hated and despised the Jew; attack like Voltaire; defend like Jean Cocteau. As I am writing the above, I recall the account given by the Rabbi Benjamin de Tudele, who, while visiting Greece during the Middle Ages, met a horde of Jews encamped upon Mount Parnassus. What a lamentable spectacle! Bands of these servile, circumcised dogs, whom Aristophanes so despised, installed among those laurels where, during the glorious times of Hellas, the God with the Silver Bow guided the sacred choir of the sister muses.

This inability to acquire a foreign language extends even to its pronunciation. The Jew who so easily speaks slang, always retains a guttural sound that never fails to manifest itself. Richard Andree has affirmed this fact in his book entitled *Interesting Observations Inspecting the Jews.* "Most of the Jews," he says, "even the educated, have a peculiar accent that causes them easily to be recognized. It is a racial mark common among the Jews of all nations."

The Jew, being thus incapable of entering into the domains of creative art, has also failed to penetrate into the unexplored regions of science. He sells eyeglasses and telescopes, but never discovers new stars in the immensity of the heavens, like Leverrier. He does not discover a new continent, like Columbus; he does not divine the laws of attraction, like Newton. The claim of the Jews, that they kept the depot of science during the Middle Ages and transmitted to us the discoveries of the Arabs, is not true. The Jews have made themselves appear learned by picking up some crumbs from the books of Aristotle. They have simply played the role of the ass in the fable, who put on the skin of a dead lion.

During centuries, they have monopolized the profession of medicine, which rendered espionage easy by permitting them to enter everywhere, but never for a minute did they think of the circulation of the blood. The Jew doctors of that period were a thousand times more ignorant in a scientific point of view than their contemporaries. They believed that the heavens were solid; that the firmament was pierced with holes from which rain fell. They formulated axioms of this sort: "A little wine and bread taken on an empty stomach preserves the liver from sixty maladies"; "It is a sure sign of too much blood when one dreams of a cock."

It is to the Aryan that we owe all discoveries, both great and small. It is to him that is due the art of printing, the discovery of gunpowder, of America, of steam, of electricity, of the circulation of the blood, of the laws of attraction. All progress has been evolved from the natural development of Christian civilization. The Jew, one must never weary of repeating it, only exploits that which Christian genius and work have achieved.

The true emblem of the Jew is that hideous bird [the cuckoo] that installs itself in the nest constructed by another. We know a Jew abroad whose life would make an interesting subject for a novel. A few years ago, he gave himself the title of General, and recently posed before the world as an archaeologist. He palmed off upon a board of mummified directors a large number of objects, many of them of more than doubtful authenticity, and pocketed for his worthless collection a princely fortune.

The Character of the Jewish Race

Having indicated the principal traits common to all Jews, let us now examine more closely the race and the species. The principal signs by which the Jews can be recognized are the following:

The famous hooked nose, the restless eyes, the close-set teeth, the elongated ears, the square nails (instead of being tapered in the shape of an almond), the flat foot, the round knees, the soft hand, almost melting with the hypocrisy of the traitor. Often, they have one arm longer than the other. Johann Lavater observes: "Physical degradation closely follows upon moral degradation. This is strongly remarked among the Jews, who, of all races of men, are the most depraved."

The Jewish tribes have preserved to this day almost intact the features that formerly distinguished them, a number of which are indicated in the

Bible. Gambetta, with his nose of so pronounced a curve, belonged to the tribe of Ephraim. To the same tribe belong the Seligmans, the Oppenheimers, and the Wormsers, which accounts for the mutual sympathy existing among them. The Stearns, who with few exceptions are of a dark and velvet-like skin, belong to the tribe of Daniel. The Jacobs as a rule belong to the tribe of Judah. The numberless Levys, notwithstanding slight differences of type, belong to the tribe of Asser.

Besides these tribal peculiarities, it is absolutely necessary to distinguish two different types of Jews: the Jew of the South and the Jew of the North, the Portuguese Jew [Sephardic] and the German Jew [Ashkenazi]. The Jews of the Portuguese rite claim to have settled in Spain during the earliest antiquity. They reject with horror all kinds of relation "with the murderers of Christ." They even claim that the Jews living in Toledo had, at the time of the Crucifixion, written to their brethren in Jerusalem to deter them from committing so great a sin. Whether these claims are correct or not, it is an indisputable fact that there exists a great difference between the Portuguese and the German Jew.

Warmed by the sun of the Orient, the Jew of the South is at times physically beautiful. It is not rare to find in him preserved the Arab type in all its purity. A few recall, with their mild, velvet-like, caressing eyes, their ebony hair, some comparison of the Moorish kings or of a Castilian Hidalgo. They are obliged, however, to keep their hands gloved, for this greedy, avaricious, low race quickly manifests itself by the curved fingers, which are ever restless, ever ready to seize or to rob.

The German Jews have none of the above personal advantages. Their weak, glassy eyes seldom look you straight in the face. Their skin is yellowish, and their hair often of the same disagreeable color. Their beard, almost always of a reddish hue, is now and then black, but of a faded black which recalls an old Prince Albert coat. He is the type of the old slave-trader, of the lowest kind of usurer. Good fortune never changes him while touching him with its wand. When one sees him driving in his magnificent carriage, one is reminded of itinerant venders in thread and needles, and of money-lenders of the Shylock kind. In a word, the German Jew is a vain, ignorant, tricky, ungrateful, low, creeping, insolent, dirty, ill-smelling fellow. The German Jewess is imperious, credulous, prone to blackmail, and seldom faithful to her conjugal ties.

The above description is given by one of their co-religionists, Mr. Herz Cerfbeer de Medelsheim. The same author brings against the rabbis accusations that we do not reproduce, because never does a Christian writer attack a priest, no matter to what religion he may belong. He leaves this task to the writers of the Jewish press.

The Jew of the South mingles a grain of poetry with his financial enterprises. He takes away your purse—it is the race that demands it—but he does it by means of certain proceedings not wanting in a sentiment of grandeur. The Jew of the North has not even the genius of commerce. He is the one who rubs off the metal from gold pieces, who, as it is said in Frankfurt, causes gold coins to suffer the operation of circumcision. His brother of the South works, moves, exerts himself. He of the North does not stir, but behind his window, motionless and stagnant, waits for success to come to him. He enriches himself though he never produces. The one is the quick, restless, alert water-bug; the other, the indolent, lazy parasite, living in inertia, at the expense of the human body.

In a word, the Jew who can be tolerated is the man of the South. But the venomous being—he who makes obscene caricatures, he who spits upon the crucifix—is the Jew of the North. The Jews of the South have suffered much more than those of the North, but they have been much less despised. Martyrdom, as it often happens, has aggrandized, as it were, their descendants; while the habit of living in public humiliation has plunged into degradation the sons of the German Jews. It must not be forgotten, however, that the true Jew is the Jew of the North.

But, excepting a few passing dissensions, both those of the North and the South are closely united against the Goy, the stranger, the Christian. Religion among the Jews is but of secondary importance. The question of race is what, above all, preoccupies them. Even among those who have abandoned Judaism, a Jew has no difficulty in recognizing his own people. He knows if there is a drop of Jewish blood in one's veins, and very readily spares an antagonist because he has discovered in him a brother who has wandered from the way.

The above point is admirably shown in *Daniel Deronda*, that marvelous study of Judaism. From one end of the universe to the other, Israel sends its emissaries to discover the fragments of the lost tribes. They are sought with eagerness, perseverance, and patience, because as long as they are dispersed, the family is not complete.

It was in order to find these lost tribes that the Jew Benjamin, who died in London in 1864, visited during many long years Egypt, Syria, Bagdad, India, China, and Persia. Another Jew, Wiener, professor at the "Lycée Bonaparte," went to look for them in South America, and the funds of public instruction were used to defray the expenses of those patriotic missions. It is for this same purpose that Disraeli made England undertake, under the false pretext of an offense to England, the war of Afghanistan, which cost the lives of so many men and the expenditure of an enormous amount of money. Mr. Gladstone, in the great meeting held on 5 October 1881, in Leeds, denounced that disastrous expedition, which resulted in alienating the Afghans from the English, and in overthrowing the moral barrier existing between England and the Russian Empire. The events of 1885, when England backed down before Russia, prove how clearly Gladstone saw the whole matter.

The main body of the Jews is divided, as it were, into three army corps. First, the *true Jews*, the *Notoires*, as the Jewish Archives call them; that is, the known Jews, who venerate officially Abraham and Jacob, and who are pleased to maintain the possibility of making their fortune, by remaining faithful to their worship. Second, the *disguised Jews*, or free-thinkers, type of Gambetta, Dreyfus, Professor Worman, etc., who carefully conceal their Jewish origin, but ridicule the Christians in the name of the glorious principles of tolerance, civilization, and liberty. Third, the *conservative Jews*, who, Christian in appearance, are united to the two former classes by the closest ties, and communicate to their comrades the secrets which may be useful to them. In the above relations lies the incredible success of the Jew.

Solidarity is the force of the Jew. All the Jews are clannish in the extreme, which characteristic we observe in them from one end of the world to the other, with an exactitude truly touching. One may easily understand what an advantage this principle of solidarity gives the Jew over the Christian, who, while ready to assist the unfortunate, has little of the sentiment of solidarity. No one can, more than myself, admire charity, that sublime flower that Christianity has caused to bloom in the human heart. That unwary charity, ardent and inexhaustible, which always gives, gives without ceasing, not only money, but its whole heart, time, intelligence. The Christians open their arms to the unfortunate. They are ready to respond to an appeal, but they do not keep close together. Accustomed, which is after all quite natural, to consider themselves at home in a country that belongs to them, they do not think of mustering their ranks in close array to resist the Jew. Accordingly, the Jew can easily attack us with surprising insolence. Today it is a merchant whose capital the Jew covets, and the entire Jewish commercial world combines to force him into bankruptcy. Tomorrow it is a writer who has wounded them, and whom the Jews reduce to despair, perhaps to drunkenness or madness. Again, there is a gentleman bearing a time-honored name, and who, unwittingly perhaps, has rudely accosted a spurious Jew baron. Plans are immediately formulated to procure for the unfortunate man a Jewish mistress for blackmailing purposes. Sometimes no efforts are spared to engage the victim into a supposed advantageous affair. His hopes are aroused by a first gain, but finally ruin and perhaps infamy are branded upon his once-fair name.

Had the merchant, the writer, and the aristocrat united, they would have escaped, they would have mutually defended one another. Each would have brought assistance to the other; but they succumbed, without even suspecting who was their cruel enemy. By reason of this solidarity, everything that happens to a Jew, even in the remotest corner of the desert, assumes the proportions of an event. The Jew, in fact, has a way of braying that is peculiar to himself—"Grow and increase, ye numberless posterity of Abraham".[5]

As soon as a Jew becomes interested in any matter, a great commotion is sure to break forth. How did Olivier Pain die? Nobody knows. His friends are sorry for him, but the public at large takes little, if any, interest in his fate. Now it so happens that Bismarck, who is desirous to have France and England estranged the one from the other, formed a plan to have Lord Lyons, who for many years had been the English Ambassador in Paris, ill-treated. Thereupon the Jew, Goedschel Selikowitcb, appeared upon the scene. He published a pamphlet entitled, *The Sheol of the Jews, and the Sest of the Egyptians.* That is all that is known of him. In return he knows the most secret things, he saw Olivier Pain shot, he affirms it upon his honor, he declares that this outrageous action must not remain unpunished. He is believed. Meetings of indignation are organized, and England and her venerable queen are both outrageously insulted. Diplomatic notes follow. Rochefort swears that he will avenge by the death of Lord Lyons the murder of Pain. Everybody is frightened. The English Embassy closes its doors.

A wretched Jew sufficed to create all this hubbub. How does the Jew manage to disturb the entire world? Nobody knows. It is his secret; it is a special gift of his and it comes quite naturally to him.

---

[5] See Genesis 22:17.

No matter to what country a Jew may belong, he will never fail to find assistance proffered to him. Country, in the sense we attach to this word, has no meaning whatever to the Jew. I do not clearly see why one should reproach the Jew for attaching a different meaning to the word 'country' than we do. To use an energetic expression of the *Alliance Israélite*, the Jew is a member of the "inexorable universality." What does 'country' mean? The land of our fathers. The sentiment of country is engraved in our heart, just as names are cut into a tree, and which each year that passes causes us to adhere and penetrate more deeply into the bark in proportion as the tree grows older, so that in course of time, both name and tree make one whole. One cannot be an improvised patriot. Patriotism exists in the blood, in the bones. Can the Jew who is continually wandering, who is a nomad, experience sentiments so lasting? No doubt one can change country, as so many foreigners do every day in America; as many Italians did at the time of the arrival in France of Catherine de Medicis; as the French Protestants at the time of the revocation of the Edict of Nantes. But that such transplantation may succeed, it is necessary that the soil shall be very like the one left. It is necessary that Christian elements shall be present in the moisture of the ground. Furthermore, the first condition of adopting another country is to renounce one's own. Now the Jew has a country that he never renounces. It is *Jerusalem*, the holy and mysterious Jerusalem[6]—Jerusalem triumphant or persecuted, joyous or afflicted, serves as a tie to all her children who every year at the Rosh-Hashanah say, "next year in Jerusalem."

Outside of Jerusalem, every country, be it France, Germany, England or America, is for the Jew simply a place in which to sojourn, and where he may find it profitable to live for a time: but of which he forms a part simply in the capacity of a free associate or a temporary member. If the reader would consider the matter in its regular and normal condition, he would be convinced that the Jew has no incentive that weighs with him to be a patriot. Why should a Rothschild, a Bischoffsheim, be attached to the France of Fontenoy, of St. Louis, of Henry IV and Louis XIV? Why should a Wormser or an Oppenheimer take any patriotic interest in this land of ours?

"By its traditions, its beliefs, its recollections," says Drumont, "France is the absolute negation of all Jewish temperament. When France has not

---

[6] Recall that this book was written some 60 years prior to the creation of Israel.

burned the Jew, she has obstinately closed her doors against him, covered him with scorn, and has branded his name with the cruelest insults."

Again, one must not judge the Jew after our own ideas of right and justice. It cannot be gainsaid that the Jew never fails to betray his employer. Cavour used to say of his secretary, the Jew Artom, "That man is precious to me, for he makes known what I intend to say. I do not know how he does it, but I have no sooner uttered a word or conceived a plan than he has betrayed me, even before leaving my office." "Why should God have created the Jews," says Bismarck, "if it were not to serve as spies?"

Sedecias poisoned Charles the Bald. The Jew Meire poisoned Henry III, of Castile; the Council of Ten discussed, on 9 July 1477, the proposition of the Jew, Salomoncini, and of his brother, who offered to have Mahomet II poisoned by his physician, the Jew Valcho. The Jew Lopez, physician to Queen Elizabeth, was hanged for allowing himself to be bribed by Philip II. The Jew Louis Goldsmith served as a spy to Talleyrand, in England, during the First Empire. The Jew Michel was guillotined for having surrendered to Russia military documents. Another Jew, a few years ago, stole the plans of the Russian War Office. Only today, 26 October 1887, the notorious Jew, Menzil Mark, one of General Boulanger's spies, stole from the commander of a garrison in Austrian Galicia the plans of three forts, and fled with them to Russia. Who does not remember the repeated attempts made by the Jewess Kaulla to seize the plans of the French mobilization? The Jew, Gustave Klootz, betrayed General Hicks, who was destroyed with his army by the soldiers of Mahdi. The renowned poet, Krazjewski, trusted himself to the Jew Adler, who sold him to Prussia, and the old Polish bard was cast into a fortress. These facts, which it would be easy to multiply, have reference not to an isolated case (which proves nothing against a collectivity), but to the entire race, the race of Abraham.

Is this considered espionage or treason by the Jews? Not in the least. They do not betray a country that they do not have; they simply engage in a business affair or a speculation. The true traitors to their country are *the natives*, who permit the Jew to thrust his nose where he has no business. "The Republican ministers" who, says Drumont, "not content with naming an officer of the Legion of Honor, Oppert de Blowitz, a German by birth, and an Englishman when occasion may demand it, take him for a confidant, communicate to him the secrets of the War Office—they are the ones who deserve blame and contempt." By what right could you prevent a Jew, oscillating between two countries, from favoring with his information the one of the two that pays him the best?

This, it is well understood, renders very difficult the study of the Jew in a criminal point of view. The evil the Jews commit, a frightful and fathomless unknown evil, enters into the category of crimes committed in the name of "the right of state." To assassinate, ruin, despoil the Christian, constitutes for the Jew an act authorized by his religion, acceptable to his God. As Eisenmenger explains it in his *Judaism Exposed*, "It is what the Jews call 'to commit a Korban.' Such a Jew, who will, by the aid of his coreligionists, reduce to despair or suicide a Christian merchant whose place he covets, will be, in the estimation of his own people, the most charitable, the most serviceable, the most disinterested of friends."

The absence of every serious statistical document, and the ability with which the Jews, who are always conniving among themselves, conceal their acts, surround, I repeat it, every research of this kind with difficulties almost insurmountable. In 1847, Cerfbeer de Medelsheim gave the following interesting figures: "There are," he said, "in the twenty-two principal prisons of France about 18,000 prisoners. The number of Jews among these 18,000 is about 110. Now, the population of France being 34,000,000, the proportion of a prisoner is about one-half per cent, on a thousand inhabitants. The Jews being about 100,000 in all, the proportion of the condemned Israelites is, therefore, more than one on each thousands of their co-religionists".[7] Today, however, the numberless Levys, Salomons, Mayers, etc., who swarm the police departments, and who occupy all offices from the highest to the lowest, never arrest one of their co-religionists, excepting when driven to the last extremity.

Maxime Du Camp, only a few years ago, in 1867, thus wrote concerning the dark ways of the Jews:

> The time served in prison by the Jew family Nathans, father,
> mother, brothers, sisters-in-law and sons-in-law, in all, fourteen persons, represent a total of 200 years of prison life. The
> Jews are to be feared, not for their desperate deeds, for they
> rarely commit murder, but for their tenacity and persistency in

---

[7] In other words, about 5 Frenchmen are imprisoned for every 10,000 people of the population, but about 11 Jews are imprisoned for every 10,000 Jews. Therefore, Jews are imprisoned at more than twice the rate of Frenchmen.

evil; for the inviolable secrecy they keep among themselves; for the wonderful patience they display, and the facility with which they conceal themselves among their co-religionists. The Jew thieves rarely put themselves in open combat against society. They are always in a state of secret and concealed animosity. One would suppose that they are pledged to vengeance, that they are in the right, and that, after all, they plunder and seize only the property of which their ancestors have so often been deprived and despoiled by ours.

Often they unite and engage in wholesale stealing, just as one would enter into an honorable enterprise on an extensive scale. They have their correspondents, their warehouses, and their buyers. It is in this way that the Nathans proceeded, of whom we have just spoken. Everything with them has a value: the lead stolen from the public sewers, as well as the handkerchiefs picked from the pockets of strangers. The chief generally assumes the title of commission merchant, and forwards stolen goods to the United States, Germany, Russia, England, Italy, and to other parts of the world. The quaint German-Hebraic jargon [Yiddish] that they speak among themselves is well-nigh incomprehensible and renders all means for their capture abortive. They are the cleverest receivers of stolen property, and conceal their nefarious doings behind the screen of a business honestly pursued.

An old Jew fireman, called Cornu, was one morning walking in the Champs Elysees, and was met by two thieves, great admirers of the old Jew's bold deeds. "Well, Father Cornu," said they to him, "what are you doing, now?" "Always the same *grande soulasse*" he replied, with an innocent air—"Always the *grande soulasse*" By *grande soulasse* he meant murder followed by theft.

Nathan, the senior, was a veritable patriarch, and was imprisoned for the last time when seventy years old on 6 May 1852. He ostensibly carried on the business of dealer in wood, and enjoyed a high reputation in his quarter. He loved art, and was the friend of artists, to whom he loaned money at the modest interest of 50 per cent. "The clan of the Nathans," says the Celebrated Cases, "has had its feminine celebrities also. Minette, or Esther Nathan, wife to Mayer, was a thief of watches, and also of money tills, and so was also her sister, Rosine Nathan, famous for her elegant manners and skill in disguises. She was twice in prison, and twice did Esther put on the rich

garments of her sister, because Rosine Nathan, had, during many years, deceived both her victims and the police, under the most astounding and divers
disguises. A society lady when circumstances required it, she had her valets,
her carriages, her diamonds and silks. She had the address and outward appearance of a great lady. She was as clever a comedienne as she was a thief.
She closely resembled Schumacher, that well-known daughter of a coach-
man, and who was one of the elegantes of Paris, and was married to the
Marquis of Maubreuil. Her brother was in prison, while his sister received
the most distinguished people in Paris."

These criminal associations of the Jews are handed down from father to
son. In the month of October, 1884, one called Mayer was arrested at Strasbourg, where he kept a central bureau for stolen securities. There was captured at his house shares stolen at Brussels, representing a value of 400,000
francs. Also, stocks belonging to Mr. Burat, a banker, valued at a million
francs; also bonds stolen from the Widow Bontemps, proprietor of the café
in the Montmartre theater, worth 200,000 francs. It would seem difficult to
conceive how Mayer could have succeeded in entering into relations with all
these thieves scattered throughout Europe had there not existed an organization cosmopolitan in its scope, and doing business on a stupendous scale.
Can there be anything more significant than the following letters, addressed
to the Paris Financial Association, concerning a famous robbery, and signed
Michael Abrahams? Commentary would be useless before the tranquil effrontery of these people who serve as agents to thieves.

> LONDON, the 27th Sept, 8 o'clock.
> To the Financial Association, Paris:
> GENTLEMEN:
>   We have this day received a visit from Mr. Samuels, who
> is the agent of the holders of your shares. He begs us to inform
> you that the shares of No. — will be returned to you upon
> payment of 35 percent, of their value. As to the other shares,
> "City of Brussels," etc., he wishes you to make an offer of so
> much per cent, before they are returned to you.
>   We believe that the shares of No. — can be had for less
> than 35 per cent. Please inform us what sum your clients are
> willing to sacrifice for the return of their property.
>   (Signed,) MICHAEL ABRAHAMS, SON & Co.

Here is another letter from the same firm, while negotiations were in progress, in the hope of obtaining better terms:

> Since the receipt of your letter of the 25th of October, we have received a visit from an agent of the unlawful keepers of your values. We are authorized to inform you that all further negotiations are at an end, for his friends will not accept the 100,000 francs you offer. Accept, gentlemen, our sincere regards.
> (Signed,) MICHAEL ABRAHAMS, SON & Co.

The murder of the watchmaker Peschard at Caen serves to illustrate still further the character of the Jew. All the accused were German Jews. Minder, alias Graft, Gugenheim, alias Mayer, and Louise Mayer all have the well-known physiognomy. Solomon Ulmo, apparently an honest merchant, but in reality, affiliated to a band of assassins, presents a most striking appearance. There is nothing more remarkable than the interior of the homes of these Jew malefactors. Murder is looked upon only as a speculation, and does not exclude domestic virtues. The family of the Ulmos lived well at Chaumont, a city that contains a considerable number of Jews. The son, according to the testimony of the witnesses, was very diligent in his business, was never seen in a cafe, and was blindly obedient to his father. The most incredible parsimony ruled in the household, the whole expense not amounting to more than 16 per month. The Peschard affair occurred on 30 August, 1857, and justice was meted out to the criminals; but had this occurred today, it would have been immediately stifled. The Jews are not pursued today, excepting upon rare occasions, and when it is absolutely impossible to do otherwise.

Hirsch, the banker, who was caught dealing in spurious banknotes which he knew to be false, was condemned, it is true, on 8 May, 1884, to a fine of 7,500 francs; but said fine, relatively light, had the character of a disciplinary penalty, of a family reprimand, as it were. Were you, my reader, to present yourself to the house of the Rothschilds with a spurious bank-note, you would be arrested, imprisoned, questioned as to your accomplices, and finally condemned to prison at hard labor. In the month of August 1885, two criminals, Gaspard and Mayer, were convicted of the murder of a trunk manufacturer and were both committed to prison. Gaspard was the unconscious instrument of Mayer, who conceived the idea of the crime, and coldly proposed the murder. But Mayer was a Jew, and consequently was pardoned, while Gaspard was executed.

When the law pretends to busy itself with the Jew, it is simply to acquit him. A few years ago, the wealthy Jew banker, Baron d'Erlanger, was in trouble by reason of peculations of his. Needless to say, that the case was thrown out of court on account of "nonresidence."

Respecting the complete impunity of the Jews, proofs gather every day under our own eyes. "Is it necessary," says Drumont,

> to recall to Parisians the little episode of that poor Spanish courtesan, so full of vitality and spirit, and who had an insurmountable horror for the very idea of suicide, but who is believed to this day to have thrown herself out of her window, when in truth she was hurled from the height of a balcony by her Jew lover, who had in his veins the blood of a barbarian, but dreamed of a princely marriage? The simple examination of the spot would have convinced a child of the utter absurdity and falsity of the theory of suicide?

In 1882 a woman, a Smyrneote, was arrested in a great dry goods store in Paris, in the very act of theft. This woman was found to be related to a Jewish actress who wearies the world with her vagaries, all done for advertising purposes. It was declared that the thief was a victim to kleptomania. Imagine a woman belonging to a Christian family, and stealing an object worth not more than ten cents in a Jew store, and you will see if she is a kleptomaniac. Sarah Bernhardt, fired with indignation on account of the book of Marie Colombier, invaded, with three companions, the rooms of her rival. She broke everything in her way. There was manifestly a violation of domicile. Did anybody prosecute her? It would have been useless.

Most of the Jew failures in business are only prearranged plans, committed with a view of robbing the Gentile. To cite but recent events, says Drumont:

> Have we not seen two Jews of Mayence, the brothers Bloch, establish themselves in 1882, on Aboukir Street, Paris, and after having received many consignments, run away in September, 1883, on the eve of a bankruptcy of 300,000 francs? In

August, 1884, a North German Jew, Mendel, established in Enghien Street, Paris, fled with more than 600,000 francs' worth of diamonds belonging to Christians who had trusted him. The Jew, John David, director of the National Credit, stole more than 3,000,000 francs, the savings of hardworking people. Twelve hundred depositors brought an action against him, but the incorruptible magistrates allowed David to depart in peace. It was true that afterward he was condemned to ten years' imprisonment, and a fine of 3,000 francs, with five years of surveillance, but it was all the same to David. The bird had flown to foreign lands to enjoy quietly the products of his theft.

There are also kings among the Jews, as the Israelite Archives call them. Ephrussi, a penniless adventurer not long ago, is today the king of wheat, as was formerly Moses Friendlander, who died in San Francisco in 1878. Moses Ranger was the king of cotton, when, in 1883, he failed in Liverpool for about $4,000,000. Spreckels is the real king of the Sandwich Islands, known also as the sugar king of the Pacific coast. Strousberg, alias Baron Hirsch, is the king of railroads. There is also a king of baccarat, the Jew W. R. Deutch, who won at the Washington Club and at the Press Club more than 2,000,000 francs.

In an old Byzantine writer we find an interesting but at the same time heart-rending account of a corner in wheat, organized by a family of Tarsus Jews, the chief of whom was called Johannes Rockefellos. The result of this corner, while it brought fabulous wealth "to the abominable clan of the Rockefellos, shattered the foundations of our prosperity, brought ruin and death to our beloved fellow-citizens, and prepared the destruction of our fair city." The people, the author informs us, finally arose as one man against the family; but the three prominent brothers, Johannes, Moses, and Wilhelm, made their escape to western Europe and there were lost. The name is certainly suggestive.[8]

The Jewesses furnish the strongest contingent to the prostitution of great cities. This fact cannot be denied, and the Archives Israelites have also recognized it. We reproduce in part the article:

---

[8] The clear reference is to John D. Rockefeller, at the time of writing one of the richest men in America. More on Rockefeller in chapter 5 below.

> For the last quarter of a century, moralists have been at a loss to explain how it is that among the women who lead a bad life, a greater number of Jewesses are to be noticed than of Christians. This unfortunately is but too true, because in Paris, London, Berlin, Hamburg, Vienna and elsewhere, among the *demi-monde*, in the public streets, and in the houses of prostitution, one meets with a greater number of Jewesses than of Christians, taking into consideration, of course, the difference in number between the two populations.

This vice, however, has a particular character among the Jewesses. It is certain that the Jew father and mother unhesitatingly sell their daughters when they are poor. The Jewess prostitutes herself for money, and she does so boldly, deliberately, without the slightest shadow of intoxication, and with the firm determination of getting married as soon as she has accumulated some money. They often marry an actor, a merchant, or a financier.

A few years ago, in a trial in Vienna, a Jew lawyer, Glaser by name, declared: "Every woman has the right to sell her body and to derive by the sale the best possible profit." The outraged public cried out in loud condemnation. The presiding judge expressed his astonishment. Glaser, however, asserted only what Semitic tradition teaches. The Jewish prostitute often serves Israel in her particular way, for she is an excellent instrument of information to Jewish diplomacy.

The Jewesses of the rich classes live, even here in New York, in Oriental fashion. They take their siesta in the afternoon, and live a sort of secret and isolated life. They are strangers to violent passions, which so often trouble the heart of the Gentile woman lost to religion. They are void of all sentiment, of the ideal, a peculiar characteristic of the Israelites.

What is the cause, the great cause of the ruin of Gentile women? It is the inspiration toward a mistaken ideal, the dream of being superior to all others, the chimerical hope of achieving independence, the thirst for living, be it only for a few short hours, in the ethereal regions of an esthetic existence of ardent love and infinite tenderness. Neither the Jew nor the Jewess has these sentiments.

A Jewess will never discuss religious questions, for the Jew knows well the danger that may arise and might cause the blindness of Israel to be revealed. The Talmud formally forbids women the study of religious subjects.

"He who teaches his daughter the sacred law is as guilty as he who would teach her indecent ways." But if the Jewess does not know the teachings of her religion, she practices it faithfully, even in the most troubled existence. Miss Ada Isaacs Menken, the actress, whom Rothschild called the inspired Deborah of her race, after having appeared for thirty consecutive nights in San Francisco, all at once stopped to celebrate the night of Kol-Nidre. No sooner did an article appear against her co-religionists than she sent an answer to defend them in *The Israelite*, of Cincinnati.

Here again we must praise the respect with which the Jews surround a girl of their race, no matter the calling she may follow. If an actress, they declare that never has the world seen any one more beautiful. They will go into ecstasy, into hysterics, they will cry with admiration as soon as she makes her appearance. If she returns to a normal life, all doors are open to her.

Virginity, virtue, innocence, purity, are only so much capital with the Jew, a capital that one must defend, but which may be regained if lost. The loss of it is only a bad bargain, over which one must pass the sponge of oblivion without the slightest cause for grief. If an artist, a merchant, or a financier ever gets into trouble, you will always find that admirable solidarity which is the only virtue of the Jew, which explains, justifies, almost legitimates his success.

If a libelous sheet ever brings an accusation against a Christian, all his former friends, acquaintances, and associates will avoid him. One and all will say, "I do not know him." But on the bench of infamy, at the feet of the scaffold, the Jew never abandons his own, and will never permit an insult that in his opinion and belief affects "the great family."

If a drama is played in which a Jew is pictured in a disagreeable light, no efforts are spared to have it fail. Once it was intended to produce at the "Gaite" a piece entitled *The Lender on Wages*, in which the usurer was a Jew. The director was called upon, the matter was explained to him, and the usurer was changed into a Christian.

Mr. Hallays-Dabot relates that it was intended to produce in the theater of "Ambigu-Comique" Shakespeare's immortal work, *The Merchant of Venice*. In this great creation, which revives the centuries of oppression, which depicts the Jew, his secret intrigues and plots against the Christian, all blended in the loathsome character of Shylock, whose sarcastic laugh and cries of despair lighten the somber side of the middle ages—everything, both time and place of action, was changed, including the low and savage type of Shylock, into a close Venetian merchant, solely to please the Jews of the metropolis. Imagine if the work of any great literary genius ever suffered such a mutilation out of respect for the feelings of the Christians.

The Longevity of the Jews

According to observations made in Germany by the Jew Meyer, the average life of the Jew is 37 years, and that of the Christian is 27, a difference of nearly eleven years.

Dr. Lagneau read a paper before the Academy of Moral and Political Sciences respecting the increase of population among the Jews compared with that noticed among Catholics and Protestants. According to the doctor, the increase of Catholics, Protestants, and Jews is [in the ratio of] one, two, three. The Jews in Russia, Poland, Prussia, Austria, and France present the most rapid increase. In the two countries last named, it is seven times more rapid than among the Catholics and Protestants.

But as the Jews, both as a race and as individuals, are absolutely different in their evolution from the Gentiles, they, the Jews, are also entirely different in a sanitary point of view. The Jew is subject to all the maladies that indicate the corruption of blood, such as scrofula, leprosy, itch, salt-rheum, erysipelas, and all skin diseases. Nearly all the low classes of the Jews have the itch. Many of the most elegant Jews whose hands we shake, are likewise affected with it, though they keep it secret. All take care not to engage a physician who is not of their religion, an example that the Gentiles ought to imitate. On the other hand, the Jew possesses a wonderful aptitude in adapting himself to all climates. "There are Jews under all degrees of latitude, from the 33rd degree of the south hemisphere to the 60th of the northern latitude, from Montevideo to Quebec, from Gibraltar to the coast of Norway, from Algiers to the Cape of Good Hope, from Jappa to Pekin." Thus spoke one of them in a transport of admiration.

Through a phenomenon that attracted attention more than a hundred times in the Middle Ages, and that has been noticed at the present day at the time of the cholera in France, Spain, Italy, and elsewhere, the Jew seems to enjoy a particular immunity with respect to epidemics. There seems to be within him a sort of permanent pest, which guarantees him against the ordinary scourge. He is his own vaccine as it were, a living antidote. The plague recedes when it smells him.

It is a matter of fact that the Jew is ill-smelling. This smell exists even among the richest, a *foetor Judaicus*, which indicates the race and assists them to recognize one another. The most charming Jewesses, notwithstanding the perfumes they use, justify the words of Martial: "*Qui bené olet malé olet.*" This fact has been a hundred times verified. All Jews are ill-smelling, *puent*, said Victor Hugo. "In 1266," relates Hugo, "in a memorable assembly that took place before the King and Queen of Aragon, to which were invited the learned Rabbi Zeckhiel and brother Paul Cyrac, a very learned Dominican, a great discussion arose, during which the Jew cited the Toldos, the Archives of Sanhedrim, the Talmud, etc. The Queen, who evidently was impressed with the great learning of the Rabbi, ended by asking him why it was that the Jews smell so bad. The consternation of the assembly may easily be imagined."

The question why the Jews smell bad has for a long time puzzled many men. During the Middle Ages, it was believed that they could be freed of this odor through baptism. Bail claims that this offensive smell is owing to natural causes, just as there are negroes to this day who exhale an unbearable odor.[9]

Neurosis is the implacable malady of the Jews. Among that people for so long a time persecuted, living always in the midst of continual changes and incessant activity, shaken afterward by the fever of speculation, and following no professions excepting those in which the mind is in continual energy, the nervous system has ended by altering itself. In Prussia, the proportion of lunatics is much greater among the Jews than among the Christians, for whilst it is 24.1 in 10,000 Protestants, 23.7 in a like number of Catholics, the Jews are 38.9 in 10,000. In Italy there is one lunatic among 384 Jews, and one among 778 Catholics.

This neurosis seems to be transmitted even to those whose mother only is a Jewess. Sarah Bernhardt, with her dark forebodings, her coffin of white satin constantly in her room, is evidently a victim to neurosis.

One must not lose sight, however, of the fact that the Jew, even in his most delirious conceptions, looks out for self. Even when he loses his head, he saves the cash-box. This disease has the Jew, strange though it may appear, communicated to our generation. For the last 20 years that the Jews have held the wires of secret diplomacy, and have reduced the once honorable office of ambassador to mere parade. European diplomacy has truly be-

---

[9] For more on the *foetor Judaicus*, see T. Dalton, *Eternal Strangers* (2025).

come unbearable and foolish. The saying of Bismarck: "Paris is the home of fools, inhabited by monkeys," can be as well applied to Germany and to the rest of Europe. There is no longer a shadow of conscience in the councils of sovereigns, nor even of justice in government. Neurosis deprives the Jew of all modesty, reflection, thought, and drowns in him the enormity of what he dares to do, and brings forth types of men altogether different from those of former generations. To these types belong those who have suddenly acquired fortunes of unheard-of proportions; types of men who lead an extravagant existence, possessing sums acquired with astounding effrontery, an effrontery that confounds all reason. The Jew always goes forward, trusting in the 'Mazzal.' What is the Mazzal? It is neither the Fate of the ancients nor is it Christian Providence. It is good luck, chance, the Jewish star. Every Jewish life seems a realized novel.

Take, for instance, the notorious woman known as Madame de Paiva. Born of a family of Polish Jews called Lachmann, she married a poor tailor in Moscow, and, quickly tiring of him, came to Paris on foot to seek her fortune. She experienced in the streets of Paris all the privations of ill fortune, all the horrors of venal love. She fell one day exhausted from lethargy in the Champs Elysées, and she swore to herself that it would be on this very spot where her mansion should rise, when fate, in which she blindly trusted, would at last relent. She went to live with the famous [Jewish] pianist, Henri Herz, who introduced her to the Tuileries as his legitimate wife. She was given to understand that her society was not wanted, and she swore to be avenged. Shortly afterward she married, this time regularly, the Marquis of Païva, who, a few months later, committed suicide. She then became the mistress of Count Henkel, one of the richest men in France. She received diplomats, bankers, authors, and artists in her fairy home in the Champs Elysées.

With the peculiar intelligence of her race which the sentiment of hatred sharpens, she organized shortly before the Franco-Prussian War a system of espionage against the French, which facilitated her relations with some world-famous diplomats, who daily dined in her house and there discussed the affairs of France. It was she who prepared the overthrow of the Second Empire, and as Countess Henkel de Donnesmarck, she bought the diamonds of the Empress, by whom she had been formerly repulsed, and caused to be built, in the interior of Silesia, by Lefuel, the architect of imperial palaces, a chateau, the counterpart of the Tuileries from which she had been expelled.

She was a born artist, and although the daughter of peasants, had the intuition and the refined conceptions of a lady. But she was not happy amid her princely surroundings, for she was a victim of neurosis. She was tormented with the idea that people wished to murder her. She forbade, under penalty of immediate dismissal, anyone to be in the park when she was present. The woman who had experienced the pangs of hunger, and had belonged to all, was more of a despot, more severe in her manners and haughtier in her demeanor than a duchess. She ruled her vast number of domestics most rigorously, and instantly dismissed a poor *maître d'hotel* for having once smiled at a funny word uttered at dinner. She was 64 years old when she died of a disease of the brain in her *Tuileries* in Silesia.

Now, if one should collect all these traits and endeavor to establish a little order in the life and career of these strange personages, there would rise a figure peculiarly Jewish.

What a subject for a novel the career of the son of the Hungarian Rabbi, who subsequently became Midhat Pasha, would furnish! Once pasha, he began, according to Jewish custom, by assisting his own people, and organized Jewish schools in the Orient, and then tried to introduce revolutionary doctrines into Turkey, the land of stagnation, and soon found means to disturb and arouse even the Turks, whom one would suppose nothing could disturb. He created the party of young Turkey, and had for adviser one Simon Deutch, a Jew, a political courtier, an apostle of anarchy, who had lived in the houses of ambassadors and princes, as well as in the beer saloons of the lowest quarters. It was under the very eyes of Midhat in his konak, overlooking the shores of the Bosphorus, that the Sultan, his benefactor, Abdul Aziz, was murdered. Midhat was disgraced, recalled, condemned to death, which he escaped. Finally he was banished to Djeddah, where he still concocted new intrigues with the Madhi, which finally made it necessary for the Sultan to poison him. There are countless lives like these among the Jews.

If you would see a true specimen of the public man among the Jews, study the career of Alfred Naquet. He claimed to have discovered, when still a mere youth, a process by which a city could be reduced to ashes. He published a book entitled *Religion, Property, Family*, in which he advocated common property in woman. In later years, he placed himself under an agent, and went from city to city preaching the adoption of divorce in France. The Jew, even when successful, always remains mean, mercenary, and tricky. Naquet, not content with degrading society, invented also a lotion to make the hair grow and become glossy. Thus Naquet was by turns a chemist, a lecturer, a manufacturer, a senator, and furthermore he was called by his people "the rampart of Judaism."

Divorce in France was an idea of the Jews. Monseigneur Freppel, a Catholic orator, declared in a public seance held on 19 July, 1884, that the movement which will end by the adoption of the law of divorce was purely a Semitic movement. "Side, if you please, gentlemen," said the distinguished orator, "side with Israel; we remain, we abide with the Church and with France."

According to the Jewish doctrines contained in the Talmudic book *Ketubot*, one is at liberty to repudiate his wife without even returning to her dowry, provided she gives to her husband forbidden food to eat; deceives him respecting the period of her sickness; walks barefooted; speaks ill of her husband's parents; talks so loud when in her husband's bed as to be heard by those sleeping in an adjoining room...

"The Jew," says Drumont, "not content with occupying a prominent place in a society which he has not created, seeks to overturn or at least to modify its laws and customs. Formerly, if a man had acquired proof that he had been robbed by his broker, in a stock operation, he could appeal to the law for protection. He could save a part of his patrimony, the dowry perhaps of his daughter, the bread of his old age. But under the law proposed by the Jews, he cannot do so now, and the poor Goy must render to Shylock his last penny."

On every occasion, the Jew's first thought is to benefit his own people. Manufacturers find themselves ruined by the Jews, despoiled of their income, and robbed of their trademarks. Formerly, the European stock exchanges were composed of an eminently honorable body of men. Today they are largely composed of tricksters, owing to the admission into them of the Rothschilds and the rest of the band of Jews. Is not this also true of the New York Stock Exchange?

The Jew has been the cause of the most dramatic events that have occurred in the world's history. He carries death and ruin with him into all the countries he invades, and into all the homes into which he is admitted. Ruin and death have been the result of most marriages of which one of the contracting parties was a Jew. The Duke of Richelieu married the Jewess Heine, and he went to die prematurely in the Orient. The daughter of the Duke de Persigny married the Jew Friedman, and ended her life in prison. De Polignac married the Jewess Mirés, and ruin invaded his home. Ruin and dishonor invaded the home of La Panouse, who married the Jewess Heilbronn.

The lawyer Bernays, who married a Jewess, was murdered by the Hungarian Jew Peltzer. The Count Batthyani married a daughter of the Jew Schossberger, and was killed in a duel by the Jew Rossenberg, while the Count's wife contracted a new marriage a few months later. In the month of February, 1883, Daniel Naquet, one of the richest Jews of the south of France, and a relative of Naquet, the hair restorer, threw himself out of the window of his house and fractured his skull. In the month of October, 1885, the rich Jew banker Primsel, the partner of Dreyfus, of guano fame, threw himself into the Seine from the top of a bridge.

Sudden death is, however, more frequent among the Jews than suicide, although the latter has increased of late with astounding rapidity, a fact which attests that neurosis is a disease with which nearly all Jews are affected. What more terrible spectacle than the neurosis of the Jew Paradol, who was made so much of, bowed down to as a great man, and yet, at the age of 40, ended his days in so tragic a manner in Washington, after leading a showy, fastidious, but empty existence, which, in many respects, recalls the career of the Jew Gambetta. There, again, the fatality common to the race strikes, in a pitiless manner, the Paradol family. The son committed suicide at the age of 20, while the daughter, to whom Madame Rothschild, for personal motives, had offered a dowry of 100,000 francs, refused to marry, and entered a convent, sorrow's last refuge.

We have enumerated only the events which occur among the upper classes, and which cause a profound impression. It would be difficult to collect the numberless tragedies enacted in the middle and lower classes; the deeds committed in the more modest spheres, where the Jew, if he does not himself commit the crime, is the instigator and the cause.

The Jew who, according to the saying of Hegel, "has been precipitated beyond nature," has sought in vain through prodigies of astuteness and patience to enjoy social life; he is always driven from it, seemingly by an invincible force.

A drama, similar to the one that took place in the palace of Mycenae, has already forced the door of the proud house of the Rothschilds, who thought that they had made a compact with fortune. The entire world spoke of the suicide of Baron Jacob Rothschild, which, in many respects, recalls the tragic death of young Belmont, the son of one of the richest Jew bankers in New York. Although the Rothschilds have made the Christians pay dearly for that death, they do not forget that the blood of a suicide leaves an ineffaceable stain, brings an irresistible misfortune into a house, and over it suspends a curse. They feel, amid their feasts, that a certain ominous bird hovers over them ready to claim its own.

Mystery surrounds the terrible scenes which are continually enacted among the Jews. In vain we may try, we cannot ascertain the motive for the extraordinary acts of either Rothschild, Belmont, Wimpfen, or of many others.

The race, although well-conditioned for rapid propagation, nevertheless degenerates. Tradition relates that a certain inhabitant of Sicily, during the reign of King William, found in the earth a bottle that contained liquid gold. He drank it and again became a youth. But gold has not effected this transformation among the Jews. Examine them where you will and you will find that financiers, diplomats, journalists, wirepullers, one and all, are a prey to anaemotrophy [i.e. a blood deficiency]. Their eyes, which roll with feverish anxiety, denote hepatic maladies. The Jew carries in his liver the secretion produced by the hatred of eighteen centuries. There are instances of heart-rending atavism among them. The race, in proportion as it leads a civilized life, returns to the primitive type of pure Orientalism. They live in rooms hermetically closed, just as the lower class of Chinese do, where reigns an over-heated atmosphere. In the immense hotels in Vienna, they constantly seek the seclusion of corners and dark, hidden places, even in broad daylight. Take into your hand the little womanish fingers of the young Jew, which end in the shape of a shuttle, and, while they still denote the peculiar penchant of the race, they no longer have the solid and curved form of their fathers. The young Jews have the sickly color of wax; they tremble under our Northern sky, and, when they can afford it, they skulk away to Bermuda or to Nice. This physical condition, in part, explains the sadness that is the distinctive trait of the Jew's character.

CHAPTER 2
DEGENERATION OF THE JEWS

In order to succeed in their attacks on Christian civilization, the Jews have to assume the disguise of the freethinker. They shield themselves from the superstitions and prejudices of the Christian faith behind those empty but high-sounding phrases, 'liberty' and 'emancipation.' At no remote period they were in the habit of celebrating secretly in their homes their religious rites, but little by little they have become indifferent in the exercise of them.

Besides the great religious feasts which tend to unite the whole race, as, for instance, circumcision, the Purim, and Bar Mitzva, there were formerly a thousand other ceremonies that closely drew together the bonds of the fraternity. A Siyoum, that is to say, the end of a chapter of the Talmud, studied either by a society or by a private person, gave occasion to a repast. When it was announced that there was Zocher at a house, that is, that a male infant had been born, the privilege was accorded even to a stranger to go and salute it. The week that preceded a marriage was spent in festivities on a large scale. The table was loaded with those sweetmeats and those cakes that Henry Heine has more than once enumerated. These ceremonies, however, are to-day among the things of the past.

But it must not be supposed that the Jews are less faithful now than formerly to the cardinal religious rites of their faith. A Jew editor of even a low revolutionary sheet, after inserting a violent article in which our institutions are savagely attacked, and our faith is ridiculed; a Jew editor, who laughs at our sacraments, at our Christian doctrines and habits, is the first to hasten to his synagogue, and there discharge his religious duties.

It is true, however, that a sort of religious indifference has entered the homes of many an Israelite. If the Jews of Romania maintain at great expense the Isrolzka family, the supposed sacred family, from which it is believed that the Messiah will at some time issue, if the Jews of Poland leave their windows open when it thunders for the Messiah to come in, the great body of the civilized Jews no longer believe in the coming of the Redeemer. They believe only in Israel, in Israel at large, which will be the Messiah, or, in other words, the great future reigning nation.

Michael Weil, a great Rabbi, says the prophecies have never made mention either of a descendant of David or of a Messiah King—not even of a personal Messiah. The true Redeemer, according to him, would no longer be a personality, but would be Israel transformed into a lighthouse of nations, built upon the noble functions of humanity, teaching truth with its books, its history, its constancy, and its fidelity to doctrines.

It does not seem necessary to answer this impudent assertion. This gang of tricksters, of manipulators of money, is to be the lighthouse of nations, nations that have produced a Washington, a Franklin, a Bacon, a Shakespeare, a Charlemagne, a St. Louis, a Goethe, a Dante, a Socrates, a Leonidas, and so many others; nations that have produced the greatest thinkers, men of the loftiest genius as well as the most admirably organized societies! The Jew must have lost his head, even if the romantic hope of his race of acquiring what numberless generations of Christians have founded, created, and produced, has been realized beyond expectation.

By means of false promises, the Jews succeed in gathering from the pockets of the poor, from the depth of woolen stockings and the pockets of old coats, the savings which the faithful wife showed with a happy smile to the husband, who feared that the time was not distant when he would no longer be able to work. With the product of these thefts, they buy historic estates, where eminent men of former times rested after having grown old in the service of their country; thereon the degenerate scions of the aristocracy disgrace themselves by bowing to and admiring these thieves and spurious Jew barons, whose coat of arms would be more appropriately impressed upon pig-pens.

But how sad to think that these men are nominated ministers and ambassadors, as in the case of Raynal Bischoffsheim and others. A feeling, however, of disappointment has come over the Jews. They seem to say, "Is this all?" In the boxes of fashionable theaters, paid for with the pilfered savings of the poor whom they have reduced to despair, on the balconies of the castles they have stolen, these victors are assailed by the cankerous thoughts which came over the biblical Schelemo on the terraces of his palace and in the alleys of his garden:

- "Man has no advantage over the beasts. Both have the same end, both return to dust."
- "A living dog is better than a dead lion."
- "The best thing for man is to eat, drink and enjoy himself."

Thus speaks Kohelet in the Ecclesiastics, the faithful adherent of Sadducean morality. The vision of death that comes with long strides, the vision of that coffin that is raised into yonder magnificent apartment, the windows of which remain veiled during seven days, the appearance of that corpse which is carried off almost in a decayed state, cast an ineffaceable shadow upon all the Jews.

The Jews avoid even to pronounce the word 'death.' We find in the Ketubot that a rabbi was reprimanded for having said in a funeral oration, "Many men will empty the cup of life." Abbaye says, "Many men have emptied the cup of life" is an allowable expression, but we must not say, "Many men will empty the cup." In the Talmudic Berakhot, Abbaye again forbids the mention of the word 'death.' The custom of throwing water before the door of a house in which a death occurred was due to this same sentiment. It was the way of announcing the death to the neighbors without employing the forbidden word.

Although the Jews have preserved the idea of one God, their belief in a future life is wavering and confused. The Pharisees had spiritual tendencies, but the Sadducees were absolutely materialistic. There is little or no mention of the immortality of the soul in the Pentateuch,[1] and the only text that clearly speaks of immortality in the Old Testament is the following verse of Daniel: "And many of them that sleep in the dust of the earth shall awake, some to everlasting life, and some to shame and everlasting contempt" (12:2).

The Mishnah forbids the discussion of these problems, and the Aggadah brings to the defense of this injunction the story of the four well-known doctors, Ben-Azai, Ben-Zoma, Akiba, and Acher, who dared to venture into the avenues of Paradise. The first died, the second became a lunatic, Acher became an apostate, while Akiba alone got out of the scrape by the exercise of his daring and good sense. In a word, the Jewish faith never puts in the first rank the doctrine of future life. The narrowness of the Jew's horizon is evident. He is destitute of the beautiful hopes that are our consolation and our joy.

Swedenborg, in whom we often find descriptions worthy of Dante, thus speaks of a particular part in hell in which the Jews abound. "In this part of hell," he says, "the Jews were in great numbers. Their presence as they came near the other spirits was manifest by a disgusting smell of rats. There the Jews run about the streets in the mud, complaining and uttering lamentations."

---

[1] The Pentateuch is the first five books of the Old Testament.

We must not omit to mention that the Jews of today are much troubled and preoccupied with the anti-Semitic movement that is apparent throughout Europe. From 1870 to 1879, they traversed a period of delirious pride. "What happiness to live at such an epoch"—*Es ist eine Lust zu leben*—the Jew Wolff wrote in the *National Zeitung* at the time when the Laskers, the Bleichroeders, the Hausemanns, the Ickelheimers, like hungry vultures, despoiled of their billions the Prussians who were, so to speak, intoxicated with glory. What happiness thrilled the band of harpies in France and New York who saw money, palaces, princely dwellings, all in their possession. But they have now lowered a little the tone of their voices, for they feel that there is a movement among the Christians of all countries which will be much stronger than the *Alliance Israelite Universelle*.

The Jew is naturally a morose being. Enriched, he adds insolence to his moroseness. He is what may be termed 'arrogantly morose.' Drumont says that hypochondria, which is only one of the forms of neurosis, is the sole gift which the Jews have made to France, once so gay, so laughing, and so abounding in strength and gayety. "The Jews are both morose and somber," said Shaftesbury in his *Characteristics*, a sentiment profounder than it appears. It is an error to believe that the Jew finds amusement in the society of his own people; an error even to believe that he loves them. The Christians seldom support one another, but they love one another, they experience pleasure in seeing one another. The Jews, on the contrary, sustain one another even unto death, but they cannot tolerate the society of one another. As soon as they are no longer engaged in business, they run off like one possessed. They do not feel at ease in the society of Christians, and a word of veneration for the Founder of the Christian religion suffices to render them ill. A pleasantry at the expense of Judas, while they may receive it with a sickly smile, really exasperates them. In fine, the following injunction written over the doors of the Ghettos in Italy is something that the Jews everywhere follow: *Ne populo regni coelestis hoeredi usus cum exhoerede sit* ("Let the people, heirs to the kingdom of Heaven, have nothing in common with those excluded therefrom.")

At times, a smile full of meaning illumines these bloodless visages at the thought of some joke played upon a Christian. The fox, in fact, is the allegorical beast of the Jew. The *Meschabot Schualim*, or *The Fables of the Fox*, is the first book put into the hands of the young Jew. Later in life he finishes his training by exercising every manner of deceit and theft upon the

Aryan. After having, for instance, like Bleichroeder, organized the expedition against Tunis [in 1881], which cost France the lives of many of her children and the alliance of Italy, he tramples upon the dignity of his victim by causing himself to be nominated commander of the Legion of Honor by an unworthy and corrupt minister.

It may seem strange to the reader if we add that, besides the above characteristics, there is another side in the Jew's nature, resembling the innocence of a child. Innocence among the Jews! You are certainly jesting!

It is not a jest. The Jew, who is the embodiment of all that is sharp, close, and most contemptible in nature, has the astuteness of the savage as well as the vanity of a child. His mouth opens with pleasure as he contemplates some cheap mark of distinction bestowed upon him, just as the mouth of the African opens, whose eyes and teeth shine with pleasure when he obtains a piece of painted glass or a remnant of some gaudy colored cloth.

Did you ever notice the Jew Freemasons when out on parade? There is among these vain creatures a childlike pleasure in wearing a costume which distinguishes them from the rest. When the Jew relates to you that he has been rewarded with some cheap medallion for vending chocolate or shoeblacking, or some other such stuff, his pale face lights up with a ray of happiness similar to that which often illumines the faces of children upon the possession of some new toy.

The Jews' Hatred for the Christians

The sentiment that dominates the corrupt and passionate soul of the Jew is his hatred for the Church and its ministers. This hatred is, after all, natural. The vow of the missionary is a permanent mockery at the wealth of the Jew, who is incapable of buying with all his gold what the poorest Christian possesses—faith and hope, sentiments absolutely unknown among the Jews. Religion among the Jews is fidelity to tradition, an attachment to the race to which they belong. But there is not a word in the Hebrew language to express *faith*. The Jewish word *emouna* means constancy, tenacity, but not faith.

Simon, alias Lockroy, may insult yonder poor missionary. Dreyfus may raise his voice against those poor sisters of charity who are ever ready to sacrifice their lives upon the field of battle or in the chambers of sickness. There will always remain to them the crucifix they wear around their necks. The fact alone that their sublime virtues and disinterestedness exist is like a thorn in the bed of the vulgar Jew Sybarite who feels himself powerless over these souls.

But if the Jews, these perpetual agitators, have well-nigh succeeded in shaking the foundations of society with the money they have wrongfully acquired, the fact remains that the day is not far distant when a new society will rise that will crush them. The day is near at hand when all their ill-gotten gains will be distributed amongst those who will take part in the mighty struggle now brewing, distributed as formerly lands and fiefs were distributed among the bravest.

In Germany, in Russia, in Austria, in Romania, in France, even in America, where the movement just begins, all classes, rich and poor, in fact all of Christian origin, agree upon one point—the wisdom of forming an anti-Semitic alliance, an alliance directed against the Jew.

"In all affairs," says Bossuet, "there is a something that prepares them, determines them, and leads them to success." The true science of history is to study the secret causes that have brought about great changes and the important conjunctures that made them occur.

From the Earliest Times to the Expulsion of the Jews in 1394

The Jews came into France shortly after the invasion of the Romans. In the fourth century, toward the year 353, they assassinated a Roman officer, who, after having governed Egypt, returned to Gaul by order of the Emperor Constantine. Among the Gauls, the Jews were no better received than they were in Rome. Nor were they better treated by the Visigoths. The council held in 465 forbade the Christians to associate with the Jews or to eat with them. Clotaire II withdrew from them the right to begin an action against the Christians, and in 633, Dagobert II expelled them from his States. They were always punished for their usurious dealings, but they always repeated the offence, and finally they became so rich that we find them in later years prominent even in political affairs. Charlemagne added a Jew to the embassy he sent to Haroun-al-Raschid. Their influence was so great that, not content with obtaining freedom of worship, they sought to pass a law that no business should be transacted on Saturday and demanded heavy import duties destined to crush their Christian competitors, while they were themselves arch smugglers, and the manufacturers of spurious goods which they palmed off as being imported. They were, furthermore, the associates of all the lowest elements of those times.

As today, their audacity in wrong doing made everybody dislike them. The Bishop of Lyons wrote a treatise entitled *The Insolence of the Jews*, which paper, were it to be done into English, would faithfully describe the life, and the low, vulgar, nauseating ways of the modern Jew, in the transaction of business.

Drawn toward the Orient by the attraction of race, the Jews unceasingly connived with the Saracens [Muslims], to whom they delivered Beziers, Narbonne, and Toulouse. Owing to this treason, each year on Easter Sunday, a Jew was chosen, three slaps were given him at the door of the cathedral, and a fine of thirteen pounds' worth of tapers was imposed upon him.

Their condition, however, gradually improved. In 1131, when Pope Innocent II went to France, the synagogue took part in the immense parade that passed before the Pontiff.

As long as the Jews abstained from ruining the country with their jobbery, their treason, and murder of Christian children, they were left as tranquil as the Christians of those times. They were as rich then as they are now, and owned one-half of the city of Paris.

A curious characteristic which denotes the incredible tenacity of the Jews, and the persistency with which oral tradition is transmitted by this people for whom centuries do not count, is their obstinacy in returning as masters to a place from which they have been expelled. The mills of Corded, which formerly belonged to the Jew Crescent, now belong to the Jew Erlanger. Nearly all the domains of the Isle of France, where the Jews used to live, belong now to the family of Camondo, to Ephrussi, and to Rothschild. The historian Jules Michelet says: "With all their rich possessions, the Jews of the Middle Ages lived as they formerly lived in the Orient. They never failed to torment the Gentiles. In times of epidemics and political ruin, they were in league with the vilest and lowest element of society."

Peter the Venerable, Abbe of Cluny, mentions the unheard-of crimes of the Jews, who profaned the churches, overthrew the altars, burned the crosses, whipped the priests, poisoned the monks, and forced them to take to themselves women by threats and torments.

The Jews committed still more dastardly crimes. The children, those candid and charming creatures in the souls of whom the purity of heaven is reflected, have always been the object of the Jews' hatred. Herod caused

them to be massacred. The Jews of the Middle Ages bled them and then crucified them. All the testimony, all the commemorative monuments raised to
celebrate a crime of which an entire city was a witness, all authentic documents, everything upon which true historic facts are founded, agree, and all
contemporaneous writers are unanimous in their testimony concerning the
assassination of Christian children by the Jews.

The peculiar faculty of the Jew of sucking dry the prosperity of a country, as soon as he is left alone, had assumed proportions beyond bearing.
Bitter complaints were heard on all sides. Philip-August, upon his ascending
the throne [in 1180], confiscated a part of the possessions of the Jews, and
cancelled all debts due to them. Napoleon was obliged to act in about the
same way. Every potentate who has the sense of right and justice in him,
every government, ought to act in a like manner. It would suffice to say to
them, "You have not acquired the millions you possess by work, but by deceit and lying. You have not created values; you have only possessed yourself of the values created by others. Make part restitution of the wealth you
have wrongfully acquired." No one would find fault that a Seligman, a Belmont, or a Rothschild, for instance, should be left with a yearly income of
half a million only.

St. Louis, "the king without fear," determined to ascertain for himself,
and carefully to examine into, the cause of the complaints and bitter animosity against the Jews. This great and good king, who had an inexhaustible love
for justice, sought to know why the Jews were the object of the hatred of all.
Upon the demand of Pope Gregory IX., whose attention was also called to
this fact, he caused the Talmud to be examined in a solemn assembly, over
which presided William d'Auvergne, and in which the rabbis were invited to
take part:

> It was in Paris, in the beginning of summer, 24 June, 1240,
> when this memorable council took place. The Court of St.
> Louis was presided over on that day by Queen Blanche. A few
> volumes, covered with strange characters, attracted the atten-
> tion of the curious, and it became known through Nicholas, a
> converted Jew, that the characters were Hebrew letters, and
> that the books were the Talmud. But soon a more interesting
> spectacle attracted the attention of the assembly. Four rabbis
> had just entered the room. They were Jechiel, of Paris; Judah,

son of David; Samuel, son of Solomon, and Moses, of Coucy, son of Jacob—the latter a famous orator known throughout France and Spain. They entered, sad and uneasy, into the palace of the king, while the assembled Jews scattered themselves about like a flock of sheep without a shepherd.

Every opportunity was given to the Jews to defend themselves, which they did with courage and ability. They, however, were forced to acknowledge that the Talmud contained precepts not only contrary to the good of Christian society, but of every civilized society. Passages were read which horrified the listeners. The book said that Jesus Christ was plunged into hell, into everboiling mud; that the Divine Son of the Holy Virgin was the fruit of adulterous intercourse with a soldier named Pantera, and that the ministers were no better than howling dogs. Other passages were read that increased the fear of the Jews and the indignation of the Christians:

- "It is right to kill the best of the Goy."
- "The word given to a Goy need not be kept."
- "Thrice every day, during their prayers, the Jews must hurl curses against the ministers of the church, the kings, and enemies of Judaism."

St. Louis displayed an extraordinary amount of moderation. As Jechiel was trembling with fear, one of the officers of the king said, "Jechiel, who thinks of doing any harm to the Jews?" The Talmud alone was condemned, and all the copies that could be found were cast into the flames.

In conformity with his paternal goodness and kindness, St. Louis took active measures against the Jews only when he was forced to do so to protect his subjects from these rapacious wolves. The Ordinance of 1254 forbids the Jews from practicing usury, from attacking or blaspheming the belief of the people among whom they live, and enjoins them to follow an honest living.

The Jews were now forced to walk carefully. The times threatened to be bad for them. Their literature shows the disturbed condition of their mind. To the light, airy verses, the suggestive and coarse songs of the period, now succeeded in plaintive elegies:

- "Alas, the daughter of Judah is clothed anew in mourning, because the shades of the evening have spread."

- "Hope in my goodness, oh, my dove! I shall praise as of old, my Tabernacle. I shall then prepare a lamp to David, my king; then shall I repress the ferocious beasts that have kept themselves in ambuscade, in order to devour thee, oh, my beautiful dove! whose voice is so agreeable."

Their schools were closed, but we must not forget that while the Jews for centuries wearied everybody with their complaints and misfortunes, as soon as they obtained a semblance of authority, they lost no time in closing the schools of others.

We must, however, render this justice to the Jews. They supported adversity in an admirable manner. During these persecutions, they stand forth almost unequalled in their heroism, patience, and abnegation. The mothers often threw their children into the flames through fear that they would be baptized.

On 26 May, 1288, on Good Friday, the Gentiles invaded the house of the rich Jew, Isaac Chatelain, arrested him and all his family. The prisoners offered to buy their liberty with gold, but it was not accepted. They were told that their lives would be spared on condition that they abjure Judaism. This they refused, and on Saturday, 21 April, 1288, the 5048th year of the Jewish era, the entire family, numbering thirteen, were cast into the flames. All faced death with intrepidity, singing the Schema and mutually encouraging one another. The wife of Isaac herself walked into the flames, followed by her husband and the rest of the family.

In order to appreciate fully this strength of character, we must go back to the times in which these scenes were enacted. Society was then absolutely religious. The Jew, by placing himself outside of this society, put himself not only beyond the law, but, to employ the expression of Hegel, "he cast himself outside of nature." What had the Jews to gain by struggling against so many united forces, when, since the fall of their temple, they had found their God deaf to all their prayers? Their energy, however, was marvelous; their courage in the face of death has never been equaled. Then, and then only, does the Jew become the personage that Michelet has painted in an incomparable page that has the life of a work by Rembrandt:

During the Middle Ages, he who knew where gold was to be found, the true alchemist, the true sorcerer, was the Jew, or the half Jew, the Lombard Jew. The Jew, everywhere thought to be an impure being, the Jew who could not touch a Christian woman without risking his life, the despised being upon whom everybody spat—it was to him that one had to apply in time of need. This prolific nation alone had what may be called the multiplying force; the force that engenders, that increases the sheep of Jacob, as well as the shekels of Shylock. During the Middle Ages, though persecuted, banished, recalled, the Jews were the middlemen, the men who stood between the royal treasury and the victims of the treasury; sucking the gold from below and rendering it to the king with an ugly grimace.

Something, however, always stuck to their fingers. They knew that they lived in constant danger, and yet in their hands was all the wealth of the country. Today they are free, and, despite the kicks they have received, they have reached their present enviable position...

Want, bitter want alone, forced the poor man to address himself to the Jew, to approach his dingy little house, to speak to the man who had crucified his children. When yonder poor man had spent his last resource, when his bed had been sold, when his wife and children slept upon the ground, trembling with fever, slowly, and with downcast head, he directed his steps toward the odious house of the Jew, and long stood before the door ere he knocked. The Jew opened with precaution the little window, and the following strange dialogue ensued: "What did the Christian say? 'In the name of God—The Jew killed this God of yours, did he? In the name of pity—Have the Christians ever shown pity or mercy to a Jew?' These are not the words wanted here. I must have a pledge." "What pledge could he offer who had nothing?" "My friend," said the Jew, "in conformity with the laws of the king, I can lend you nothing. No, this bloody garment and this bit of iron will not do. The law prevents me from advancing money upon such objects. But you can offer yourself as a pledge. I am not of your race. My right is not the right of a Christian. It is an old right. Your flesh will do for me. Blood for gold."

The Jews were more harshly treated by Philip the Handsome than by any of his predecessors. The edict of 1306 expelled them, and decreed the confiscation of their property. The Jews kept up their courage, and determined to be avenged.

It is an incontestable fact that the Jews entered into a compact with the King of Granada and the Sultan of Tunis, whereby they organized a conspiracy known as the "Lepers' League" [in 1321], composed only of persons stricken with leprosy. This was done with a view to poison the wells and public fountains, and in this way spread death, create one of those crises, one of those vague periods of uneasiness and of trouble, which have rendered possible the terrible upheaval of 1793 [the French Revolution], so profitable to Israel.

Proofs abound, and the existence of a general uprising of the leprous is attested by all contemporary authors, one of whom says:

> With our own eyes we saw a woman afflicted with leprosy, and who, fearing to be arrested, cast behind her a bundle of rags, which was immediately brought to court, and upon being opened, there was found in it the head of an adder, the claws of a toad, and something resembling the hair of woman, steeped in a dark and fetid liquor— a fearful thing both to see and to smell. The whole was thrown into a blazing fire, but as it did not burn, it was clear that it was a virulent poison.

Another writer says:

> There were many opinions, of which the most prevalent was, that the Moors of Granada, seeing themselves so often worsted, conceived the plan of avenging themselves, and entered into a plot with the Jews to destroy the Christians. But as the Jews were already suspected, they applied to the lepers, who were easily persuaded to form the said league. The Jews advised these miserable fellows that, as they were held in so despicable and degraded a condition, it would be well to compass the death of all Christians, or at any rate spread leprosy among them.

The historian Michelet also relates:

A well-known leper, seized with fear, confessed that a rich Jew gave him money, and also certain drugs composed of human blood, urine, and human flesh, called the body of Christ. All this was dried and battered down, and then a weight was attached to it, and the whole was thrown into the public fountains and wells.

Is it astonishing that the lepers were thus instigated by the Jews? Do we not see in this the habitual manner and method pursued by the Semite in his work of revenge? The lepers, the downtrodden people, the pariahs, the moujiks of Russia, are to the Jew only ready-found instruments that he arouses, agitates, deceives, and lets loose upon society, with fat promises and big words, and that he afterward abandons to their fate. Pay no attention to this singular mixture of urine and human blood, but suppose that the ingredients are petroleum, nitroglycerine, or dynamite, and you will be in the full tide of the modern movement—a movement headed by the Jews who preach the use of fulminating cotton [guncotton], or by those like the Jewess Jessa Heilmann, who in Russia preaches dynamite, or the Jew Johann Most, who, in America, preaches anarchy, and then conceals himself under a harlot's bed; all these dastardly crimes are the peculiar business of the Jew. Did not the Jew Mezzeroff, only the other day, here in New York, in a public lecture, advise bomb-throwing as the only means left to the Irish to obtain their rights from the English? And are not the greater part of the criminal anarchists in Chicago of the Jewish faith? The Aryan temperament does not adopt this method of revenge. The Aryan will thrust a knife into you, or kill you with a revolver, but he understands nothing of this peculiar chemistry. During the last Cretan insurrection [of 1897], the Jews threw poison into the wells around Chania, and many Greek volunteers died from the effects.

The hatred of the crucifix is a dominant sentiment of the Jew. King Jean the Good [John II, r. 1350] tried to win their loyalty by generous concessions. But the Jews continued in their evil doings, and in their unaccountable intrigues and jobbery. They began anew to ruin the country, and it is also positively asserted that they strangled Christian children on Good Friday. The people of those times, who were less patient than those of the present day, rose against them, the preachers denounced them from the pulpit, and in the course of time, the kings were compelled to adopt stringent laws against them.

Charles VI issued, on 17 September, 1394, a rigorous decree of banishment, and forbade them, under penalty of death, to remain in his kingdom. Two years were allowed the Jews to wind up their affairs, after which time they were obliged to quit France. This date of 1394 is one of the most important, not only as regards French history, but also as regards Christian civilization. Former kings exercised both mildness and severity toward the Jew. But now it has been proved that the Jew could not become acclimatized to the soil of France. The most diverse races—Celts, Gauls, Gallo-Romans, Germans, Franks, Normans—have been fused into that harmonious whole which forms the French nation of today. They smoothed down their differences, and have mutually tolerated one another's faults. The Jew alone was not able to enter into this amalgamation. The people therefore said to him, "My friend, we cannot get along together. Let us separate, and good luck to you."

This may be termed 'intolerance,' but it is intolerance only in the sense that science applies to the word when it says, "The subject cannot tolerate this matter." France could not tolerate the Jew, and accordingly expelled him. She will receive him back after many long years, but she will be sick of her bargain, which will inevitably cause her ruin.

Owing to the elimination of this vermin, France, which was still plunged into the horrors of war, attained, with an almost astonishing rapidity, a degree of almost incredible prosperity.[2] She again became the great European nation, and ruled with her arms, letters, arts, exquisite courtesy, taste, and with the charm of her benevolent, kind, and social nature. She became the arbiter, the model, the envy of the world. She counted among her sons famous generals, illustrious statesmen, incomparable writers. She met with triumphs and reverses, but her honor remained spotless. She was not exempt from vices, but her vices were not those which degrade; and when she rushed to arms, it was neither for the sake of the Mexicans nor for the Tunisians. At home, her people were, if not rich, at least happy, because the Jew was not there to bring havoc with his corruption, his fanaticism, and his parasitism. Beginning in 1394, the glorious time when the Jew was banished, France kept on the road of prosperity: in a word, she *ascended*. From the year 1789,

---

[2] A remarkable situation: banishing the Jew resulted in a cultural and political flowering in France, similar to what happened in England when the Jews were banished in 1290 by Edward I and in Germany in the 1930s when Hitler pushed them out. All this suggests that such a situation would likely recur in the modern nations today, should another banishment occur.

the ill-omened year when the Jew was received back, France moved unceasingly on the downward track.[3]

What became of the Jew from 1394 to 1789? Nobody knows. He disappeared, he vanished, he burrowed like the groundhog, or, like the hunted rabbit, changed his place of action, modified his plans, cooled his ardor. He seems to have plunged into the dreams of tradition, to have been absorbed in the study of the *Zohar* or of *Sefer Yetzirah*. He became an alchemist, a magician, and claimed to foretell the future by questioning the stars. The one thought which preoccupied him throughout this time was how to act. Both France and Spain had closed their doors against him. Spain, which the Jews surrendered to the Moors, expelled him [in 1492], and in a short time afterward the chivalrous Spaniards foot by foot reconquered the soil of their country, and being rid of the Jews, they were enabled to add glorious pages to their history, such as we find during the reign of Philip II [ca. 1550].

The Jews naturally considered Germany as their land of promise. Germany was, at that time, divided into a number of small principalities, hence the royal authority was less powerful than on the other side of the Rhine. But Germany hated the Jew as much as France did, and now and then did not hesitate to burn a few of them.

James Darmesteter says that the Jew was also occupied at that time in laying bare the vulnerable points of the Church, and that he brought to this task the formidable sagacity of the oppressed. He was the adviser of the unbeliever. All freethinkers, all whose minds were dissatisfied, diseased, came to seek him in their darkness. The Jew was at work in his great workshop of

---

[3] As Timayenis might have predicted, France would continue to decline in the 20th and 21st centuries. That nation suffered badly in World War One, even in victory, and continued to lose colonies and world influence through and after World War Two. The Jewish population there rose to 100,000 (0.2%) by 1914, and to 300,000 (0.7%) at the start of WW2. Today France is about 1% Jewish, with at least 600,000 Hebrews living there. France is also heavily populated by Black Africans, with that population rising from a few thousand in 1900 to nearly 100,000 by 1930, to over 5 million today, or about 10% of the nation. Further decline resulted from Muslims, who numbered under 100,000 in 1950 but today constitute some 10% of the French population, or about 6.5 million people.

After being crushed by Germany in 1940, France continued its political and cultural decline, and today is mired in social and political problems—its only remaining influence due to a UN Security Council veto privilege and a small nuclear arsenal. Between Jews, blacks, and Muslims, France is a sociological disaster; further decline is inevitable.

blasphemy. It was he who forged the poisonous and corrupt arms of irony—shafts which he bequeathed to sceptics and libertines, and the sarcasm of Voltaire may be considered as the last expiring echo of his work.

Protestantism served as a stepping-stone to the Jews to regain a foothold in society. In 1520, the very year when Luther burned the Bull of the Pope at Wittenberg, the first edition of the Talmud was printed in Vienna. Luther, however, was far from being the friend of the Jews. He was crueler toward them than any Catholic priest has ever thought of being:

> To ashes, to ashes with all the synagogues, and all the houses of the Jews. Let them be all packed into stables, let all their treasures and goods be taken away from them, and let them be used for the maintenance of converts. Let the Jews and the robust Jewesses be forced, to the severest labor. Let their books of prayer be taken away from them, and be it forbidden them under penalty of death to ever pronounce the word of God. Let there be no mercy or pity shown to the Jews. Let our princes drive them out of their provinces. Let the ministers inculcate into the minds of their hearers hatred of the Jew. Had I authority over the Jews, I would call together the most learned and the richest of them, and would threaten to have their tongue cut to the very roots, in order to prove to them that the Christian doctrine does not teach one God only, but a God in three persons.

These were the words of Luther, the apostle of Protestantism.[4]

Protestantism, however, was profitable to the Jew. It gave him the opportunity to enfranchise himself, and permitted him to remain in Germany, where he again exercised his usurious nature, from which the Church, with a maternal solicitude, during many a century protected the Aryan.

The picture of that epoch of transition is curious to study on account of its analogy with the movement that takes place today. People then lost the taste for work. They sought enterprises which promised large returns for as little work as possible. The number of drinking places increased to an alarming extent. Farmers became poor, and were forced to sell their products at any price. Corporations were impoverished; in fact, the whole population

---

[4] See Luther's *On the Jews and Their Lies* (2025; Clemens & Blair).

stood face to face with ruin. The greater part of the people threw themselves into the fever of speculation, and, as it always happens, the majority were ruined, while a small proportion only became wealthy.

In the meantime, the Jews were constantly conniving among themselves and casting longing eyes toward France. But the times were not as yet propitious for Israel. Louis XII imposed upon the countries newly-acquired by France the same decree of expulsion as was promulgated by Charles VI, which act of his won for him the surname of Father of the People.

A few Jews expelled from Spain succeeded in finding at that time a domicile at Bordeaux. But with what great precaution they had to act! What a number of disguises they had to assume! It is to the credit, however, of this colony, to say that they repaid their hospitality to France by giving to the world Montaigne, and it is a fact that for at least 150 years, they abstained from exercising their faith in any form whatever. The letters-patent granted by Henry II authorizing their sojourn were delivered not to the Jews but to new Christians.

Another band tried to enter France by another way, and in 1615 it was found necessary to enforce anew the edict of expulsion, which, however, was not strictly carried out, as the Jews, during the minority of Louis XIII, had come into France in considerable numbers. They had a powerful protector at court, one Concino Concini, who was surrounded by a great number of Jews, and who was engaged in many an act of corruption, wrongdoing, and deceit. The history of that man reminds us of the life of Gambetta, who may be considered as a second incarnation of Concini. Fortunately, France in those days had men who considered a hostile citizen more dangerous than a foreign foe. A simple captain named De Vitry, sword in hand, and attended by three soldiers only, stood on a bridge and there hindered the passage of Concini, the insolent adventurer, who was advancing, followed by a numerous escort, resembling a regiment. "Halt, there!" cried De Vitry. "Who dares speak thus to me?" said Concini, and, as the presumptuous foreigner accompanied his words with a significant gesture, De Vitry took careful aim and pierced his brain with a pistol shot. Upon this, he entered the palace of the king, and said, "It is done." "Much obliged to you, my cousin," replied Louis XIII to the humble captain whose courage alone had just made him a relative of the king. "You are a marshal and a duke, and I am happy to be the first to salute you with your new title."

Heroism today, however, does not enter into our relations with the Jews, who are permitted to undertake everything, and slowly but surely to undermine the foundations of our prosperity. Scarcely was Concini killed when the order was strictly enforced for the Jews to disappear. The only Jew who remained in France was Lopez, who claimed that he was a Portuguese and formerly belonged to the Mohammedan faith. The poor fellow ate pork to such an extent every day that he fell sick, but he succeeded in allaying all suspicions regarding his nationality. He was a dealer in bric-a-brac, then in diamonds, then a banker, later an ambassador, and finally counsellor of state. He was at once a Proust and a Bischoffsheim.

Henry IV saw in Lopez an excellent instrument with which to create trouble in the home affairs of Spain. The death of the King put an end to this plan, but Lopez was not discouraged, and returned to the business of a diamond broker, in which he acquired such skill that uncut diamonds were sent to him from every part of Europe, which he ground in a manner not before known.

Richelieu, whose genius reminds us of that of Bismarck, employed Lopez as a spy, and entrusted him with an important mission to the government of Holland. The nature of the Jew both in prosperity and adversity remains unchanged; his instincts are always the same. If a Jew were crowned king, he would find some means to sell the jewels of the crown. Lopez did not neglect the furtherance of his private ends during his extraordinary mission, and on his return to Paris announced a sale of bric-a-brac which was more loudly advertised than the one by Sarah Bernhardt. He bought in Holland a thousand different curios, said to have come from India, and their sale brought him fabulous wealth.

For a Jew, however, Lopez was an honest man. He was accused of being a spy of two governments, but it was shown that he served only one, which fact alone may well raise a doubt in the mind of the reader as to his being a veritable Jew. He displayed his wealth with the bad taste so common among his people. He had a beautiful house, of which he constantly boasted. But what is there astonishing in this? Baron Hirsch, the well-known Jew banker, in the course of a dinner, said to his guest at the time when strawberries were served, in the month of January: "Do not hesitate to eat as many as you like. The cost is dear, but I do not mind it." This same Jew said to Lavisse, Professor of History at the Sorbonne, who was engaged to give private lessons to his son: "Pray smoke this cigar. It is true that you cannot afford to smoke as good at home, for it cost me fifteen cents." Lopez died in

Paris in 1649, and was buried according to the rites of the Catholic faith—a faith which he ostensibly exercised during his residence in Paris.

By carefully concealing their origin, the Jews ceased to be regarded as the pariahs—that degraded class in India of whom we are told that, before a native exchanges a word with one, he places his hand before his mouth. Holland offered to the Jews an asylum, and there we find them in great numbers.

Alone of all races, the Jew can exist in every climate, but at the same time he cannot exist without doing injury to others as well as to himself. With his love for wrong-doing and intrigue, his mania for unceasingly attacking the religion of Christ, the Jew is exposed to certain temptations to which he is always the victim. This, in part, explains the continual persecutions of which he has always been the object. As soon as he enters into relations with the Germans, noted for their love of the abstract; or with the French, so fond of change; or with the Slavs, so given to dreaming, he cannot restrain himself. He invents socialism, internationalism, or nihilism. He hurls upon the society that has received him revolutionary doctrines, and finally all join in driving him away.

It is remarkable, however, that the Jew has been powerless to make much of an impression on either the English or the Dutch. He perceives by instinct, through his long proboscis, that it would be useless to attempt anything against these two peoples, so wedded to their own customs, so firm in their traditions, so attentive to their interests. He contents himself with proposing certain affairs, which are minutely discussed by the natives, and only entered into when they are good; but he abstains from relating fabulous stories, and does not create either a loan or a commune.

Holland, which is a matter-of-fact country, averse to that chivalrous ideal which is also so antipathetical to the sons of Jacob, was the cradle of the modern Jew. For the first time in his existence, the Jew found there not the splendid success which intoxicates and destroys him, but the calm of long duration, the regular and normal life.

It is Rembrandt whom we must contemplate, study, scrutinize, ransack, analyze, before we clearly understand the Dutch Jew. Throughout his life, Rembrandt lived constantly with Israel. His studio, replete with countless bric-a-brac and objects of art, was a veritable storehouse, resembling the shops where second-hand goods are sold. The eye, on entering his place, for a moment remained bewildered, but from the extreme end a sordid old man, with a hooked nose, slowly arose. It was Rembrandt himself. His work is of

Jew color, yellow, of that earnest, fervid and warm yellow which looks like the reflection of gold laid upon an old rowel of the Middle Ages, forgotten in a corner. How life-like are the Jews painted by Rembrandt! They seem constantly talking of affairs as they emerge from a synagogue, ever occupied in discussing the value of a florin, or of the last consignments received from Batavia. They wind their way, stick in hand, with the air of a wandering Jew, who feels as if he had reached a spot where he can for a moment rest.

Owing to the, relatively speaking, quiet life which the Jews led in Holland, their condition seems to have improved. In England, Cromwell was the jealous protector of the Jews. It was he who lifted the decree of banishment that weighed upon them. Meantime the Jews were tolerated in Metz and Strasbourg, which proves that there is no victory without its inconveniences, for the conquest of Alsace brought into France a considerable number of Jews, whom the country could well have afforded to do without. About that time, the French authorities insisted that the old usages affecting the Jews should be relaxed, because many of them were employed as military contractors. This change benefited the Jews, whose numbers now amounted to upward of 20,000, and who possessed property estimated at from four to five million of our money.

Louis XII had extended to the territory of Provence the ordinance that expelled the Jews from France, but many among them followed the advice given them by their co-religionists in foreign lands, and pretended to be converted to the Christian faith. In Avignon, which was at that time a Popish district, the Jews of France had found almost complete liberty and comparative security. Avignon, during the Middle Ages, may be called the Paradise of the Jews. From time to time, of course, popular uprisings took place against them, owing to their cruel usury, but the Pope always intervened to appease the people.

In Avignon, as elsewhere, the Jews did not scruple to commit acts of dishonesty and scurrility toward the Christians. For a long time, there could be seen at the entrance of the Church of St. Peter a holy water font, which recalled one of their offensive acts. This font was entitled "The Font of the Beautiful Jewess." A Jewess of rare beauty had penetrated into the church on an Easter Sunday, and spat upon the holy water. For this act of hers, she was publicly scourged, and a commemorative inscription recalled both the sacrilegious act and the punishment imposed.

The Jewish colony at Bordeaux prospered to a remarkable degree. As to Spain, after the defeat of the Moors, the people of that country followed the example of France, and eliminated from their bosom the elements that were the cause of continual trouble. On 30 March 1492, King Ferdinand of Aragon and Queen Isabella of Castile, upon the advice of the illustrious Ximenas, issued a decree which ordered all Israelites to leave the country. The years following their expulsion may be considered the most glorious in Spanish history.

A few Jewish families, thereupon, sought refuge in Portugal. There they found a precarious existence, and shortly afterward they were again expelled, and Montaigne, whose parents were among those persecuted, related the heart-rending circumstances of this new exodus in a chapter that aroused more feeling than any other page of the sceptic.

Montaigne and Dumas, both of whom are of Jewish extraction on their mother's side, are the only two French writers really worthy of being called writers that the race of Israel has given us, both of whom, however, are impregnated with Christian blood. Without seeking to establish a comparison between the two, which would be strained—between the laughing and light mockery of the one, and the bitter repartee of the second—it may be affirmed that both have been destroyers, both have put in relief the vices and weaknesses of humanity, without proposing any loftier aim for man to strive for. Both were gigglers, and morose at the same time; both void of illusions and destroyers of the illusions of others.

No writer has ever been more occupied with religious questions than Dumas. None has ever penetrated more deeply into the depths of the human heart. Had his robust and virile intelligence been enlightened by the truth, he would have rendered immense services to the world. He himself seems to have had the feeling of what he was losing and of the harm he caused to others by his unbelief. He never lent his ears to any proposals, vile temptations, or to a desire of being on good terms with the so-called freethinkers, of whom he often spoke with scorn, but he was unable to take the one decisive step. He was born blind, and he remained blind to the end of his days. Vain were his efforts to escape from the fatality of the race.

We have already stated that the Portuguese Jews have never been able to enter France as Jews, but as new Christians. "It is impossible" says a document written in 1767, "to conceive of a plan formulated with greater skill and cunning, than the one for the establishment of the Jews at Bordeaux.

That lie of being new Christians was well-calculated to please his Christian majesty."

It is true that these Portuguese Jews always protested with energy whenever they were spoken of as Jews. In the year 1614, fearful that active measures would be adopted against them, they addressed a petition to the king, stating: "For many years we have been living at Bordeaux, and, owing to the bitter jealousy of which we are the innocent cause on account of our prosperity, we are accused of being Jews, when in truth we are good Christians and Catholics." They scrupulously adhered to all the outward practices of the Catholic faith. Their births, marriages, deaths were inscribed in the register of the church. Their contracts were preceded by the words, "In the name of the Father, the Son, and the Holy Ghost."

After having lived in this manner for nearly 150 years, the Jews remained as faithful to their belief as on the day when they first set foot in France. As circumstances favored, by degrees, they more openly returned to Judaism, had their children baptized in their faith, and old marriages were celebrated anew according to their own rite. A large number of Jews also, whose families had for two centuries officially practiced Catholicism in Spain, crossed the frontier, in 1686, and came to Bordeaux to be circumcised, and remarried according to the Jewish faith. The persistency, the stubborn vitality of Judaism, which nothing ever impairs, over which centuries glide without making any impression, and which maintains itself in all its entirety from father to son in the intimacy of the home circle, is certainly a most curious phenomenon for an observer.

In 1839 an English Jew wished to communicate with his co-religionists in Spain, and after a great deal of trouble, obtained a letter of introduction to a few Jews in that country. He arrived at the house of a Jew in a certain city in Spain, the name of which he discreetly does not mention. On entering the parlor, he found it full of statuettes of saints, silver crosses, and other sacred images. He made himself known, but his host, after welcoming him, begged him to say not a word that might compromise him, because the people of the country believed him to be a zealous Catholic, and both his own son and daughter were ignorant of the fact that he was a Jew.

At midnight, the chief of the family and his visitor descended into a subterranean passage. There they met a small society of Jews, the existence of which no one suspected. The well-known lamp was suspended from the ceiling. Toward the East stood a box covered with black velvet, containing the rolls of the Pentateuch, and a copy of the Prophets, while upon a table of bronze were engraved the Ten Commandments. Side by side with the box was a Jew calendar, containing a list of the illustrious men among the Jews who, without being known as such, had played an important part in the affairs of Spain. In the center, upon a table covered with a piece of black marble, were the prayerbooks of the Jews.

There was only one tomb in this whole place. Obliged to bear the humiliation of being buried in a Catholic cemetery, and to endure the prayers of the priest, the Jews succeeded in having the body of their rabbi escape this profanation, and had it buried there. At the death of each member of the community, the Jews deposited a small piece of stone near the venerated tomb.

Both the stranger and the Spaniard conversed a long time in this sanctuary of their common hopes, and then through a small hole they noticed the day about to break, and the hour for morning prayers close at hand. "We must not quit the synagogue without having raised our hearts toward the God of our fathers," said the Spaniard. The bell of a neighboring convent struck its silvery and clear notes. A light movement was heard in the house above. It was the young girl who hastened to church to be present at the first mass.

Ten years later, the same traveler returned to Spain. But instead of the humble house of his co-religionist, he found in its place an imposing palace. They sat at the table, and a prayer was offered in a loud voice. The young girl was now openly a Jewess.

The Jews have now taken almost exclusive possession of Spain. This explains the reason why Spain withers from the effects of incessant revolutions.

Among the numberless foreign Jews who wormed their way into France in 1789, a great many installed themselves without beating of drums or sound of trumpets, and lived the life of ordinary mortals. But when occasion presented itself, the old hatred against Christianity, which had remained dormant among their fathers, was rekindled among the sons, who are falsely taken to be freethinkers, but who have never failed to break down the doors of sanctuaries and otherwise injure our institutions.

A document of 1733 affirms: "The Jews employed good-looking country girls for servants, whose honor they violated in order to use them for nurses to their own children, while the babes born of the girls were sent away as foundlings." The Goy, the son or daughter of the Goyim…everything is created to enrich and amuse the Jew.

Bordeaux was, however, a very narrow territory for the Jews. It was Paris that they coveted and where their ambition centered. In 1767 they tried to take advantage of a decree permitting foreigners to join the great body of native tradesmen. The merchants of Paris, one and all, energetically protested against the admission of Jews. They protested vehemently against the equality sought to be established between Jews and foreigners. The foreigner is open to ideas common to all civilized people; the Jew belongs to no class of civilized beings; he is a pilferer.

The petition of the merchants was couched in the following terms:

> The admission of this people into a well-organized, law-abiding society threatens to be dangerous. The Jews can well be compared to wasps who introduce themselves into hives in order to kill the bees, and then open their stomachs and suck the honey from their entrails. It is utterly impossible to attribute to the Jews qualities befitting a law-abiding citizen, for they are nowhere reared in the principles of what may be termed legitimate authority. They believe every government to be an usurpation of their rights. They consider all values as being rightfully theirs, and the subjects of all countries as having robbed them of their possessions. There is a peculiar philosophy current in our day, which seeks to justify the Jews by reason of the trials they have undergone, trials imposed upon them by the Christian sovereigns of Europe. We must either regard the Jews as guilty, or reproach the sovereigns, perhaps the predecessors of your majesty, for a cruelty belonging to the most barbarous centuries.

The merchants of the eighteenth century were less stupid than those of the present day, who allow themselves to be driven from their homes, to make room for thieves who never cease to plot and rob those who foolishly permit the Jew to be established among them.

This celebrated document of the merchants seems, as it were, the last will of the old type of merchant, so upright, so conscientious, so foreign to all the ways of shameful effrontery always employed by the Jews in the transaction of business, and which made every city in Europe to be looked upon by the tourist as a true den of brigands.

All strangers who visit Paris are bored to death by the Jews. They run about like particles of quicksilver. They are on the lookout, like a hunter for his prey. They disappear and, quick as thought, they reappear to meet in some frequented thoroughfare.

The document further stated:

> Fortunes are rarely made rapidly in commerce, when practiced in good faith, as it ought to be. The Jews in a short space of time amass enormous fortunes. Can it be that they arrive so rapidly to a high degree of prosperity by extraordinary business capacity? The Jews cannot boast of having in any way benefited the countries where they have been tolerated. All work demanding constant and laborious application is shunned by them. But to profit by the discoveries of others, to counterfeit the productions of their competitors, to exercise every sort of usury, to receive stolen goods, to buy from everybody, even from a thief or an assassin, to introduce into a country forbidden goods, to offer to unhappy debtors resources that bring about their ruin, to engage in every low act of corruption and extortion, are the means constantly resorted to by the Jews, to further their worldly interests.
>
> To allow a single Jew to be established in a city would be to leave the door open to the whole race; would be to array against every merchant the forces of a powerful corporation that would not fail to crush the business of every firm and consequently of the entire city. The most vigorous laws that could be enacted, the combined vigilance of magistrates and of the police, nothing, in fact, would be able to prevent the exercise of their cupidity and of their rapacity.

The document ends with these words: "It was once asked of a philosopher whence he came? He answered that he was a cosmopolitan, that is to say, a citizen of the world. Another said: 'I prefer my family to myself, my country to my family, the world to my country.' Let the defenders of the Jews make no mistake. The Jews are not cosmopolitans. They are citizens of no country. They prefer themselves to all the rest of mankind, they are the enemies of man, whom they aim to enslave."

This document made a deep impression, and on 7 February 1777, the Jews were refused admission into Paris. The Jews engaged one Lacretelle to defend them, but they chose a singular defender, for their advocate thus wrote about them:

> The Jews, who are accustomed to the scorn of everybody, make their way in the world by adopting only the most base and corrupt methods. A Jew never hesitates to sacrifice his reputation if he can by so doing acquire even the smallest sum of money. His whole art consists of the art of cheating. Usury is his arm. It is a monster that in silence and in darkness disguises itself in a thousand forms; continually calculating the hours, the minutes that increase his gains...

Finally, toward the end of the eighteenth century, the Jews after persistent efforts succeeded in worming their way into Paris, where, however, their existence was very precarious. They were obliged every month to have their permits to remain renewed, or their departure could be demanded at once. A single incident will suffice to give an idea of their miserable existence: They were not allowed to have a cemetery of their own. They interred their dead in the back yard of a miserable inn, in a spot called La Villette, and paid the innkeeper fifty francs for permission to inter the body of every distinguished Jew. The proprietor pitilessly exploited these pariahs, insulted them in their dearest beliefs, had oxen and horses killed and skinned on the ground he allowed for their burial, mixed the flesh and bones of the animals with their dead bodies, troubled them in their funeral ceremonies, and finally threatened no longer to receive their dead.

What a contrast between that time and the present! Behold these miserable men who furtively wormed their way into an obscure corner, without a place to weep or to offer the last prayer of the widow and of the orphan! ... "Oh, Eternal Rock of the world, God who livest and. forever existest, Thou who art full of pity, Thou who pardonest the offences and effacest the iniquities, I implore Thee for the soul of him who has just died." Behold them today! They are the financial despots of every city through the streets of which they glide like shadows. They own palaces, they rule the Goy.

This burial-ground of bygone days still exists in Paris, in Rue de Flandre, No. 44. In the backyard, which looks like a farmyard, hens, turkeys, and geese wade in a pool of murky water. The people living in this neighborhood do not know even of the existence of the cemetery. No spot is more suitable for meditation. The black wall around it crumbles piece by piece. The grass grows dry and thin in this sterile enclosure, in which here and there a few scrawny trees cast their shadows. The humidity has eaten into the tomb-stones covered with Hebraic characters and has rendered most of the inscriptions illegible. The place is now used as a receptacle for garbage, and in the corners are heaps of empty bottles and bits of old iron. Amid the scanty verdure, a few inscriptions are still to be seen. "Here reposes the well-beloved Judith Delvallee Silveyra, thirty-six years old, born at Pantin, near Paris, on the 9th of Tristry, 5563rd year of the creation of the world."

One is moved almost to pity to think of those clan-destine funerals of bygone days. True, the Jews have also been insulting to our dead the moment they in their turn were masters; still one is moved, and involuntarily takes a keen interest in their efforts to obtain a tomb in that France that in later years was destined to be theirs. Not till 31 March 1785, were the Jews permitted to buy at Montrouge a piece of ground to receive their dead. It continued to be their cemetery until the year 1804.

Louis XVI sought to improve the condition of the Jews, and the following interesting anecdote is related:

> One day in the year 1787, Louis XVI, happy, smiling and in good humor, went hunting, surrounded with all the splendid pomp which accompanied even to the chase the ruler of the most beautiful kingdom upon the earth.
>
> Suddenly, in the environs of Versailles, a place which to this day awakens in one's mind an idea of greatness and of melancholy majesty akin to the impression of the setting sun, the king saw four old men of strange appearance carrying a coffin covered with a rough piece of cloth. A small number of people of Oriental type, hooked nose and humble mien, followed. Upon the order of the king, the captain of the guards accosted the funeral train, and informed his majesty that they were Jews transporting the body of one of their co-religionists to the cemetery at Montrouge...
>
> Pity took possession of the honest heart of the king who, although of a weak nature, was never known to commit a

wicked or cruel act. The remembrance of those poor Jews
whom he met on his way haunted him in his palace where he
ruled in the splendor of his power. He summoned his Prime
Minister and won him over to his generous ideas. A commission was nominated with authority to devise means to better
the condition of the Jews, and a number of prominent Israelites were invited to assist the commission in their work.

This king, who busied himself with the misfortunes of
others, had already been doomed by his implacable enemies,
the revolutionists, to the scaffold, and his body—the body of
the Christian king who first of all kings interested himself in the
Jews, was mutilated, and was delivered to the Jews without
even being covered with a piece of rough cloth, and by them it
was cast into a ditch full of burning lime in Anjou Street.

Did the Jews of those times feel any sorrow at the fate of their friend, the
unfortunate monarch? The Jew newspapers contained only brutal allusions,
and in recent years during the anniversary of the execution of the King, the
paper *La Lanterne* of the Jew Mayer, and *La Nation* of the Jew Dreyfus,
announced that "the happy event" will be celebrated with concerts and other
amusements.

During those times, the Jew, though admitted nowhere, was to be found
everywhere. The strength of the Jew then was his apparent weakness, just as
his weakness today is his apparent strength, so cynically displayed—a seemingly colossal strength, but which rests upon no solid foundation, for a few
clicks of the telegraph will any day suffice to confiscate his unrighteously
acquired riches.

Marie-Therese was the implacable enemy of the Jews. She renewed
against them the laws of former years. She compelled them to wear a long
beard and to have a small piece of yellow cloth sewed upon the right arm of
their coat sleeve. On 22 December 1744, the following royal edict was
promulgated at Prague and throughout the kingdom of Bohemia:

1st. For various reasons, I have decided no longer to tolerate
the Jews in my Kingdom of Bohemia. I therefore demand that
on the last day of January, 1745, all Jews depart from the city

of Prague, and if any shall be found, the soldiery are hereby commanded to drive them hence.

2nd. That ample time, however, may be given them to arrange their affairs and to dispose of their effects, a month will be granted during which they may remain in my kingdom.

3rd. At the expiration of the above time, all Jews must quit the Kingdom of Bohemia.

How powerful the Jews were at that time, and with how great a force they exercised their authority—which since the foundation of the *Alliance Israelite Universelie* manifests itself daily with constantly increasing freedom and insolence—is evidenced by the earnestness with which certain kingdoms in Europe intervened in their behalf. Baron Van Barmenie, the ambassador of Holland, was requested to defend their cause. The English plenipotentiary, Thomas Robinson, addressed also a note to Marie-Therese. They succeeded, however, only in obtaining a postponement of the decree of banishment to the end of March. On that day 28,000 Israelites had to quit Bohemia.

Efforts to revoke the edict were renewed, and owing to new and repeated representations and remonstrances entered into at the same time by Poland, Denmark, and Sweden, the Jews finally succeeded in their efforts and were allowed to remain in Bohemia. The Jews in Holland and Belgium struck a medallion to commemorate the joyful event.

As soon as a favorable opportunity presented itself, the Jews pitilessly avenged themselves upon Marie-Antoinette for the rebuffs and heavy taxation imposed upon them by Marie-Therese.

Never since the Crucifixion has severer torture been inflicted on a human being than was inflicted on Antoinette by the revolutionists, goaded on by the Jews, who always spoke of her as the Austrian.

Soon after the abolition of the decree against the Jews in Bohemia, another decree appeared in France permitting the Jews to re-enter France. The Jew was in France! This news circulated from city to city, everywhere reawakening hope, even in the most distant ghettos, and giving cause for thanksgiving in all the temples and synagogues. On 21 October 1793, a Hebrew song was sung in the synagogue of Metz, to the air of the Marseillaise, proclaiming the triumph of Israel.

The ancient Cabala was finished; the new Cabala began. The Jew was no longer the accursed sorcerer whom Michelet depicted performing his witchcraft in the shades of night. He had transformed himself. He could now operate in the full light of day. The pen of the Hungarian Jew journalist replaced the wand of the magician. The magical mirror was broken. To the fanatical apparitions of former years, illusions of a peculiarly strange nature succeeded—illusions unceasingly feeding the poor dupes with the deceptive image of a happiness that constantly flees.

Why should anyone blame Shylock, who asked for only a pound of human flesh? The Jew of today does not care for a pound of Christian flesh. He wants the entire body, aye, he wants the bodies of hundreds of thousands of Gentiles who rot upon battlefields fought solely to benefit Israel.[5]

What are a few ducats? It is millions that henceforth the Goy is going to sweat. The Jews now handle gold by the shovelful. They found banks, institutions of credit, invite subscriptions to loans of all sorts, national loans, foreign loans, loans of war, loans of peace, loans of Europe, Asia, Turkey, Mexico, Russia, Honduras, Columbia, etc.

This transformation is complete, and this time the magical charm has entirely succeeded. By a singular hallucination, this serf, this pariah, in a word, the Jew, who has been more of a slave than were the beasts of burden of Pharaoh, considers himself today the most free, the most enviable, and cleverest of men. The outcasts of old are now our Rothschilds, our Seligmans, our Hausemans, our Wormsers, our Oppenheims, our Nathans, our Henriques, our Schenks, our De Cordovas, etc.!

What has this transformation cost? Formerly an American, an Englishman, or a Frenchman, whether a laborer in the fields or in the cities, was happy and peaceful as long as his associates were of the same race, as long as there were no Jews around. At eventide, the peasants danced, accompanied by their bagpipes; mechanics had their fraternal corporations and meetings in which feeling allusions were made to the memory of a dead companion. Look now at the workman of our large cities. He listens to the Jew, who like the serpent of old advises him to revolt against the existing state of affairs. He bends like the Jews of the pyramids over his work. He has become a

---

[5] A remarkable anticipation of World Wars One and Two, the Vietnam War, both Iraq wars, the US-Afghan War, the "war on terror," and ongoing conflicts with Iran and Russia—all fought by Gentiles, to the benefit of Jews or Israel.

slave, very like the slave of ancient times, who, according to Aristotle, was but a living machine.[6]

Is it necessary to arouse this human machine? Is it necessary that these victims whom the Jews have taught that there is no heaven, should free themselves, if but for a moment, from the frightful reality that weighs them down? The Jew offers them burning alcohol. Instead of innocent beverages, the Jew offers adulterated mixtures, mixtures which give the victims the delirium tremens at the end of a few years, but for a time galvanize the dormant organization.

The Jews During the French Revolution and the First Empire

The Jew during the Revolution was constantly on the move. He planned and connived in order to exert a powerful influence in a society, the framework of which was, as it were, now in ruins. The occasion was favorable. The scaffold had been erected that took off the heads of many of the most honest and the most intelligent men of that eventful period. The Jew had no longer to fear the vigilance of which he was the object in that old society where young and old knew one another from having prayed together in the same church, and were besides held together by a thousand traditional ties.

From its very beginning, the Revolution had—like the present Republic of France, which the Jews have organized—the character of an invasion. The native French element had disappeared, like today, from the Republic, and the Jews seized upon the important positions and terrorized the country, as they do today. "All the turbulent elements," says Henri Forneron, "all the outlaws, had centered in France." Switzerland, for example, sent Marat, Hulin, Claviere, all leaders of murderous bands. These outlaws were welcomed, like brothers, by the Jews in Paris, who now claimed to direct the destinies of France and of mankind.

Who has not heard of Jean-Paul Marat? The counterfeit of his repulsive figure is to be seen in Madame Tussaud's establishment in London. Marat, who was afflicted with leprosy, a disease peculiarly Jewish, had for adviser and inseparable companion the notorious Jew, Pereyra. The true name of Marat was Mara. The family was expelled from Spain. They went first to Sardinia and thence to Switzerland, where, being unable to openly practice

---

[6] *Politics*, I.4.

Judaism, they embraced Protestantism. Marat was, by birth and instinct, a true son of Judah, and a prominent figure in doing the work of the guillotine. The nature of Marat could not deceive the careful observer. It was the Jews' neurosis. No Gentile would advocate in London, Berlin, and St. Petersburg, as Marat did, the killing of 200,000 people without distinction of age or sex. No Gentile would dare advise it. The Jew alone dares to counsel it and to do it.

This unique audacity, this unparalleled impudence which we meet with in all the enterprises of the Jews, comes of the venom instilled centuries ago into their blood. The religion that teaches the Jews that they are superior to all other men, that they must annihilate everything foreign to them, and that everything upon the Earth belongs to them, is the source of the delirious conceptions peculiar to the race. It is the basis of their theories and the cause of their seemingly incomprehensible aberrations.[7]

The common phrase, "the revolting Marat" does not half express the idea sought to be conveyed. No doubt his mouth—in which the lips were hardly discernible, being contracted as if by lockjaw—was ferocious, but his eyes were beautiful. True, they sparkle with fury in the Marat of Tussaud, but they are mild and soft in the pictures painted by Boze and Madame Alais. Examine carefully at the Musee Carnavlet the bust of Marat, and you will perceive the pure type of the Jew, a hallucinator, a victim of neuropathy. You will discover, as in the case of Robespierre, of Guiteau, the assassin, whose ancestors were French Jews, and of many other actors of like tragic scenes, the lack of symmetry in the two sides of the face that betrays the maniac.

The wax figure taken almost immediately after the fatal wound inflicted upon Marat by Charlotte Corday, which figure is to be seen in Madame Tussaud's *Musee*, gives the same impression. Here we have the hand with its tapering fingers, a hand not of a murderer who strikes from instinct, but of a methodical scoundrel, of one who acts from theory and cold deliberation. Death has spread suddenly upon the face the domineering nature, the basis of the Jew's temperament, moroseness mingled with sadness.

No doubt there were other persons besides the Jews who at that time denounced and sent many a good man to the scaffold. But if a patient research were to be made among the official archives of the period, if one would inquire into the time certain persons and families entered France, the

---

[7] The combination of misanthropy and of a God-given right to rule the world results in a uniquely pernicious Jewish supremacism that persists to this day. All these elements are documented in the Old Testament and the Talmud.

Jew would occupy a prominent place, and a hereditary hatred for Christianity would be traced to families of pure Semitic origin.

The first act of the Jews, who were now anxious to prove themselves worthy of their emancipation, was to steal the crown jewels. The sight of these treasures, patiently accumulated during generations, and which consisted of royal crowns, cups offered by Suger, jewels given by Richelieu, magnificent and glorious souvenirs, divided hastily on the bank of the Seine, secreted underground or thrown into a pool of water, dragged into the vilest resorts, concealed in tatters, is the very image of the brilliant past of the unfortunate France, now delivered to a horde of Jews. The theft of the crown jewels nourished for a long time the commerce of the German Jews.

The bulletin of the criminal tribunal of those times says: "One of the first persons found guilty of the theft of the crown jewels was a Jew named Louis Lyre, a native of London, twenty-eight years old, ostensibly a merchant. ... He was found guilty of having participated in the robberies committed during the nights of the 11th, 13th, and 15th of September, and to have sold in the course of the same month to a certain Moyse Trenel pearls and diamonds, his share of the theft. He made a will on 13 October 1792, and at half-past ten in the evening of the same day, he suffered death, displaying a courage and a coolness worthy of a better cause." Another Jew, Delcampo, alias Deschamps, was also executed.

All the Jews in Paris were implicated in the robbery of the crown jewels. "The crown jewels," says Drumont, "have never been in luck either with the Republicans or the Jews. The first Republic allowed them to be stolen. Under the present Republic, the Jew Lockroy entered into an agreement with certain gentlemen with hooked noses who congregate in the basement of the cafe 'De Suede,' to pass a law authorizing the sale of all these souvenirs of bygone glory."

It was the Jews also who at that time organized the systematic pillaging of the churches and the destruction of all the masterpieces inspired by faith and executed by genius. Those stormy years were admirably suited for the Jew to satisfy both his hatred and his cupidity. The silver of the churches passed into his rapacious hands. The public treasury received no benefit whatever from his wholesale spoliations. Drumont continues:

> The Jews often bought entire churches with a handful of assig-
> nats (paper money of the French Republic), and when tranquili-

ty was restored, they let them to the Christians at an exorbitant rental. France was their prey, and Jean-Baptiste Capefigue, in his *History of Great Financial Operations*, thus describes the situation:

> The Jews entered Paris like hungry wolves. At first they were timid and ostensibly engaged only in selling second-hand clothes, cheap wares, and in mildly exercising their old trade of usury. They were not yet sufficiently strong to establish banks, which were in the hands of the Genoese. They were satisfied with buying and bidding in, in connivance with auctioneers, the furniture of castles, the relics of the churches, and with lending to the old aristocratic families that were banished a few louis on good values, and at an appalling interest... Left alone, in a short time they will be masters of the industrial and financial markets.

How true the words of Capefigue! Wherever a Jew has established a bank, he has changed the existing order of things. Whenever the Jew enters into a business transaction with a Gentile, his first thought is to swindle and ruin him. The greatest financial catastrophes that have occurred in Europe have been the work of the Jew. America, by reason of its vast extent of territory and exhaustless resources, has not as yet keenly felt the wounds inflicted by these fellows. But hardly a day passes that we do not read in the newspapers accounts of their peculiar operations. To conceal their tracks, they often, by mutual arrangement, institute suits against one another, while their aim is to ruin the Christian. Thousands of examples could be cited to prove the truth of this statement, but one will suffice, which we copy from the *New York Times* of November 8, 1887

> The Fifth National Bank in St. Louis closed its door at 1:15 pm today. I. B. Rosenthal, Joseph Specht and Marcus Wolfe are directors of the bank [no comments are needed as to their origin]. Marcus Wolfe [poor fellow] brought two suits of attachment against I. B. Rosenthal, aggregating $71,000, and it is thought that Rosenthal was indebted to the bank to a consid-

erable amount. The bank is situated at 700 North Broadway, and has a capital stock of $390,000. The usual deposits amounted to about $400,000. On Friday they had to meet a heavy run, and as the depositors continued to withdraw their funds, the bank closed its doors a few minutes before one o'clock. Henry Oderstolz [another one of the seed of Jacob] is president, and C. C. Crecilius [of the same stock] cashier... Within the last month, the stock of the bank has sold at 105, and this morning it found a ready market at 95.

The Jew of 1800 was less accomplished than the Jew of today. He was half brigand and half banker, or rather, he began to be a brigand before he established himself as a banker. To illustrate the above, it is necessary only to recall the career of the famous Jew Michael, the assassin, whose grand-daughters married dukes and princes, without, however, obliterating the sinister reputation which to this day clings to them. Michael enticed to his castle in the suburbs of Paris a family of noble French exiles, whom he strangled in order to obtain the money and valuables they carried. Acquitted by a jury which he had bribed, notwithstanding the overwhelming proofs, which have disappeared together with the briefs of the trial, he was nonetheless looked upon as guilty by the public.[8]

In the meantime, the Jews were watching the political horizon. They waited for a Cromwell, who was so favorable to them. He came.

Was Napoleon of Semitic origin? Disraeli said he was, and the author of *Judaism in France* is of the same opinion. It is certain that the Balearic Isles and Corsica served as a refuge to many Jews banished from Spain and Italy. These exiles, it would seem, were converted to Christianity, and, as has been the case in Spain, they took the names of Orsini, Colonna, and Bonaparte, Christians that served them as godfathers. The historian, Michelet, has spoken of this matter three times. "I said" he says in his *Nineteenth Century*, "that an Englishman sought to make people believe that Bonaparte was of Jewish extraction. As Corsica contained formerly a vast number of Jews who settled there from Africa, it seems that Bonaparte may have belonged to the Moors more than to the Italians."

---

[8] The reference to a French Jew named "Michael" is unconfirmed.

Napoleon was just the man to act the important part that the Jews expected of him. From the very start, the Jewish capitalists adopted him. All the wealthy Jews of the time may be said to have been in silent partnership with him during his first expedition into Italy, when the treasury of the country was empty. His early exploits were greatly exaggerated, and the enthusiasm inspired by his achievements having been fanned to fever-heat by the Jews, won for him the entire country. We have had a repetition of this sort of excitement in the case of Gambetta, who, although really dishonest, swayed all France with his eloquence; still France looked on him, for a time at least, as the predestined man.

Napoleon acquitted himself of all obligations he had toward the Jews, for he granted them the free exercise of religion and the full enjoyment of political rights.

A great council, composed of the most prominent rabbis, took place on 4 February 1807. Its sittings lasted until March 4 of the same year. This council was well calculated to awe the imagination of the descendants of a race so long proscribed. For the first time since the destruction of the temple [in Jerusalem in 70 AD], a Sanhedrim collected the members of that wandering family. The representatives of Israel were moved by the solemnity of this spectacle. One of their first acts had truly something noble in its character, altogether foreign to everything expected from that race.

They recalled the long persecutions, the long years that had passed—years replete with keen sufferings. They remembered that for years only one man had spoken in their behalf, had unceasingly declared that we ought to respect the liberty of their conscience, and had set the example of tolerance by according to the Jews in his kingdom better treatment than they had had elsewhere. This man, always the same in doctrine, always the same in his goodness, was the vicar of Christ [i.e. the pope].

The popes have always accorded to the Jews their august protection. In the seventh century, St. Gregory protected them throughout the entire world. Alexander II warmly congratulated the bishops of Spain for having taken under their protection the persecuted Israelites. Innocent II and Alexander III took active measures in their behalf; Gregory IX interposed for them in France, England, and Spain, and forbade, under penalty of excommunication, anyone from troubling their feasts. Clement VI granted them an asylum at Avignon; Nicholas II wrote to the Inquisition not to force the Jews to embrace Christianity, and Clement XIII granted them permission to bring up their children as they wished—a kindness which the Jews repaid by stealing the children of the Christians as soon as they were able to do so.

After many years of persecution, the Jews, at last finding themselves left in peace, wished to thank the pontiffs, who had so often interested themselves in their affairs and made themselves the advocates of the proscribed race. These thanks the members of the Sanhedrim expressed in an address, which is certainly an honorable page in Jewish history. The address was as follows:

> The Israelites of the Empire of France and of the Kingdom of Italy, at their Synod held on the 30th of last March, penetrated with gratitude for the successive benefits that the Christian clergy have rendered in past centuries to the Israelites of the various States of Europe—
>
> And full of gratitude for the welcome that the several pontiffs have extended to the Israelites in various countries, when barbarity, prejudice and ignorance incited the people to persecute and expel the Jews from the bosom of society—
>
> Decree, That the expression of these sentiments be recorded in the proceedings of this day, that they may forever remain as an authentic testimony of the gratitude of the Jews for the benefits conferred upon preceding generations by the Christian clergy.

It behooves us to compare the address of 5 February 1807, with the account of the infamies committed by the Jews of Rome, as related by two converted Israelites, who subsequently became priests—the Abbes Leman—in a pamphlet entitled: *Letter to the Israelites throughout the world, respecting the conduct of their co-religionists in Rome during the captivity of Pius IX in the Vatican:*

> On the 20th of September, 1870, the Pontifical Zouaves, defenders of Rome, received orders from Pius IX no longer to continue their heroic defense. Thereupon they left the ramparts and assembled, sad and isolated, in the Vatican. But as they were crossing the bridge of St. Ange, numerous bands of Jews heaped insults upon them, forcibly took away the packages

containing their travelling outfits, and pretending that robbery was not their actual motive, but that it was done for political reasons, cast the packages over the bridge into the Tiber. Below, however, were their boatmen, who collected into their boats everything thrown from above. The Jews afterward pillaged the barracks and took away arms, uniforms, even the furniture, and the planks. Last year, 1872, acts of abomination and ferocity were again committed by the Jews—acts that beggar description. They cursed and struck the peacefully disposed Christians as they were leaving the church; turned sacred things into ridicule, insulted the priests, soiled the images of the Madonna, and threw into the crowd balls of lead, which resulted in the shedding of blood.

Only a year or two ago, did we not see the Jew Levy, author of a blackmailing pamphlet against the Pope, declare that the anti-clerical congress, which he had organized, would meet next year in Rome, in order more keenly to defy the august captive in the Vatican? This is the way the Jew generally returns favors.

In 1807 the hearts of the Israelites overflowed with gratitude. The thanks voted in Hebrew to Napoleon seem instinct with the breath of biblical poetry:

> Napoleon, all kings have vanished before thee. Their wisdom has been bewildered, and they have reeled like one intoxicated. At the battle of Austerlitz, thou hast shattered the forces of two emperors. Death marched before thee. Thou hast marked his path, and never once did death turn from it. The past generations that death has devoured, that hell has swallowed, at the report of thy exploits have exclaimed: Among warriors, among heroes, never has one resembled thee. God has chosen Napoleon to govern *his* people. Napoleon alone has done as many great deeds as have all the heroes of past centuries.

The Jewish Synod advised the Jews to conform to the laws of the country, and to do everything in their power to win the esteem and the good-will of their fellow citizens. Vain words! The Synod did not succeed in changing the

Jewish temperament. Nothing in the world's history has ever made any impression upon the Jew.

The struggle against Judaism was carried on even during the reign of Napoleon, but it was carried on unperceived, on account of the terrible events which were then crowding upon one another. Through a phenomenon that will be the perpetual astonishment of history, Napoleon, the little sub-lieutenant of artillery, occupied the place of chief of an empire, an empire impregnated with the spirit of absolute authority, impregnated with the traditions belonging to hereditary monarchy. This parvenu, we are forced to acknowledge it, was the last sovereign who truly governed France.

Eminent men of that period acknowledged that it was wrong to grant to the Jews equality of rights. No one would have found fault had Napoleon sought merely to ameliorate the condition of the Jew; to have been inspired, for instance, with that Roman wisdom of old, which distinguished between the Roman citizen and the public slaves of the Roman citizen. The Romans allowed their slaves the free enjoyment of their property. They even allowed them to display an arrogant luxury, but half of their property, after their death, belonged to the State. Had such a law applied to the wealthy class among the Jews, to families like the Rothschilds, the Ephrussi, or Baron Hirsch, who reduced Romania almost to pauperism, it would give excellent results. It would cause to revert to the public treasury part of the ill-gotten gains of these usurers, without, at the same time, preventing this race from exercising their vocation. Even during the most ill-fated period of Rome's history, the freedman was not admitted into the curia of a provincial city. The Roman people never believed that a foreigner, even though naturalized, could be the equal of the sons of the old citizens who had founded Rome's greatness.

At the time when equal rights were granted to the Jews [in 1791], an illustrious Frenchman, whose lofty and serene intelligence was proof against every fanatical influence, expressed himself clearly upon this question in a document of not more than 30 pages, which is a masterpiece of impartiality and good sense:

> The [French] Assembly has thought that in order to render the Jews good citizens, it would suffice to have them participate, without special conditions being imposed upon them, in all the rights enjoyed by the natives. Experience has unfortunately proved that if the Assembly has not lacked in philosophy, it

has lacked in forethought, and that in certain cases new laws cannot be promulgated without detriment.

The error arises in this case from the fact that the Assembly has not clearly understood the suitableness of the Jew to enjoy full civil rights. The Jews formerly had their territory and their government. But from the moment they were dispersed, they began to wander over the globe, seeking a retreat but not a country. They have existed among all nations without ever uniting with any. This order of things is owing to the nature and strength of the Jewish institutions. Various nations may have one common object, as, for instance, that of maintaining their liberty. But each nation has an object which is peculiarly its own. Aggrandizement was that of Rome, war that of Lacedaemon [Sparta], letters that of Athens, commerce that of Carthage, and religion that of the Jews...

Religion ordinarily is related to things which affect the conscience. But among the Jews, religion embraces everything which constitutes and molds society. To this end, the Jews form everywhere a state within a state. They are neither Frenchmen nor Germans. They are Jews, and Jews they will remain...

It follows that it would not have been unwise or unjust to have submitted to exceptional laws this kind of a corporation which, by its institutions, its principles, and its customs, has remained constantly separated from society at large.

The Jews of those times had not yet entered upon those gigantic financial movements which, they said, "would be the glory of the nineteenth century" and which movements consist in causing the gold of the universe to be circulated and "scooped in." The Jews of those times were satisfied to follow their ancestral and time-honored business—usury—and freed of all fetters, and armed with equal rights, they practiced it without let or hindrance.

Unhappy Alsace writhed in the grasp of these vampires. She prayed, supplicated, cried, agitated, and finally threatened. The honest Kellermann, who had led so many heroic charges, felt his courage abandoning him before the wave of German Jews who seized upon the unfortunate province which he governed. Driven to despair, he poured his sorrows into the bosom of the

Emperor Napoleon, to whom he wrote in 1806: "The usury of the Jews is frightful. They repudiate the receipts for loans returned to them, which receipts I myself know to have been duly signed by them, averring that they are forgeries." The Emperor, notwithstanding his many services to Judaism, was now forced to issue the following decree on 17 March 1808:

> Henceforth, and beginning with the 1st of July, no Jew will be allowed to engage in business of whatsoever sort or nature, without first having received an official permission from the governor of his district, which permission will not be granted but upon strict examination and careful investigation, and only when it has been fully ascertained that the said Jew has not practiced usury, or has not been engaged in any illegal traffic.

Besides the above decree, Napoleon issued another, requiring that as many of the Jews as had no family name or a first name should at once take one. He forbade them to have for a family name one from the Old Testament, or to take the name of a city, for which the Jews had a great fondness.

A commission was appointed with orders to give names to the Jews, and the Jews succeeded in bribing the petty officials, who were appointed to see that this decree was carried out, by paying them a small sum in consideration for which the commission gave them a beautiful name, as of a bird, a flower, or a name of good omen. The Jews called themselves the *evening breeze*, or the *morning perfume*, for instance, the name Rosenthal means *valley of roses*; Wohlgeruch, *good odor*; Edelstein, *precious stone*; Goldader, *a vein of gold*. Those who refused to pay were given ridiculous or disagreeable names, as, for instance, Galgenvogel, *a jail bird*; Saufer, *drunkard*; Weinglas, *wineglass*.

The most common name among the Jews is that of Mayer. It is very ancient, and figures both in the Old Testament and in the Talmud. It pleases the Jews, for it evokes in them the image of something that shines. The true name is Meier, meaning resplendent, brilliant, and it comes from a word meaning light. Cohn, Kahn, Kohn, Cahen, Cahun are very ancient derivatives of the Hebrew word *Cohen*, meaning a priest of the family of Aaron. The first names prevalent among the Jews are generally translations of Hebrew names. Maurice corresponds to Moses, Isidore to Isaac, Edward to Aaron, James to Jacob.

The Jews, in consequence of the new measures adopted against them, limited themselves to uttering doleful complaints. But the divorce, as it were, was complete between them and the Emperor. Napoleon, leaving aside the question of his origin, was in many respects the opposite of the typical Jew. In a discussion before the Council of State, he said: "Nobody complains of the Protestants or of the Catholics. People always complain of the Jews. The fact is, that the evil done by the Jews does not come from individuals, but from the very constitution of that people. They are the grasshoppers and the worms that ravage France."

Beginning with 1810, the Jew, who up to that time had sustained Napoleon, now that he had nothing further to expect from him, took side with his enemies. The mighty Emperor had henceforth opposed to him that mysterious money-force that no one can successfully oppose, not even a Napoleon.

Judaism, which is unequalled in its power to push forward, to extol and to launch any form of enterprise, is likewise unequalled in its power to destroy, to undermine, to sap, and to ruin. When the Jew is an enemy, be it to the chief of an empire or to a private person, to a journalist or to an artist, each feels himself suddenly surrounded by a thousand Lilliputian wires which impede him in every step he may take.

The enemy of the Jew is crossed and thwarted on all sides, as Disraeli so well expressed it. Traduced, dishonored, demoralized, he does not know which way to turn, nothing succeeds, and he does not understand the reason of his repeated failures. To defy this occult power, before which even a Bismarck retreated, there needs upright men who have meditated upon the words of Christ, "Blessed are they who are persecuted for righteousness' sake: for theirs is the Kingdom of Heaven."

No doubt Napoleon's expedition to Russia contributed to his downfall. But sooner or later, the financial Jewish coalition would have ruined him. The future banker of the Holy Alliance, Rothschild, displayed, when the catastrophe neared, unparalleled activity.

When evening fell upon Waterloo, when the Emperor tried in vain to penetrate the last square, one of the Rothschilds who watched at Brussels was immediately informed of the defeat. This information came from the Jews who followed the army, and who did so in order to kill outright the wounded soldiers, and to rob their bodies. Were he to arrive first in England, he could make an immense sum of money, estimated by some at £20,000,000. He ran like a deer to Ostend, but a frightful tempest well-nigh rendered the passage across impossible. Perplexed for a moment at the waves which roared with fury, the banker, notwithstanding the danger, gave the order to depart. "Do not be afraid," he might have said to the boatman; "thou carriest more than did the bark of old. Thou earnest the misfortune of Caesar and the fortune of Rothschild."

"Bonaparte was dead" wrote Michelet. "Of the century of iron was born the century of money. Owing to the loans contracted, loans apparently made to prepare for war in time of peace, the Jew was the man of the hour. Then sprang also the famous Jew Rodrigues, who, under the name of St. Simon, founded a new sect, wrote a new gospel that tended to cast a cloak of respectability over the Jews, which, though light in itself, covered many of their sinful acts... The Jews created reservoirs into which capital incessantly poured."

People and kings were no longer anything but puppets, the strings by which they were moved being held by the Jews. Christian nations have heretofore fought for country, glory, and their flag; in future, we shall find them fighting their battles for the sake of Israel, with the permission of Israel, and for the satisfaction of Israel.

The Jews—The Rulers of our Epoch

In 1790 the Jew arrived in France. Under the First Republic [1792-1804] and under the First Empire [1804-1814], he rambled about aimlessly, seeking a place. Later, under the Restoration and the Monarchy of July, "he sat in the parlor." Under the Second Empire [1852-1870], he slept in the bed of others. Under the Third Republic [1870-1940], he began to drive the natives from their homes, or, at the least, he began to force them to work for him. "In 1890," says Drumont, "if, as I wish to believe notwithstanding past follies, there is still concealed among the Gentiles a sufficient amount of strength to snatch us from death, the Jew will return to his starting point, after restituting in a wholesale manner what he took 'in retail' from the too trusting and hospitable Aryan."

All the blood shed upon the scaffold, and upon the fields of battle, battles which recall the genius of Napoleon and the tenacity of Wellington, all ended in what may be termed "a settlement of accounts." All that formidable human movement that cost the lives of thousands of Aryans had just been settled in the *Judengasse* of Frankfurt. The man of the time was a Jew, a tricky Jew, known to the world as the great financier, Rothschild. The Aryans had killed one another during the previous 25 years in order to raise to eminence a Jew of loathsome mien, who, while they were fighting, quietly gnawed upon ducats.

While he collected into his hands all the private treasures of Germany and of England, Rothschild placed his capital at the disposal of the French Government. But, like Matre Jacques in *L'Avare* of Molière, he changed role according to circumstances. He was by turns the most implacable of creditors and the most accommodating of lenders. How is it possible to dispute the validity of a loan with one who so readily obliges you?

Under the pressure of this accommodating Shylock, France had to pay, even to the last cent, the most impudent claims, the most fraudulent accounts, the most chimerical debts. Every damage, real or imaginary, that an army of 1,500,000 had caused during its march across Europe, had to be settled by the Restoration, but engrossed by the filthy hands of the subordinate Jews, through whom these claims had passed before reaching the neater but equally avaricious hands of Rothschild. At the call of Israel, the dead seemed even to rise from their tombs, and France had to pay the accounts of a regiment of German cavalry which a certain unheard-of general had collected to assist France. These operations powerfully aided the plans of the Jews, from whom these claims were redeemed with interest, claims that the Jews had obtained for a mere nothing. The Jews were everywhere busy in ferreting out these claims, for they knew that there was one in France, one of their own, who treated of affairs of state directly with the ministers.

James de Rothschild, who in former years was installed at Rue de Provence, was no longer the obscure moneylender of bygone days. He was an Austrian baron, raised to this position by Metternich. The Duchess of Angouleme was surprised and shocked at the proposal once made to her to admit Rothschild's wife to her presence, a shrug of her shoulders eloquently expressing her disgust. But notwithstanding the rebuff of the Duchess, Rothschild himself was already a power in the financial world.

The Jews on the other side of the Rhine, who were still timidly trying to establish themselves in Paris, looked upon the house of the Rothschilds as the mother of French Judaism. With that spirit of solidarity that animates the race, the Rothschilds assisted the newly-arrived Jews, furnished them with the means to exercise their trade of petty usury, and at the same time received from the new-comers valuable information, and organized that secret Jewish police which has not its equal in the entire world.

The Restoration [1814-1830] had not perceived the danger of this Jewish invasion, and the Jews were accordingly able to follow out their silent work. To the little synagogue in St. Avoie Street, with which they were content until the year 1821, now succeeded a pretentious temple in Victory Street, a name in which the Jews claimed to see a favorable omen.

It was in 1818 that the Semitic question was again brought to the attention of the Chambers. A courageous citizen, the Marquis de Lallier, demanded, in a petition, that the decree of 1808 should be extended against the Jews for the period of ten years. The petition passed without a dissenting vote. But secret influences were brought to bear that put an end to a further mention of the subject.

The Jews, we must admit, then displayed great political acumen, for they induced people to speak as little about them as possible. The crowding and noisy Jews of today did not then exist. In proportion as they are today cynical, grossly blasphemous, dazzled by their triumphs, imagining themselves to be already completely our masters, to an equal extent under the Restoration, they were patient, humble, and content to wait. It was enough for them to be allowed to wait.

The number of bankers of purely French origin was then very limited in Paris, for, as Toussenel says, "It is so repulsive to France, that great and generous nation, to follow the ignoble traffic which forces man to lie, that it had been found necessary to import the Judah to exercise it." Opposed to the Rothschilds and the Jew Barings stood forth the distinguished French financiers, Casimir Perier, Lafitte, and a few others, who occupied in the financial world an honorable position. Had these few Aryans united, they would from the very beginning have stopped the establishment of the Jewish bank, which introduced theft and ruin into the markets, for the French bankers were in close relations with ministers who were not like those of today, promoters of stock-swindling operations. They were men who never lent their names or influence to launch forth mines without mineral. They were irreproachable men who, upon leaving the offices entrusted to them, kept for their patrimony only a name upon which no suspicion could be breathed. But petty grudges, as it often happens, stifled patriotism among the native bankers, and the Jew bank was allowed to be established.

With the rule of Louis-Philippe [1830-1848], the reign of the Jew began. Under the Restoration, one could approximately compute the number of Jews. Every Jew was obliged to have his name registered. In 1830 Rothschild succeeded in having this law annulled. As Toussenel says: "There was no longer a reigning power in France, for the Jews kept it enslaved."

During this reign of the Jews, an imperishable masterpiece appeared—the book, by Toussenel, entitled *The Jews, the Kings of the Epoch* (1845). A philosophical and social study, the work of a poet, of a thinker, of a Christian, this admirable work by Toussenel has to this day remained without an equal. Toussenel had in him what the saints possessed to an exceptional degree—hatred and love: the love for the poor, the suffering and the humble; hatred for the swindler, the thief, the trafficker in human flesh. In that eloquent work of Toussenel, the Jew is depicted in his hideous nakedness. His filthy bargains and swindling operations are clearly told. The everyday life of Rothschild is drawn in all its rottenness, as well as that of the Jews Leon Say, John Lemoinne, Aaron Raffalowich, and of others who obtained official positions and concessions through blackmail and bribery.

Jewish exploitation is also displayed in this book in all its cynicism. We find ministers of state appropriating for the construction of the Northern Railroad 100,000,000 francs, an enormous sum for those years, and when no more resources were available, the ministers turned the railroad over to the Rothschilds for a term of 40 years for exploitation in consideration of a ridiculous sum. We find in the same book the career of the Jew Fould, who caused the death of one hundred persons by his refusal to repair an engine which had been time and again condemned. This Fould was the son of a bootblack, whose curious origin is as follows:

During the last century, there lived in Nancy the Jew banker Cerfbeer de Medelsheim. He was the father of eight children, of whom four were boys, to whom he tried to give a liberal education, by which the boys profited little, as they placed pleasure above their duties.

Under the window of this banker, there was a little Jew bootblack, who blacked the shoes of those who entered the house of the financier. Medelsheim noticed this boy, who picked the papers thrown into the street, and tried, pencil in hand, to teach himself to write and to count. He was delighted to see his application, but at the same time he was pained at the laziness of his sons, whom he often reproached, and cited to them the example of the poor little abandoned waif, who acquired by himself the instruction which professors, dearly paid, in vain tried to impart to them.

Opening the window, he called in the little fellow, and said to him: "Put yourself there, my child; you are studious and wise. Henceforth you will partake at this table of the instruction given to my sons, and I hope that you will be benefited?"

The young bootblack was installed in the mansion of the banker, and profited by the instruction so liberally granted to him. In course of time, he became footman, then the factotum of the house, and later was promoted to the position of cashier. He married one of the chambermaids of Madame de Medelsheim, and finally decided to establish himself on his own account as a banker in Paris. His benefactor advanced him 30,000 francs, but the amount did not last long, and the new bank failed. Another sum of 30,000 francs was advanced him, which did not improve matters. Finally a third sum of an equal amount was brought by post to him, by Madame Alean, a granddaughter of Medelsheim, and niece to General Baron Wolfe. This time fortune smiled on Fould, and did not abandon him. He associated with himself his son Benoit, who married a Miss Oppenheim, of Cologne, and hence the firm name, Fould & Fould-Oppenheim, so well known. His other sons were Louis and Achilles, the latter the friend and minister of Napoleon III!

In Toussenel's book, monopoly, or the Jewish feudality, is described in the following manner:

> It is a pity that Montesquieu failed to define the industrial feudality. We might have expected upon this subject some piquant revelations from the witty thinker who said, 'The financiers sustain a State as the rope sustains the hanged.' The industrial, financial or commercial feudality does not rest either upon honor or upon honors. ... It has for basis the commercial monopoly, the character of which is insatiate cupidity, the mother of swindles, bad faith and coalition, stamped with the mark of falsehood and of iniquity...
>
> If anarchy claims to strike the rich and respect the poor, it is not the same with the despotism of commercial feudality.
>
> Monopoly invades the hut of the poor as it does the palaces of princes. Every kind of food is suited to its voracity. Like the subtle mercury, which, both by its weight and its fluidity, introduces itself into all the pores, like the hideous tape-worm whose parasitical circlets follow in their circumvolutions all the viscera of the human body, in the same manner, monopoly, which is personified in the Jew, causes its suckers to run to

the extreme ramifications of the social organism, in order to pump out of it every substance which can strengthen its tentacles. The tone of monopoly is egotism, which seeks in vain to dissimulate its nature under the cloak of a hypocritical philanthropy. Its device is, 'Everyone for himself.' The words country, religion, and faith, have no meaning for these men who have a moneybag in the place of a heart.

Country the Jew has not. Where gold is to be found, there is his country. Monopoly, I repeat it, is personified in the Jew. The religion of the Jews tramples under foot Christ, and spits in his face in order to acquire the exclusive right to traffic with the Japanese.

No one better than Toussenel has depicted the conquest of all Christian governments by the Jews: "The Jew," he writes, "has struck all governments with a new mortgage, a mortgage that Christian States will never pay off with their revenues."

Europe is a fiefdom to the domination of Israel. This universal dominion, which so many conquerors have dreamed of, the Jews have in their hands; the God of Judah has kept his word with the prophets, and given victory to the sons of Maccabees. Jerusalem has imposed tribute upon all states. The products of all workers pass into the purse of the Jews, under the name of interest on the national debt.

If the German Jews, represented by Rothschild, have, in a short space of time, succeeded in swallowing up the greater part of the public fortune, we must acknowledge that they have been powerfully aided by the Portuguese Jews, of whom a vast number belong to what is termed the St. Simon sect. Capefigue thus defines this wonderful sect, one of the most interesting developments of the human mind: "The spirit of this particular school, and that of the Jews at large, have this in common, that both aim to speculate, to enrich themselves. But the spirit of the former sect at times lights up, becomes passionate, almost poetic. It is often occupied with the theory of social advancement, while Judaism at large is content with its swindling operations, speculations, and money grabbing."

The Rothschilds do not belong to the Simon sect. In the immense city of Paris, they have always remained the same as in their frame house in the

Judengasse of Frankfurt, where for years they patiently waited until some-one knocked at their door, to open it and ask what pledge was brought.

A well-known and, relatively speaking, respectable family in Paris is the family of the Jew Isaac Pereire. They live in a simple style, and do not even have a box at the opera, although they are wealthy enough to build an opera-house. They do good quietly, but they do it, and without noise. They belong to a family infinitely more honorable than the Rothschilds, and they do not have, like these scions of the Ghetto, a mania for always putting themselves forward, nor the vulgar impudence to deride, with their insolent display, families whose names stand forth gloriously in the pages of history. The attitude of the family of Pereire has won for them due consideration, and they are far more respected than the Rothschilds, who, with all their ridicu-lous pretensions, are scoffed at and despised by even those who associate with them.

During the inauguration of the Northern Railroad in France, a few fa-natics cried "Vive Rothschild!" But at once, hisses and booings were heard. At Versailles, the immense crowd that had collected burst into laughter be-fore the *Smalah d' Abd-el-kader*, in which Vernet represented Fould running off with the cash-box.

At that time, people dared what very few would dare today. Rothschild was openly attacked, and an amusing and witty work, containing anecdotes representing the swindling operations of the Jews, found readers by the thou-sands. In 1835, a book was published, written by one Renault Becourt, enti-tled *Judaism Unveiled*. We have succeeded in finding only a prospectus of this book because the Jews cause all books to disappear in which they are judged somewhat severely. The author cited the progressive encroachment which during the last fifty years has assumed such formidable proportions. "Ever since the enfranchisement of the Jews," he said, "their numbers have so much increased that in the provincial towns where formerly only a score could be found, they are today counted by the thousands. ... What have these usurers let escape their grasp? Ask the unhappy merchants who were formerly well off where their property has gone to." It is evident that the possessions of many merchants, who have been reduced to poverty, must have gone some-where. The Jews did not arrive covered with gold from the interior of Germany.

There still existed newspapers which overwhelmed their operations with their bitter sarcasm. In vain, the *Archives Israelites* took Heaven to witness as to the virtues of Israel. The earth responded by enumerating its misdeeds.

At that period, a writer of great originality, Petrus Borel, published an article in the *Journal du Commerce*, apropos of a representation given by the Jews "amid trumpets of advertising." He handled them without gloves, with the refined insolence of the scholar, whose pen leaves blue stripes. Poor fellow! The Jews, according to their custom, persecuted him during his life. They tracked him like the hunted deer. They deprived him of the petty position he held in Algeria whither he had gone to escape them. Owing to these intrigues and persecutions, Petrus Borel, the great writer, died of lethargy.

CHAPTER 3
FROM THE GERMAN REVOLUTION TO THE PARIS COMMUNE

The German Revolution of 1848 was the only one not favorable to the Jews —omitting, of course, the coming one, which will be infinitely less agreeable to them, the good one, the one that will be made against them. What saved Rothschild at that time was the fact that the notorious Jew Michel Goudchaux, formerly a dealer in spurious stones, was Minister of Finance. Rothschild was an interesting subject to contemplate. From November 1847 to February 1848, he solicited subscriptions to a government loan of 250 million francs, and during these few months he not only succeeded in placing the entire loan, but realized for himself the modest benefit of 18 million francs. With the avidity that distinguishes him, Rothschild was unsatisfied with this. He cynically refused to pay the amount of 170,000,000 which he still owed to the government on account of the loan, and announced that he had failed. The course the government had to pursue was clear. It had only to arrest this fraudulent banker and to imprison him in Mazas, which prison had just then been constructed. But the Jew Goudchaux, the Minister of Finance, took care to protect him. He considered valid the theory of Rothschild, that the word given to a Goy does not bind the Jew. He not only protected the defaulter who had failed to carry out his engagements with the government, but employed him again for a new issue of 30,000,000.

History does not furnish an example of such unparalleled robbery. The Aryan was black with coal-dust, died of hunger in the streets, all shops were closed, and finally when victory came to him, he had succeeded—in doing what? In strengthening the position of the Jew Goudchaux. In the midst of so much heart-rending misery, one thought only pervaded the compassionate soul of the Jew. Goudchaux still remembered that in the treasury, which was supposed to be empty, there still lingered a few shares of the loan issued, and he himself brought them to Rothschild, for which theft he was well rewarded.

This revolution, however, well-nigh brought about the annihilation of the Jews. As soon as the Republic was proclaimed, the peasants in various sections of the kingdom attacked the houses of the Jews, and took back portions of the property of which they had been robbed. When they were brought before the jury at Strasburg, they were acquitted amid cheers, and were carried off in triumph.

Unfortunately the movement was isolated. No anti-Semitic organization was then in existence to urge upon the oppressed to act in common, and the attempted emancipation of the Christians did not succeed.

Upon the restoration of the Empire, the Jew Achille Fould, in his capacity of Prime Minister, brought about the marriage between the Emperor and the Empress, pronouncing, no doubt, in Petto all the forms of malediction that the Talmud contains over the head of the child that was to issue from this union. This was the unfortunate Imperial Prince, who was inveigled by a Jew into an ambush in Zululand and lost his life.

With the return of order in France, a considerable number of Bordeaux Jews came to Paris. The Jews of the South displayed the qualities peculiar to their race, which qualities we have already indicated. They were powerfully assisted by the gold that constantly accumulates in the vaults of Rothschild, as if heaped together by the silent rake of an invisible partner.

The Jews of the South when they reached Paris built magnificent residences, but refrained from joining the Rothschilds in their nefarious designs, whereat the Rothschilds became dissatisfied and well-nigh effected the ruin of Pereire, one of the most prominent Jews of the South. The Rothschilds invited the Jew capitalists of Germany to join them in their conspiracy against Pereire, and the German Jews crossed in masses over into Paris.

From the beginning of 1865, everything has been in the hands of the German Jew. He became the master of the world. A few should be specially mentioned. The Jew Offenbach and the Jew Halevy deride in General Bourn the chiefs of the French Army. The Jew Kugelmann conducts a printing establishment, whither flock the Jews of all stations, who talk loud and who impart to ears ever open, ever ready to catch a whisper, interesting news, or useful information, which is quickly communicated to the public press, now exclusively owned by the Jews. All government positions, high and low, are in their hands.

During the reign of Napoleon III [1852-1870], it was the Jew Adrien Marx who occupied the place formerly held by Racine, that of historiographer of France. It was the Jew Jules Cohen who directed the music in the Chapel of the Tuileries. It was the Jew Waldteufel who conducted the orchestra at the court balls. Now follow me to the confessional, into which no one, not even the Emperor, dares enter, and you will there see a woman kneeling before a priest, and confiding to him the anxieties of an empress and of a mother, concerning the war about to take place. This priest is the German Jew, Jean-Marie Bauer. Never has the Jew interloper produced a type so complete, so eminently qualified to interest the writer who in later years will try to paint this strange century.

One fine morning, this suspicious convert arrived in France. He took it into his head to supplant the venerable Abbe Deguerry, chaplain, during many years, to the Empress Eugénie de Montijo, and to occupy this post of confidence so coveted by all the priests of the country. He succeeded! Did he succeed in this through hypocrisy or by the display of eminent virtues? By no means. He relied, like all Jews, solely on his impudence, and on his belief that one may dare everything where a Goy is concerned. He organized those famous ecclesiastical luncheons where future councilors were invited, and where suggestive songs were sung. "Our Paradise is a beloved bosom." This Jew convert, dressed by Worth, wore the costume of a charlatan, displayed a luxury and a variety of lace work that made many a woman dream of him.

The siege began. This Jew acrobat, in violet stockings and shoes, such as are worn by jockeys, was appointed chief chaplain of the ambulance corps. He was always to be found at the outposts, and his enthusiasm to minister the dying soldier was so great that it brought him sufficiently close to the enemy to enable him to throw useful information into their lines respecting the besieged city.

When all was ended, he laughed in the face of those he had duped. He left his priestly robes in the greenroom of an obscure theatre, produced pornographic publications about the demi-mondaines of the Second Empire, and nightly showed himself at the opera, where, strangely enough, honorable men still admitted this unworthy priest into their boxes. At last, when he found his luminosity growing dim, he went to Brussels, where he married.

The poor Empress paid cruelly for her thoughtlessness in choosing such an intriguing personage for a confessor. The Empress was the first to set a fashion that generals, writers, diplomats shortly afterward adopted. One and all confessed to the Jews.

The Prussian Jew banker, Bleichroeder, was in the pay of the Prussian Government, and was its acknowledged spy during the late Franco-Prussian War. Under such conditions, one must not be surprised at the crushing defeat

France suffered. The Jews were enlisted on the side of the enemy, hence France succumbed.

It may be interesting, however, to know that the plans of the Jews nearly miscarried at the last moment. The thoroughly good-hearted, far-seeing sovereign, Napoleon III, resisted as long as he could the pressure of the Empress, who, spurred on by the Jew Bauer, said to the Emperor, "This is my war." On the other hand, William, the Christian monarch, felt his conscience trouble him as he thought of the hundred thousand men who that day were quietly cultivating the earth, and yet within a month would lie dead upon the field of battle. To the last moment, the Empress supplicated the Emperor to maintain peace.

William did what no other sovereign perhaps would have done in his place. The candidature of Prince Hohenzollern to the throne of Spain was withdrawn. The German Jews, in their despair, had recourse to a lie. A Jewish agency, the Wolff News Agency, announced that the French ambassador had been insulted by the King of Prussia, and the Jewish press immediately spread the news, as follows: "France has been insulted; the blood boils in our veins. Our ambassador has been outraged." The result of this lie was the declaration of war.

The Paris Commune

The first spy caught at Matz, at the beginning of the Franco-Prussian War, was a Jew. On 19 August 1870, a newspaper, *Le Nord*, stated: "The greater part of the spies caught are Jews. This ignoble business could not be better pursued than by the children of that despicable race, who had the bad fortune to produce in Judah the perfect type of perfidy and treason." In a word, the Jew was the scourge of the German invasion. Another French newspaper, *L'Illustration*, in its issue of 27 September 1873, wrote:

> So long as the battle rages, the Jew keeps far in the rear. He fears the shots. But when the enemy retreats and the field of battle is abandoned, then the German Jew appears. He is now the master, and the king of the bloody field. His and his only are all the dead bodies. The soldiers designate him by the characteristic name of 'the vulture.'

Like a phantom, he goes from group to group, quietly robbing the dead. To see him running hither and thither, bending his fiendish face, lighted with a hellish expression, one would involuntarily turn aside. With an avidity that beggars description, he seizes everything that he can carry off. How and then a group is seen hovering like vultures about a dead body. Then suddenly they fall upon it, and strip it of everything of value ... Sometimes a groan is heard, a wounded soldier pleads, but the vulture has no time to occupy himself with sentiments of humanity ...

The German Jew forms, besides, an essential part of the German forces. Stealing is only his private business. He holds an official position—that of a spy. After the battle, it is he that brings to headquarters all papers found upon the bodies of superior officers. His business, however, is not a sinecure. ... He goes in advance of the army, inquiries into the resources of a city, informs himself about the position and the forces of the enemy. Sometimes, if caught, he is shot. But this is a rare occurrence. In the first place, the Jew takes every precaution and rarely incurs any risk. But if, notwithstanding these precautions, he falls into a trap, he is never at a loss to extricate himself. He betrays the Germans as readily as he does the French. Hereafter he keeps both sides informed as to their respective affairs, and finds this business immensely profitable.

But the triumph, the dream of this low and revolting being, is an armistice. Both sides are then sufficiently at *peace* for him not to fear either rope or bullets. Both sides are still sufficiently at *war* to enable him to exercise his 'honest profession.'

When peace was signed and the German Army entered Paris [in 1871], the Jew vultures, happy, their faces wreathed with smiles, as if they had taken an active part in all the battles of the war, marched behind the white Prussian cuirassiers. As is well known, it was the staff officers, the Emperor's own bodyguard, and not the army, that first entered the city. This imposing body was on that day performing the duty of scouts, and marched in slow, measured steps, casting anxious looks to the right and to the left, upon the small crowd of spectators who lined both sides of the Elysees. These mounted men were nearly all of lofty stature and powerful build, and they appeared upon their horses like experienced horsemen of the racecourse. They wore, one and all, the brilliant uniform of Prussian cuirassiers. With their helmets of imposing aspect, their breastplates adorned with armorial bearings, they looked like legendary heroes, as they rode forward on that eventful day in the month of March. The bearing of these aristocratic soldiers was in keeping with their military dress. Their complexion was clear and red. Their whole aspect was grand. They rode upon bay horses, and their heavy moustaches were curled up in true military fashion. Their blue eyes looked fierce, and recalled the picture of the ancestors of these men as drawn by the ancient historians. The impression they made was one never to be forgotten, recalling the mounted figures sculptured upon the facade of the castles of Heidelberg. Every one of them presented the type of feudal Germany—the age of iron, the reign of force, the military Middle Ages.

This little escort, in the midst of which the King of Prussia could be seen, advanced with precaution, as it has been stated. To enter into Paris, the hot bed of revolutions, after a siege of five months and a half, justly seemed fraught with danger. It was like entering a volcano. Before risking the army, the royal bodyguard was feeling the territory, from fear, no doubt, that, notwithstanding the precautions taken, some hidden mine, charged with dynamite, might burst under the invading forces. It was the King, the princes, the generals, who on that day were doing the work of the Uhlans.

This detachment was immediately followed by another. But this time it was not a military force. It was a civil procession which presented an appearance not less curious than the one we have described. Behind these centaurs, clothed in iron and glittering with steel, marched a crowd of queer beings, clothed in long coats. Their elongated faces, their hooked noses, their disheveled hair, their dirty beards, and their broad-brimmed hats, presented the type, the unmistakable type of the Jew who follows the German army, and whom the soldiers call 'vultures.'

After this double-procession had passed, nearly an hour elapsed before anything occurred. The delay was caused by the well-known Jew, Ernest Picard, who had the kindness to welcome the conquerors with a banquet in which champagne flowed without stint.

When the banquet was over, the bodyguard resumed its march. But now it wheeled around, and marched back again through the Champs-Elysees until it came before the army, which was ready to enter. Again we saw the centaurs followed by the sons of Israel. But their appearance was not the same. Breakfast had produced its effect. The wine had illumined their faces. Their attitude was arrogant and assured, because no danger was to be feared, and no mine threatened to explode. The German cuirassiers move up the avenue. But now a sorrowful episode occurs. A poor French workman, mad with patriotic grief, plunges his knife into the chest of a horse. The man is seized and turned over to the Jews, who tear him to pieces.

Here we must say a few words concerning the French workman so often mentioned in accounts that have heretofore appeared about the Commune. We have visited nearly every country in Europe, Asia, and America, and after a careful examination into the industrial condition of the working man, we are prepared to say that nowhere have we seen a happier and more satisfied being than is the French workman. Owing to his ardor and his gayety, to his patriotism, which was so conspicuously displayed during the siege of Paris; owing to his loyalty, his disinterestedness, his love of fair play, he is an obstacle in the path of the covetous German Jew.

The Paris Commune [of 1871] offered an excellent opportunity to kill as many of these working men as possible. Denounced by the leaders who goaded them to acts of violence, as, for instance, by the notorious Jew Barrere, who afterward became Minister Plenipotentiary, these unfortunate men filled with their bodies the streets, the avenues, the squares, the gardens, and the parks of Paris. Perhaps some of my readers saw these workmen during the second siege on their way to the ramparts, marching in good order past the house of Rothschild, and never for a moment thinking of entering it, half clothed and half fed though they were. To the low German Jews, who governed Paris at that time, the palace of Rothschild was an object of veneration, and without much difficulty they inspired the same respect for that mansion in the poor dupes around them.

The Aryan, need we repeat it, is a being of faith and discipline, and holds to these sentiments even in times of revolution. He is born to be the intrepid and devout crusader, the soldier of the veteran guard, the obscure and interesting victim of even the Commune.

The French Commune consisted of two classes. The one was the unreasonable, thoughtless, but brave class. This class was mainly composed of native Frenchmen. The other was the invidious, thievish, and low speculative class, composed wholly of Jews. The French Communists fought bravely and were killed.

The Jew Communists stole, assassinated, and lit fires with petroleum to conceal their thefts. Certain Jew merchants, established at Turbigo Street, organized devastation in the spirit of commercial-enterprise, and subsequently retired to New York with a fortune of two or three million francs. Like the Jew fireman, as the anecdote has it, the Jews practiced the *grande soulasse,* only murder followed by theft was this time combined with incendiarism.

The Commune had two results. First. It enriched the Jews at the expense of the Gentiles. The Communists never touched a Jew's property. Not one of the 150 houses owned by Rothschild was attacked.

Second, an important result for the Jews. It caused 30,000 Frenchmen to be killed by Frenchmen. The Germans in exchange for the protection they had granted the Jews asked of them only one service—the destruction of one of France's glorious monuments. The Vendome Column, constructed of the cannon taken from the Germans, was an object of constant annoyance to them. Notwithstanding their easy victory over the nephew, they were still wroth at the invincible Imperator whom they saw draped in the mantel of a Roman Emperor, standing upon one of the world's greatest monuments.

But although masters of Paris, their Aryan descent would not allow them to lay violent hands upon the Column. They respected the monuments of the victories won by France, as well as the statues of her heroes. But what they themselves abstained from doing, they let the Jew do, as if perchance to prove that the Jew may at times be useful. Maxim Du Camp, in his book, *Convulsions de Paris* (1878), thus relates the events of that day:

> Suddenly a man appeared upon the top of a building, agitated a tricolored flag and hurled it into space, in order to indicate to all the assembled multitude that the commemorative emblem of the French Revolution, of the First Empire, of the Kingdom of Louis-Philippe, of the Second Republic, and of the Second Empire, then disappeared from history and was to be succeeded by a new era, symbolized by a rag of the color of blood, called the red flag.
>
> The man who had the honor to throw to the wind the flag of France was worthy of his mission. He was called Simon Mayer, the same who had taken part in the murder of General Lecomte and of General Clement Thomas. This noble action of his found its sweetest reward at that hour in the presence of

the members of the Commune who stood there attentive and delighted. The sound of a clarion was heard—a deep silence reigned throughout the streets. Everybody kept quiet, and a sort of fascination kept all eyes riveted upon the column, around which heavy cables were wound. It was a little after five o'clock when it fell with a thud... From time to time, a few cannon shots fired at a distance sounded as a farewell.

A man betrayed the God who came to bring to the world words of comfort and of love. He was called Judas, and he was a Jew. A man betrayed a woman who had trusted in him. He was called Simon Deutz, and he was a Jew. A man gave the signal to destroy the monument of the old glories of France. He was called Simon Mayer, and he was a Jew. Out of that sublime trinity—God, woman, genius—out of that triple form of the ideal—divinity, beauty and glory—out of all these, the Jews made money.

Accordingly, the years 1873 and 1877 saw the complete triumph of Israel. From one end of Europe to the other, a Jew hosannah took place, which reverberated to the remotest corner inhabited by a Jew. The Jews now repeated, but on far more gigantic proportions, what Rothschild had done in 1815. They enriched themselves by loaning to the Frenchmen the money which they had obtained from the Prussians, and which money France had paid the latter. Out of every five millions paid by France to Prussia, four at least remained in the hands of the Jews.

The king of the time was Bleichroeder, for whose sake France later undertook the expedition to Tunis. He was rewarded by Bismarck with the iron cross; but we must not forget that while Germany employs the Jew and sometimes rewards him, she keeps aloof from him in all matters pertaining to the honor and the dignity of the country. When the son of Bleichroeder wormed his way, nobody knows how, into a body of officers of the Hussars, deafening hisses arose as soon as he presented himself before them. They spat in his face, and he had to flee precipitately. Never will the German officer, who keeps sacred the traditions of the old Teuton Cavaliers, admit to their ranks a man whom they dare not trust, and who, for the sake of money, will not hesitate to betray their flag.

The Jews after the Commune

The Commune [of 1871] drew to Paris all the wanderers, all the adventurers, all the low, swindling mass of the Israelite race. They established themselves in many once populous quarters which the Commune had left empty.

The admirable solidarity of the Jews, and their spirit of intrigue, enabled the newcomers in a short time to openly assume the direction of the affairs of the city of Paris. First of all, they sought for a false Messiah, and they quickly found him in Leon Gambetta.

Little attention was paid by them to Mac-Mahon. Faithful to their inexcusable infatuation for the half-foreigner, the conservative French element instead of applying to a brave general of pure French stocky like Ducrot, who would have saved the country from that hideous crowd of Jew adventurers, put its confidence in Mac-Mahon, that arrant idiot who said Thiers "never spoke, and always lied."

Mac-Mahon was of the pure mastiff type, and may well be considered a representative of the Celtic race when in power.

"The Greek," wrote Paul de Saint-Victor, "was the child of genius of the Aryan family." It may be said of the Celt that he is the black sheep of this same family. The Celts have had heroes, prophets, poets, but they never have produced a great statesman. Now and then, at long intervals, there springs from this race some extraordinary being, almost legendary. The devotion, the spontaneity, the enthusiasm, which manifests itself throughout this race, sometimes produces men of an almost superhuman inspiration. But all these precious gifts are neutralized by an absence of the faculty of order. As a social organization, the Celts, left to themselves, have never been able to get beyond the clan. Ireland received her deathblow from the family divisions perpetuated from generation to generation. Although the Irish are eminently qualified to accomplish exceptional exploits, they are lamentably deficient in continuity.

Mac-Mahon on the field of battle had all the bravery of his race, but all its faults when in power. He was astonishingly grotesque as President; he allowed himself to be driven from a position that was impregnable, if intelligently defended, and finally he shamefully backed down before a handful of lawyers who trembled every time he sought his handkerchief, believing that he was going to seize his sword. He had neither the subtleness nor the ability of Thiers, nor had he the sentiment of authority, the respect for his word, nor the tenacity in maintaining his rights, that a German would have had. Thiers called him "the disloyal soldier" and he merited this appellation, for he abandoned all who had trusted in his promise to fight to the very end.

The great misfortune of France, at that time, was her slowness in putting at the helm of government true representative men, instead of leaving the management of the ship of State to a motley crowd of Jew speculators. The Jews were masters of the situation, and they soon gave abundant evidence of the authority they had and of their ability to win over to their side men in whom the populace blindly trusted. At the Berlin Congress, France, for the first time since the Franco-German war, was brought face to face with Europe, which, but a few years previously, had allowed her to be mercilessly mutilated.

Now who was entrusted with the task of representing France? William Henry Waddington, an Englishman, a man with all the instincts of the cosmopolite Jew. Waddington had relatives everywhere excepting in France. He had many cousins in Germany. His sister married a Prussian diplomat, and one of his uncles was a colonel in the English army.

Public demoralization was so complete that no one protested against his being chosen, no one in fact paid any attention to the matter. The people were as in-different as when the Prussian Jew Spuller was appointed Secretary to the Government of National Defense. Worse still, not a murmur was heard against the attitude assumed by Waddington at that memorable Congress. The policy that ought to have been followed was manifest, and any intelligent and patriotic man would have followed it from instinct.

Russia, on account of the latent antagonism existing between her and Germany, is, if not the natural ally of France, at least the only nation upon which France can count. The Czar Alexander rendered to France a signal service in 1875 by opposing the brutal attitude of Germany toward France. What possible harm could the treaty of San-Stefano do to France, even had it been favorable to Russia?

We saw, however, the strange spectacle of a French Minister of Foreign Affairs [Waddington], nominally a Frenchman, espousing with burning zeal the interest of England, urging her to seize Cyprus, and smilingly assenting when England announced her intention of driving France from Egypt and adding that country to her numerous possessions.

In return, Waddington asked for only one thing—the emancipation of the Jews in Romania! Notwithstanding the lies of the Jewish press, it is well known that the Romanians are a brave, hospitable nation, a nation of artists, descendants of the ancient colonists of Trajan, and that they love to recall that their name even shows the near relation existing between them and the sons of ancient Rome.

The Italian type has assumed among the Romanians a sort of Oriental grace, but at the same time virile and poetic in the extreme. They love to sing in the evening by the light of the stars those original and weird melodies, the strange rhythm of which lingers in the ear. In a word, if the Jews did not exist among them, they would have been perfectly happy.

The Jew in Romania does not constitute a fixed malady. He is a sort of continual influx impossible to stop. The great reservoirs of Judaism in Galicia and the neighboring provinces of Russia incessantly exhale upon that unhappy land their miasmatic matter.

These Jews have been time and again described in books of travel. They wear long, filthy cloaks, embroidered with metallic gimp, from which vermin fall wherever they pass, thus offering a constant danger to public health. The Jews have made this country, in which they believe their Messiah will be born of the Isrolka family, what they have sought to make France. They gnaw, suck, exhaust unhappy Romania. They monopolize the sale of strong drinks, and little by little they take all the money and all the products, thus destroying the prosperity of the country. If a farmer sets foot in one of these drinking places, he is lost forever, for everything he has passes from his hands. The clothes, the beast of burden, the farm, the field, the marriage ring, everything is sold to satisfy the Jew. The farmer, stupefied by the poison poured out to him, signs a paper authorizing the Jew rum-seller to charge any drinks that the farmer may ask for. This paper is not presented to him until a long time afterward, when he is no longer in a condition to pay. Then the Jew vulture falls upon his prey, and a confederate buys for a mere nothing the little domain of the poor fellow.

"These Jews," says Ernest Desjardins, in his book *Les Juifs de Moldavie,* "do not wish either to work or to cultivate the soil. They will not assume any responsibility, they will not submit to law, to the regulations of hygiene, and they refuse to handle the plow, the pickaxe, or the gun. In a word, they refuse to handle anything except money."

These Romanian Jews have, let it be mentioned to their credit, had the frankness to acknowledge their aversion to the profession of arms. The *Archives Israelites* of the year 1865 published a petition of the Jews sent to the

Senate in Bucharest, couched in the following terms: "As we Jews are, generally speaking, cowards, and have not even the courage to shoot at a rabbit
—a reason why we have lost our country, and have been for the last two
thousand years in a position inferior to all other peoples—we cannot be useful to a country as soldiers."

These were the clients whom Waddington turned over to France, to the
stupefaction of Bismarck, who, in his brutal way, burst into laughter when
the French Minister brought this question upon the tapis. An old revolutionary, Bratiano, a man who, during his exile, had been the ardent friend of all
the persecuted, said before the French Chamber: "Gentlemen, during my
political life I have passed through many vicissitudes and through many misfortunes, but nowhere have I felt so unhappy as in Berlin, owing to the attitude taken by Waddington."

At this time, the Jews exulted, and the notorious Jew, Adolphe
Crémieux, the chief man of the Republic of France, at a meeting of the Israelite Alliance, said in dithyrambic accents: "My faith is unbounded in the
continued prosperity of our situation, which today is so exalted. Ah, allow
me to attribute the cause of this to the noble, the loyal, and the pure attitude
that our Minister of Foreign Affairs, *our* Waddington, displayed in Berlin."

The word 'our' either explains the origin of Waddington, or at any rate
it shows that the French Minister of Foreign Affairs was theirs, because they
had paid him. Owing to the attitude of Waddington, France acted the ignoble
part of a brutal policeman, who, without provocation, handcuffs an innocent
man solely to permit the Jew to empty his poison into the mouth of his victim.

Subsequently, Waddington was appointed ambassador to Russia, and
the following almost incredible act of his shows his love for the nation that
trusted him. Acting upon the advice of Bismarck, who was desirous to have
France commit an affront to the government of the Czar, Waddington abstained from sending an invitation to M. de Giers, the Russian Minister of
Foreign Affairs, to the official ball given by him. This is a fact, and it was
mentioned in the newspaper, *Le Gaulois*, in its issue of 22 June 1883, in an
article signed by one of the best-informed political writers of the day. How
delightful to see France, on the eve of bankruptcy, pay 250,000 francs to an
Englishman who thus insults the only power which has preserved a shadow
of sympathy for France.

Waddington was subsequently appointed Ambassador to the Court of
St. James. He not only acquiesced in the occupation of Egypt by England,

where formerly for a long time French influence preponderated, and consented to the reducing of a debt owed to France and guaranteed by all the Powers, but he also assented to the issuing of a loan by England to take precedence of all existing loans. This loan enabled England to repay the damages that she had caused by her unjustifiable and barbarous bombardment of Alexandria. When Waddington's action became known, France, acting upon the advice of the Powers that had guaranteed her own loan in Egypt, refused to ratify the agreement made by her ambassador.

While the Jews had Waddington to protect their interests abroad, they had at home Gambetta, in whom the dearest hopes of Israel were centered. Gambetta was the creature of the Rothschilds. He never did anything unless for them, through them, and with them. Acting upon a plan perfected at a meeting held at the residence of Rothschild, and to which a number of Jew bankers of Berlin were present, it was agreed to precipitate France into a new war with Germany.

The dream of the Jew ever since France foolishly opened her gates to him has been to reduce her to the condition of Poland, to force the Frenchman to wander, like the Jew, upon the earth, without a country and without a home. The plan agreed upon promised to succeed; it promised to throw France into complete disorganization, but just as everything seemed to favor the Jews, Bismarck ceased to menace France, and even refused to avail himself of the proffered advantages.

With that peculiar gift of foresight that great men possess, the Chancellor perhaps saw that if France were broken up as a nation, how severe a judgment would be passed by the historians of this, the greatest event in history. Even the remorseless Bismarck could not bring himself to decree that France, that chivalrous and generous nation, should be crushed by a crafty German diplomat at the instigation of the Jews. Evidently while Bismarck listened to the Jews, the remembrance of the maledictions uttered against those who dismembered unhappy Poland haunted him. He determined that his memory should at least remain pure from a like stigma, and resolutely refused to take part in such an affair, though it promised to be successful.

Baffled in his efforts, Gambetta organized, in connection with a notorious Jew, now one of the foreign ambassadors of France, the war in Tunis. The reader has perhaps seen, in books of travel, descriptions of the Jewesses in Africa, who, half reclining upon cushions, hold their hands, covered with rings, upon their big stomachs of flabby flesh. Incommoded by their rotundity, which assumes frightful proportions at the age of thirty, glistening with fat, these Jewesses have but one passion—to see the heavy necklaces around their bloated necks grow heavier with the gold coins that are attached to it.

It was in connection with one of these Jewesses, a mistress of the aforesaid ambassador, that the plan was first concocted to force France into war, to murder her soldiers, who longed to return to France after the time of their enlistment was over, and to sing again, at the time of harvest or of vintage, the joyous songs that lulled them in their infancy.

Is it necessary to recall the frightful scandals that gave rise to this war, to mention the name of the Tunisian Bey, who, in return for his complacency to the lover of his wife, was rewarded with the Cross of the Legion of Honor? Respect for the feelings of our readers forces us to pass over this fetid affair in silence, the loathsome details of which scandal have been published time and again in the *Intransigent*.

Before leaving this affair, we must briefly describe the sufferings endured by the French soldiery, solely that a flock of hungry vultures might fall upon a country with unparalleled rapacity. Who has not felt his blood boil on hearing a description of the march of that little army, under a burning sky, without a tree for shelter, without water, and with nothing but a desert before them? True, water was carried upon camels, but it was never at hand when wanted. And when at last it came, it was warm and unfit to drink. What else could be expected of the military contractor of this expedition, a Jew, Chelma by name, who in a few months pocketed a fortune of three million francs?

The sufferings of the troops seem almost incredible. There were men that suddenly uttered incoherent words, or suddenly burst out laughing— they had become maniacs. Others dropped like a stone. When lifted they were—dead. A coffin was quickly improvised, and what a coffin! Provision boxes were used into which the body was thrust, and buried in the sand, where in the night the jackals dug it up and feasted upon it. Every isolated soldier was lost. If made prisoner, he was delivered as a toy to the women of the tribes, who put him to death slowly, by sticking into his flesh pins reddened in the fire. "One of my own relatives," says Drumont, "who returned dying from this expedition, related to me the impression of horror which he experienced at the sight of an officer whom nobody could recognize. The unfortunate man, with eyes plucked out, ears cut, his virile parts frightfully mutilated, in vain tried to trace his name upon a paper with a pencil that was put into his hand." What a picture for the avenging pen of a great writer.

But does not this fetid atmosphere begin to weigh upon you? Well, enter the house of the Jew Abraham Camondo, and there perhaps you will find the Jew Martin Munkacsi, who entertains his guest with petty American scandals. If you prefer, August Belmont, the correspondent of the Rothschilds, will give you a description of the mansion of Baron Hirsch, who, the public press informs us, has just given $20,000,000 to Jewish charities. There you will find the fountains ever spouting. There you will find the wonders of art embellishing his domain. Life is after all worth living. The Baron muses over the gains, the millions he made out of the Tunisian enterprise.

With an expressive shrug of his shoulders, Gambetta said before the Senate: "After all, how many men were killed in the Tunisian War? Only 1,500 Frenchmen; that is all." The fact remains that 15,000 is the official figure given by the military doctor, who remained at his post throughout the war. "We defy anyone," says Drumont, "to contradict this figure."

A few years ago, a syndicate, composed of the Jew, Edgar May, president of the Franco-Egyptian Bank—which institution has also a branch in Alexandria, Egypt, and makes advances to the Fellahs at the moderate interest of 33 per cent—and of the Jews Dietz-Moniu and Bozerian, capitalists, with whom were joined several other Jews, occupying prominent political positions, but of the same stamp, planned the expedition to Tonkin [present-day Vietnam]. No patriotic or honest reason could have prompted these Jews to urge France to undertake this expedition. Their pretext of colonial policy is too absurd to need any comment. Colonial projects can only benefit nations that are embarrassed by too great a population. It is the height of folly for France to engage in colonial projects, since the number of births in France is inferior to that of any other great nation. On the other hand, the fertile land of Algeria, still uncultivated, lies before the very gates of France, because nobody wants to go there, a fact which shows the uselessness to France of distant possessions.

The Spaniards, the Italians, and the Maltese were far more numerous in Tonkin than the French. Again, we must consider that France's commerce with South America amounts every year close to 920,000,000 francs, and she has never troubled herself with colonies in that quarter. Her commerce with Algeria amounts to 306,000,000 only, a country which cost her the lives of so many men and the expenditure of an enormous amount of money. The total value of goods ever exported from France in a year to the French settlements in Oceanica never exceeded the sum of 618,567 francs. The amount of goods exported to all the distant French colonies would not reach in a year the sum of 47,000,000 francs. These facts show that in the space of ten years, the inhabitants of Tonkin, who are the poorest people in Asia, and who live exclusively on rice, would not buy goods amounting to a million francs. "I defy," said Vice-Admiral Duperré, a man thoroughly acquainted with Tonkin, "anyone to show me a Frenchman capable of earning in Tonkin, as a workman, a sufficient amount of money to enable him to pay his passage back to France."

M. Alcide Bleton, who was sent to Tonkin by the minister of the French Navy, entrusted with a commercial mission, declared, in a published report, that he saw absolutely nothing that could be exported from Tonkin or imported into France. All that could be done, according to him, to make a little money, would be to construct barracks for the European employees, and to establish laundries.

At a time when Germany so savagely grinds her teeth, and is a constant menace to France, the idea of killing the best of soldiers in order to wash the dirty clothes of the natives of Tonkin is an exceedingly original conception.

But these arguments have no weight with the Jew. It was enough that he saw in this expedition a chance to enrich himself at the expense of the Goy. The Jews set to work at once. The Jew senators thundered in the Senate: "We will never live to see the flag insulted. National honor above all. We will never quit Tonkin, even if it would cost us the lives of 50,000 men." The promoters of the expeditions were still more enthusiastic. "They were ready to sacrifice their last penny for the honor and glory of France." A company was formed, a circular was issued, claiming that the company had obtained the right of absolute control over all the territory in Tonkin, for the space of 99 years. They promised the construction of railroads, the opening of new roads, the establishment of banks and of a steamboat line carrying the "proud flag of France." Ferry warmly recommended the patriotic plan submitted to him by "the distinguished" French financiers, Dietz-Monin, Bozerian, and the rest of the crowd of Israel.

Was Ferry bribed? No. The Jews have a way of their own to obtain a wished-for signature. They sent to the daughter of Ferry, as well as to the daughters of other prominent men in the Senate, whose signatures were desired, a number of dolls, on the first day of the year, and lo! these dolls had, by mere chance, around them diamonds worth not less than 50,000 francs. These luminous diamonds covered a multitude of their dark designs.

Then came the Jewish press, which announced the plan in the following words: "The gold in Tonkin is so abundant that in certain districts, the natives raise ducks solely in order to collect in their excrements—which, in the course of time, have become valuable guano beds—the gold they have swallowed while paddling in the rivulets."

Proudhon said of the Jews, "They live solely on what others have produced." We have shown that the Jew is a negation. He creates nothing, and he thirsts for everything. He is, therefore, fatally condemned to seek where he can find. In other words, in the purse of the producer. The details of the frauds practiced by the Jew syndicate, of their gigantic swindles, and of the sufferings inflicted upon the innocent investors, who were led to invest their savings mainly upon the recommendation of Ferry, are unimaginable.

Need we now relate the details of this war [of 1884-1885], entered into without perceptible reason, and actually waged for some time before it was formally declared? All this time, Frenchmen died by the thousands. They were killed by bullets, died of typhus fever, of cholera, and succumbed to the climate. The hospitals were full of people and without medicines. Finally the whole ended in the foolish flight before the Chinese at Lang-Son; a flight calculated to deprive the French army of the little prestige that still remained to it.

We are appalled when we reflect that these things occurred only a few years ago, that human beings were found who deliberately planned it all, and that the Assembly was foolish enough to approve. Nothing, perhaps, could give a clearer idea as to how easily poor humanity can be gulled and how much it can endure. These scoundrels who have been the cause of the death of so many men now quietly enjoy their ill-gotten millions.

Jules Ferry, at the time when the Lang-Son defeat was announced, was heartily laughing with Raynal, who, it seems, amused him by relating to him the hideous mutilations that the soldiers suffered. One would not believe Ferry capable of so much cynicism, if the official documents of the Assembly on that day did not expressly mention the fact that Ferry was there laughing with the Jew Raynal.

The career and fall of Ferry is one of those pages in history calculated to move the reader to indignation. This lying lawyer, who killed more men than a conqueror, who killed by famine in a defense of the city of Paris criminal in its hopelessness, who killed by unjust court-martials in 1871, who killed by the war in Tunis and in Tonkin, is now constantly tormented, as by a phantom, with the fixed idea that he will one day fall living into the hands of the people who will make him pay well for all the evil he has done.

At the news of the defeat at Lang-Son, the masses seemed paralyzed with disgust. They learned the truth too late. It is in one of those nervous hours when all the movement of the city seems to be centered in the forum, when journalists, compositors, mechanics, merchants, all the citizens, in fact, with bleached face and anxious looks speak all at once, that one realizes how many noble qualities still exist among the masses of the Aryan type. Then one can see how the masses realize their responsibility. The workmen had not read the *London Times*, which affirmed that the Rothschilds had guaranteed the Chinese loan, and had thus furnished these barbarians with the arms with which to fight France.

Spontaneously, however, groups of people were formed at 11 a.m. at the corner of Lafitte and Lafayette streets. They became indignant, they noisily discussed the affair, and suddenly an ominous cry was heard: "On to the house of Rothschild," "On to the house of the traitor." "Fortunately," says the newspaper *Le Gaulois*, a Jew publication, "cool heads intervened and dissuaded the people from putting their intention into execution." We do not share in the opinion of this newspaper, but the reader must not fail to notice that almost instinctive manifestation which is like the cry of public conscience. He must not fail to notice this lucid moment, this expression of public indignation, which the newspapers quickly hushed up.

Patriotism still exists at the hearthstone of the Aryan, even if the Jewish press, time and again, has declared that 'country' is only an empty name. It seemed as if all the proletarians communicated by thought with the unfortunate soldiers lost thousands of miles away; with the soldiers surrounded by numberless hordes and drowned by the surge of barbarians.

In what a tone, a tone stifled almost with tears, they asked the journalists, whom they supposed knew something, for news! How they ran about crying, and asking of everybody if at least the flags had been saved!

The flags! What is called 'society' troubled itself very little about them. A veritable flood of feasts and of balls was announced immediately following the news of the misfortunes that befell the country. "Easter week," announced *Le Figaro*, "is the veritable ball season." The Jews were wild, with joy. They threw their doors wide open. The papers announced "a grand ball this evening at Baroness Hirsch's," who, in order to celebrate, it seemed, the victory of the Celestials, wore a laurel wreath. Madame Henry Sneider also gave a ball, as did also Madame Solomon Goldschmidth, the Rothschilds and all the other Jews in Paris.

Lang-Son proved a veritable windfall to the Jews, and the Exchange had found again the glow of its former days. "One should have seen the Exchange," wrote Octave Mirbeau, a journalist,

> at the sight of which one's heart was stirred with disgust mingled with indignation. Every time France is in peril, every time her blood flows from her flanks, the tears from her eyes, there are thousands of men of prey who fall upon her, who precipitate themselves upon her body to gather her blood and her tears, and like hideous alchemists seek to transform them into gold. From the recesses of what dens, from the vaults of what banks, from what galleys, and from what ghettos were these miserable Jews let loose? With twisted mouths, widely tossing arms, eyes fired with the prospect of rapine, they ran about, trampled upon one another, trod upon one another, clamoring like barbarians with cries more deafening than those uttered by the Chinese victors.
>
> These Jews wished that the disaster had been more complete, the defeat more crushing. They spread sinister news, as if the reality were not already sufficiently painful, and the sorrow cast upon the city sufficiently mournful. It was not enough for them that our army had been butchered, and that not a soldier would perhaps return to the country that now wept for him. They invented stories of revolt in Paris; they swore that men wore killing one another in the Assembly and in the boulevards. In proportion as stocks fell and the government securities went down, the faces of these brigands were illumined with a smile akin to the one seen in the faces of the Jew vultures who, after the battle, amid the broken cannon and the twisted guns, rob the wounded and despoil the bodies. I swear that I, for a moment, wished to see the cannon sweep down this band of jackals, and to let fall, one by one, the stones and the columns of that cursed building, the Exchange, that insolently rises like a perpetual insult and treason to the country.

And during the time when these men reveled in pleasure, our heroic soldiers, without succor, without hope, were fighting, perhaps, their ferocious enemy in his native defiles, where soon their bodies will lie in the burning sun of a pestilential atmosphere.

The reader must, by this time, have come to the conclusion that when the Jew rises, the Gentile falls, and when the Jew falls, the Gentile rises.

The Jews today possess one-half of the capital in circulation upon the Earth. Nobody was heard to offer a word of protest when the Jew banker Stern said in a well-known club: "I do not know how the devil the Christians will manage to live ten years hence." No man was there to reply to this cowardly remark: "Five hundred resolute men in the avenues of New York or Paris, assisted by a regiment surrounding the banks of the Jews, will teach you how the Christians will be able to exist."

CHAPTER 4

THE JEWISH ELITE OF FRANCE

We read in an article published in *The Political and Literary Review*, that Gordon, the apostle-soldier, during his travels in Egypt, met the Jew Reinach, with whom, as it often happens in travelling, the Christian hero joined in conversation, nor did Gordon scruple to express his opinion of what he thought of Disraeli, and of all other statesmen of his kind, whom he called 'mountebanks.'

'Mountebanks' is the precise word to be applied to politicians of the nature of Gambetta, Lasker, and Cremieux. The diplomacy pursued by men like Richelieu, Colbert, Bismarck, is simple. In the diplomacy pursued by the Jews, one constantly finds a formidable display of pompous words, such as liberty, equality, and fraternity, that conceal plans to further individual interests—in a word, a semblance of emancipation and of amelioration, which invariably means the most intolerable persecution and the most impudent extortion of money.

Among these mountebanks, the Jew Cremieux, who only a few years ago held the helm of the French ship of State, which he well-nigh succeeded in swamping, occupied a place apart. Gambetta, with his inexhaustible loquacity and his frothy allurements, was withal a demonstrative personage, or, as Drumont describes him, "a showy being, like a doorkeeper, constantly occupied in exhibiting his form, which he padded out with cotton."

Never has a Jew shown himself more odiously indifferent to the interest of "country" more thoroughly occupied in furthering his own interests and those of his race, than did that miserable old Jew, Cremieux, during the dark hours of France, at the time of the late war, when he promulgated the decree ordering the emancipation of the Jews in Algeria.

Cremieux could not have been ignorant of the trouble he was about to make, in a country where the greatest possible care should have been exercised to keep it at peace, so as not to weaken unhappy France, powerless as she was to resist the enemy that oppressed her on all sides. He was, on the contrary, admirably informed of the situation; he knew the hostility that existed between the Jews and the Arabs whom, in order to arouse, during the campaign in Italy, one had only to say to them: "Yonder enemy in front are Jews." Cremieux, by issuing a decree naturalizing the Algerian Jews, purely and simply betrayed France while serving the interest of his race.

In 1870, at the time when the decree was issued, this measure had a character peculiarly odious. The Arabs had heroically done their duty during the war. These "black devils," as the Prussians called them, were always in the thickest of the fight, and won the admiration of the enemy at Wissei-bourg and at Woerth.

The French general, Albert Duruy, related the fantastic impressions which these Arabs produced with their savage cries, their joy at the mere mention of the word 'gunpowder,' their manner of rushing forward like tigers. When at Wissembourg the scattered sharp-shooters received orders to maintain their position till the last moment, in order to protect the retreat, General Duruy involuntarily bent his head under a hail of balls. Suddenly he felt a hand of iron upon his shoulder, and a thundering voice exclaiming, "Lower down, lower down." It was an Arab who smiled, as if laughing at danger, and displayed his white teeth, which shone with peculiar light in his copper-colored face.

These Arabs, who so heroically fought on the side of France, after having for so long a time fought against her, merited some signal reward. Rome emancipated the slaves who had fought in her behalf during the social war, and some proclamation, honoring with the title of friends and citizens those who had shown themselves worthy of the name, would have produced a lasting effect upon the Arabs in Algeria. But the Jews of France did not consider the matter in this light.

By the side of the Arab who fights, there lives in Algeria an abject race which exists only by shameful traffic, which grinds down to the uttermost the unfortunate Arab who falls into its claws, which enriches itself by robbing its fellowmen. It is to this dastardly race that the sympathies of a government, ruled over by a Jew, of a Christian government, were enlisted.

What sort of being is the Jew in Algeria? Nothing of what we see here can give us an adequate idea, because Jewish usury, which has attained in certain countries incredible proportions, cannot be compared with the usury practiced in Algeria upon the Arabs.

A letter of the late Emperor Napoleon, addressed by him to Marshal Mac-Mahon, Duke of Magenta and Governor-General of Algeria, may be cited as presenting one instance in a thousand:

In the month of November 1861, two farmers of the tribe of
Djebela (district of Mostaganem), sorrowfully tried by several
consecutive years of drought, were in want of grain. The principal members of this district, together with the two farmers,
applied for aid to an Israelite of Mostaganem. The Jew consented to give them what they wanted at the exorbitant price of
thirty-six francs the quintal (hundredweight). This was to be
returned to him not in money but in produce, on the year following, at market value. Now, in the month of August, 1862,
grain was worth seven francs the hundredweight, and the people of Djebela had to render him nearly six quintals for one. In
other words, they had to borrow at 600 per cent.

The following article was published in the newspaper *La France*, in July
1884, at the time of the Semitic troubles in Algeria:

Usury is really frightful. The Turcos and the Spahis, on the
eve of receiving their pay, borrow of the Jews one franc,
agreeing to pay two on the following day. This continued for a
year would make 100 francs cost the borrower 3,650. Owing
to these acts the Jew is looked upon with scorn and contempt
by the native Arab, which is easily understood. He can enter at
any hour of day or night into the tent or the house of an Arab.
Their women will not even take the trouble or think of veiling
themselves, which is a strict Mohammedan custom. No woman
of the Turkish faith ever appears before a stranger unveiled. But
these women do not consider the Jew to be a man. An Arab
would deem himself forever dishonored were he to kill a Jew.
If an attack is made upon a caravan, the Jews have only to
make themselves known, and their lives are at once spared.

At Bou-Saada, one may see the Jews squatting down upon filthy hides
covered with grease, spying for the Arab just as a spider watch for the fly.
They call him, surround him, and try to loan him money, for which they
plead with him to sign a certain paper. The poor Arab feels the danger, hesitates, and refuses. But his passion for drink urges him on. The Jew shows the
money with peculiar signs that a Jew only can make. The Arab thinks of the

good times he can have with the money thus proffered. He yields, grasps the piece and signs the greasy paper, which may well be called his death-warrant. At the end of six months, he will owe 10 francs; at the end of the year, 20, and at the expiration of three years, 600. Then the Jew will sell the poor Arab's farm if he has one; otherwise his camel or his horse; in a word, everything he may possess. Even the chiefs of the Arabs rarely escape the claws of these rapacious devils, who are the scourge, the disease, the never-healing wound of the colony, "the great obstacle in the way of the civiliza-tion of the Arab."

When the French army is called upon to reduce to subjection a rebel-lious tribe, a horde of Jews follows it, buying for a mere nothing the booty captured, which they sell back to the Arab as soon as the French army has withdrawn. If, for instance, a flock of six thousand sheep is seized, in a fara-way district, the question arises what is to be done with these sheep? Drive them into the city? They would die on the way, for how can they be fed when there is no water in the territory that must be crossed? Again, it would require a vast number of men to guard such a flock. Perhaps twice as many as the entire army counts. Kill them? What a massacre, what a loss! The Jews are there, who plead, who beg, who ask to buy them at two francs each—sheep that are well worth twenty francs apiece. Their wish is granted. Next day the original proprietors redeem the sheep at five francs each.

The Jew is master of all the south of Algeria. There is hardly an Arab that is not indebted to a Jew, for the Arab does not like to pay what he owes. He prefers to renew his due bill at 100 or 200 per cent. The Jew throughout the south lives only by his unlawful usury, and the real merchants of the place are the Mozabits.

Mr. Onesime Reclus, in his admirable book *France, Algeria, Colonies*, thus speaks of the Algerian Jew:

> The Algerian Jews have been naturalized in block, at the time
> when we were struggling against the disciplined armies of
> Germany. Certainly the Jews did not merit it, occupied as they
> are solely with usury, jobbery, and swindle. Not one among
> them plows, waters the garden, or prunes the vines, while very
> few are artisans among these descendants of the supplanter
> Esau. Not one of them ever risked his life in battle, like those

brave Arabians, who won for themselves, time and again, the name of hero while fighting the fortunes of France.

Were these Jews, at any rate, ever noted for their love of France? Never! At the beginning of the conquest of Algeria, they served as spies, both for the French and for the Arabian hero, El Hadj Abd-El Kader, keeping themselves in an attitude of neutrality, until at last fortune favored the side of France.

While the poor Arabians were sacrificing their lives in behalf of France, during the Prussian War, the Jews in Algeria, on the contrary, rejoiced at her defeat with the most indecent cynicism. At the news of the disaster of Sedan [in 1870], the Jews were, so to speak, intoxicated with joy, stamped their feet with happiness and danced in the streets. A touching incident occurred at that time. The bust of the unfortunate Emperor was dashed by the Jews upon the pavement, when a few native Arabs picked up the pieces reverentially. What a spectacle, to see the sovereign who possessed a beautiful kingdom, left only with a few faithful Arabs, who still remembered that he once paid them a visit, surrounded with all the splendor of power, took an interest in them, and earnestly sought to free them from the usury of the Jews! The above facts, however, only strengthened the Jew Cremieux in his vile design. He felt, as he himself expressed it, "Joyful as he never before felt in his life, being enabled to grant to thousands of his co-religionists the title of French citizens."

The Arabs, of course, revolted, and Admiral Gueydon says: "This decree was the cause of the insurrection. The natives were extremely angry. They were astounded to see raised to the dignity of French citizens that scurrilous people whom they always considered as servile, contemptible and miserable cowards. 'Why should this preference be shown to them?' they justly exclaimed. 'Have the Jews ever, like us, shed their blood in the Crimea, in Italy or in Mexico? Have they left 10,000 prisoners in Germany?'"

Another French admiral remarked:

> When the Arabs were informed of the Cremieux decree, their wrath was changed into profound scorn for the French. The proud spirit of the Arab was roused to its highest pitch at the idea that the Jew was preferred to him. The French they considered in the same light as the Jews. The insurrection broke out when the Muslim population found out, toward the end of

January, 1871, that the Jews were chosen to perform the functions of jurymen. Then only did they understand that they
might become the inferior of the Jews in the eye of the law.
Then did the brave chief of the Arabs, Mokrani, summon his
Arabs to arms, and send back the cross of the Legion of Hon-
or, an act by which he made it known that he preferred death
rather than submission to the affront cast upon his race by
placing the Jews above the Arabs.

Side by side with the Jew Cremieux, who betrayed the trust that France re-
posed in him, let us place the noble, loyal figure of the Arab, Si di Mohamed
Ben-Ahmed-el Mokrani, the enemy of France. Mokrani may be considered
the complete personification of those grand Arab lords whom Fromentin so
admirably described in his books.

Passionately fond of beautiful arms and spirited horses, warlike and
majestic in the stirrups, brave and dignified as they bade welcome to their
guests at the entrance of their tents, pompous and full of display when they
treated with the French officers, these Arab chiefs, after years of resistance,
had been fascinated, as it were, by the bravery of the French soldier. They
were proud to wear upon their cloaks the Legion of Honor, this flower today
withered, this emblem today prostituted, but which formerly signified courage, talent or virtue. A terrible enemy, a sincere friend, Mokrani, by a feat of
arms worthy of the heroic times, won, in a hand-to-hand contest, the Cross of
the Legion of Honor, by killing, with his own hand, the agitator Bou Bar-
ghla, surrounded though he was by his partisans. When a French officer
handed to him the decree of the Jew Cremieux, he spat upon it and returned
it to the envoy with the words, "I shall never obey a Jew."

This man, who had in him the most generous instincts, refused to attack
France while at war with Germany. He chivalrously waited before declaring
war until the French could dispose of all their forces. It was then that he returned his decoration to General Augeraud, and, while he courteously
thanked him for the past consideration shown to him, he now declared war,
the note ending in the following words:

If I continued to serve France, it was because she was at war
with Prussia, and I did not wish to increase the difficulties of

the situation. Today, however, peace has been established, and
I mean also to establish my freedom.

Mokrani fell like a hero. He sought his own death, for he was unwilling to
serve France now so degraded, or to fight a country which he so loved—a
country of which he had been the guest. It is an Arab custom that an unbroken friendship must ever exist between men who have partaken of the same
food. To break bread with an Arab is to cement a friendship which will remain unbroken until death. To make sure of his death, he left—this hero
without an equal—his horse, which perhaps might have snatched his master
from peril. He met the French Zouaves, and, at the head of his hesitating
column, marched forward, until a ball struck him upon the forehead.

Sidi Mokrani kept his word. He did not obey the Jews.

Among the French soldiers, whom the fatality of the times had reduced
to the sad necessity of drawing the sword in behalf of those who live by theft
and usury, many wept and perhaps envied the fate of the brave Arab chief. It
was the sons of Christian mothers who were obliged to sacrifice their lives in
order to assure to the usurers, the thieves of Algeria, the rights that had been
accorded to them, but which they themselves did not have the courage to
defend. General Bouzet says:

> The Jew cannot become a soldier. War is not at all his ele-
> ment. But if the Jews are arrant cowards, they are without pity.
> The Arabs who had surrendered themselves, trusting to the
> pledged and written word of the French officers and generals,
> were murdered by the Jews, and thus the renown and good re-
> pute of the French army was vilified and destroyed forever.

A poor Arab had preserved on his person the letter of pardon written by the
French general, and believing that a French soldier would never break his
word, he handed it to the officer who commanded the platoon of execution.
The officer, instead of obeying the voice of honor, instead of executing some
of the miserable Jews in place of the conquered heroes, gave the word "fire,"
in obedience to the command of the Jew Cremieux, a command which violated the pledge of the French officers. The poor Arab, fell, waving over his
head, as if by way of silent protestation, the lie written by the Frenchman.
What is still more revolting is the fact that the brave Arabs were excluded

from the amnesty that was granted to the other natives. Amnesty was granted to the Jews who had assassinated, pillaged, burned; but no amnesty was extended to the men who fought for the sake of securing their liberty.

It is interesting to see how this question was finally disposed of by the National Assembly. Do you think that among the Gentiles who form the majority, there was found a man to rise and point out with scorn the fanatic old Jew, Cremieux, who in the interest of his own people had caused the frightful insurrection that cost the lives of so many Frenchmen? Do you imagine that a voice was raised to render homage to the Arabians killed in the war with Germany, for the defense of a country that had deprived them of liberty? If you do, you are sadly mistaken. No one dared to displease the Jews, no one dared to proclaim the truth and to show things exactly as they are. The people of today are different from the people of old, who met death while affirming their opinions.

Cremieux succeeded. He took advantage of the disasters of France to push forward his own people. It is the peculiar method of Jewish diplomacy, such as they have continuously pursued since 1791. Be it war, peace, insurrection, reaction, they seek always their own aggrandizement, and they constantly advance while the Gentiles recede.

Before dying, Cremieux expressed the wish that the following simple but eloquent inscription should be placed upon his tomb:

> To Isaac-Adolphe Cremieux,
> President of the Universal Israelite Alliance.

The great work of Cremieux was *L'Alliance Israelite Universelle*, and he was right in saying that this institution was the most beautiful and the most wonderful ever founded in modern times. The Alliance, such as it actually exists, dates only from the month of July, 1860. Its first great assembly took place on 30 March 1861, but in reality the Alliance had at that time already been in existence for many years.

The Constitution of the Assembly is simple. Every Jew can become a member of the Alliance upon the payment of the modest fee of six francs a year. The Alliance is governed by a Central Committee, composed of 60 members. The Central Committee resides in Paris, and its members are chosen for nine years by the entire membership of the Alliance. They in turn elect every year a President, two vice- Presidents, a Treasurer and a Secretary, who manage the affairs of the Alliance.

A lodge, so to speak, may be instituted in every place where the society numbers ten members, and it has liberty to act as its members see fit in all purely local matters, for which, however, the lodge must assume the entire responsibility. The lodges correspond with the Central Committee, to which they communicate all matters of interest to the Jews, and in return they are kept informed of the progress of the Alliance.

Mr. Moses A. Dropsie, of Philadelphia, is an honorary member of the Central Committee, and Mr. Isaacs S. Myer, of New York, is also an honorary member of the same Central Committee.

The capital of the Alliance is of course unlimited, but the ostensible figures at the disposal of the association are given as one million francs.

With few exceptions, and for obvious reasons, the entire European press is friendly to the Alliance. But the Jews have a hundred other papers that address themselves solely to the sons of Israel, and a few of which we cite below. *Les Archives Israelites, L'Univers Israelite* of Paris; *La Famille de Jacob,* of Avignon; *The Jewish Chronicle, The Jewish World,* of London; *The Jewish Messenger,* of New York; *The Wiener Israelit, The Lebanon,* of Mayence; *The Volkszeitung, The Vochenschrift,* of Magdebourg; *The Allgemeine Zeitung des Judenthums, The Vessilo Israelitico,* of Casale; *The Corriere Isrealilico, L'Educatore Israelitico, The Famiglia Israelitica, Ben Chanonia, Ben Hanania, Der Orient, The Maggio, l'Ariel of Jerusalem, The Speranza,* of Smyrna, *The Jaetz,* of Bucharest, etc.

The Alliance is absolutely foreign to the idea of a country in the sense we attach to the word. A few words of Cremieux sum up the spirit of the institution more clearly than we could ourselves express it: "The Alliance is not a French, German, or English Alliance, but an Alliance of the Jews. This is the reason why it progresses, and why it prospers."

L'Alliance Israelite treats as an equal with the great European powers. It sends notes, protestations, and often an ultimatum, which sovereigns receive with exemplary docility. As soon as a Jew is imprisoned for theft, even in the remotest corner of our planet, the ambassadors, the consuls, the dragomans become excited, aroused, exchange notes, and protest. This is the reason why the Jews move heaven and earth to have in the Diplomatic Corps men of their own race, as, for instance, Roustan, the French Minister at Washington.

The sacrifices that the Jews are ever ready to make for the good of Israel may also be seen in the princely manner with which they have endowed and founded schools in the Orient. It is certain that this money has been obtained from the Gentiles, but the actions of the Jew must not be judged by our ideas, with which we have nothing in common. From the profits made on Turkish bonds, Maurice de Hirsch gave a million to the Jewish schools in the Orient; from the profits made on the Honduras affair, the Jew Bischoffsheim founded a school for girls, known as "The Bischoffsbeim Institute," etc. The Jews have today in Syria, Morocco, Tunis, Mesopotamia, and Jerusalem 36 schools, with more than 7,000 scholars, of whom 5,400 are boys, and 700 girls.

Baron Hirsch—The Upper Class of the Jews

Baron Maurice de Hirsch lives in Paris. He is the true type of the cosmopolite Jew. He occupies a better social position than the Rothschilds. He is the Baron, if you please, while the Rothschilds are the Barons. The Rothschilds claim to present a collectivity, the Baron keeps aloof, stands aloof, and even abstains from a too close association with his own family, which he leaves, as it were, in the obscurity of twilight. He is the Sultan, and his family is his harem.

But the Baron has not the pride and the haughty airs of the Rothschilds, whom one hesitates to approach even when he meets them in the same parlor. A self-satisfied parvenu, Hirsch is infinitely more open, more plain-dealing, easier in his manners than the Princes of Israel, in a word, less ridiculous. He is, no doubt, insolent, but his insolence is bantering and familiar. He has a puffed, red face, wide, dilating nostrils, and he enjoys life, when he is not a victim to the liver complaint, so common among the Jews. He is a good sort of fellow, with a grain of raillery.

This difference of manners noticeable between him and the Rothschilds is easy to be explained. The Rothschilds have inherited a social position that was achieved by their parents, who experienced the first rebuffs. They believe themselves to be scions of the aristocracy, "to belong to the aristocracy." Hirsch, on the contrary, believes that the aristocracy belongs to him. Hirsch has, unassisted, step by step, by his own exertions, gained that place in the fashionable world that he occupies today. He knows the current price of every conscience.

Like Bismarck and Gambetta, Hirsch also is a despiser of man, but the contempt the Baron feels is unalloyed. If Bismarck truly estimates all the cowardly acts of the diplomats and politicians who kneel before him, he cannot and does not disregard the noble traits of humanity when he thinks of the thousands of obscure heroes who have sacrificed themselves for the glory of Germany. If Gambetta had around him the most contemptible examples of human servility, he was not forgetful of the fact that in the beginning of his career many disinterested and guileless men supported him, believing that they were assisting in the triumph of a principle. Hirsch never in his life has seen a human being that has applied to him for any other purpose than to ask for money.

Hirsch has arisen in proportion as France has been dragged down. Only a few years ago, even the respectable middle classes scornfully refused his invitations, but today the noblest aristocrats feel happy in ascending the famous steps of his palace which the architect signed just as Raphael might have signed one of his masterpieces—Emile Peyre Fee.

It was on the top of these steps that the Baron said one day to his son, while looking down upon the dukes, princes, and marquises who were ascending them: "Twenty years hence they will all be either our sons-in-law or our janitors."

There are a few persons who look upon the house of Rothschild in the same light as that in which the old French nobility formerly looked upon the royal house of France. It is a bizarre and curious destiny, this destiny of the Rothschilds, a family that for the present we will touch upon only as respects their social connections.

We have already mentioned the eloquent but laconic shrug of the Duchess d'Angouleme, at the proposal made to her to admit Mme. Rothschild to her parlor. It was necessary to invoke the aid of all the European diplomats in order to obtain for the Rothschilds admittance, not to the court (had this happened all the chamberlains would have forthwith sent in their resignations) but to the receptions held in the Tuileries during great festive days, and to which, as a matter of fact, respectable men have never been refused admittance.

Three times the head ushers refused admittance to the Rothschilds when they attempted to enter the Tuileries on those festive occasions; three times they repeated the attempt, with an engaging smile, as if nothing had ever happened.

We produce the interesting details of a little episode in the case of Esther-Rebecca de Rothschild that occurred not many years ago:

One of the modern lights of ancient Zion, the wife, daughter and sister of honest Israelites, devoted to the worship of the golden calf, believed herself entitled to treat kings as her equals. She ordered her horses to be harnessed, and herself to be driven to the Tuileries. But there—cruel disappointment!—she was refused admittance.

Stung to the quick, she returned home. Tears flowed from her eyes. 'Jerusalem,' she cried, 'Jerusalem, what an offense to your people!' Extraordinary couriers were sent immediately to the courts of Germany to make known this great event. Kings were agitated, councils were summoned, and diplomats discussed the affair. Metternich seized his pen. The ambassador of Austria hastened to the Tuileries.

Finally pride yielded—the double doors opened, and the baroness entered the charmed circle. Then everywhere Israel was joyous. The mountains leaped like rams, the hills like lambs, the harp, which was left hanging on the willows, quivered anew under the fingers of the daughters of Zion. The chosen people once more celebrated the passage of the Red Sea.

Speaking of the Red Sea, it reminds us that red is the color that the circumcised Croesus is partial to, and it is in a red uniform, adorned with the epaulets of colonel, that James is in the habit of assisting in all the national festivities. His faithful Rebecca, the chosen one of his heart, the angel of his affections, lately accompanied him to the ball given by the city. This pearl of Israel was set between two Christian diamonds that shone so brilliantly that they dimmed all her luminosity.

These sentiments of repulsion lasted for a long time. In 1846 it was proposed to give at Baden a ball in honor of the recent arrival of a foreign potentate. A committee of three was appointed to regulate details, among whom was Maurice de Haber. The other two refused to have for a colleague a Jew, although this colleague was Haber, the millionaire banker of Cologne, and also allied to the family of a marshal of France, to the family of Grouchy. M. de Haber sent his seconds, but the two gentlemen refused to fight with him, although they expressed their willingness to do so with any one of his friends. They considered it a disgrace to cross swords with a Jew.

"The strange feature of the affair," said the *Archives Israelites*, "was that M. de Haber no longer belonged to Judaism, but to Protestantism. Mlle, de Haber, his daughter, was a convert to Catholicism for the sole purpose of marrying M. de Grouchy."

Jewish tenacity and Jewish patience in enduring affronts, and the Jews' manner of feigning not to be aware of them, are the causes of their social success. James Rothschild the elder was invited into society much as a clown would be invited. He amused people with his stories and puns.

He was niggardly in the extreme. One day a gentleman went to the elder Dumas to ask for a loan of 500 francs. The generous old man was, to use his own expression, "dry." The matter, however, was urgent. Dumas took his pen and wrote to the Baron James Rothschild a letter sparkling with wit, asking the loan of twenty-five louis. The man of millions did not even reply to him. A few months later, the autograph mania struck Paris. "Then these papers have a value, have they?" asked the Baron, of a friend. "That depends." "Let me see, I have one that I will show you." He produced that of Dumas. Immediately they offered him ten louis for it, which he accepted.

Dumas, however, avenged himself by a witty saying. One day, at a fair given for charitable purposes, a lady asked the Baron to put something into the charity platter. "But I have already put in something," said the financier. "I did not see you," said the lady, "but I believe you." "And I," said Dumas, "saw him, but I do not believe him."

Even his co-religionists censured his greediness and avarice. *Les Archives Israelites* tells us of a lesson that he received from Marcus Prague, a very zealous Israelite. One day during the Yom-Kippur, James Rothschild was requested to bring out the Sepher from the Ark. He asked Marcus Prague to take care of his prayerbook. The Baron noticed that the latter examined with interest his prayer-book, which was splendidly bound. "My Machsor seems to please you," said he. "How much will you give me for it?" "How, Baron," replied Prague, who was a zealous follower of the law, "in such a place and upon such a day would you transact business?"

He never heeded rebuffs. The following severe lesson was once given him by the distinguished aristocrat, d'Orsay: One day the Baron was playing whist at a gentleman's house, and accidentally let a louis fall on the floor. Immediately he stopped playing, seized a candle from the table and was about to hunt for his louis. "Do not disturb yourself, Baron," said one of the gentlemen present, who was no other than d'Orsay, "pray put the candle on the table. I will give you a light." And he quietly lit on the candle a bank-note of a thousand francs, with which he assisted the Baron to find his louis.

Today, however, the Rothschilds do not fear to meet an aristocrat of the independent spirit of d'Orsay. Aristocracy, at least such as figures in news-papers, is literally groveling at the feet of the Rothschilds, the Seligmans, the Belmonts and others of the same class. The aristocrats deem themselves spe-cially honored when they are entertained by these Jews.

This degradation is, however, more common among the Americans and the French, for we know that in Russia and Germany, the Jews are seldom admitted into the refined circles of society. In the beginning of 1884, Mad-ame Ephrussi went to St. Petersburg, and, owing to importunities and influ-ence set to work long before her arrival there, the Empress of Russia was prevailed upon to permit Madame Ephrussi to be presented to her at the Winter Palace. "The Master of Ceremonies," relates the *Political Corre-spondence* published in Vienna, "asked how he should introduce the Jewess to her Majesty." "You will introduce her to me," said the Empress, "when she gets ready to leave." Consequently, the daughter of Alphonse de Roth-schild (Madame Ephrussi) was presented to the Empress when she was about to leave the salon where the Empress was entertaining several ladies with her well-known gracefulness. As for Madame Euphrussi, who on that day was covered with a veritable mine of rubies, the Empress did not even look at her or exchange a word with her.

A few years ago, the Austrian Government, which, by the way, is fi-nancially in the hands of the Israelites, refused to receive A. A. Keiley as Minister from the United States, because he was married to a Jewess.

We have already seen how the German officers received the son of Bleichroeder. We give below an account of the manner in which the German correspondent of the newspaper *La France* describes the reception accorded to the daughter of Rothschild by Berlin society, in March, 1884:

> Speaking of anti-Semitism, here is a hitherto unpublished sto-
> ry now going the rounds of the salons of Berlin. The daughter
> of Rothschild, the banker, was presented this winter at court,
> but at the first ball that occurred there, nobody paid her any at-
> tention or exchanged a word with her. In short, she was ig-
> nored by everybody; not even an invitation to dance was given
> to her, at which, upon her return home, she shed bitter tears.

Nevertheless she again made her appearance at the next ball given at the Old Castle, where she again met with exactly the same reception.

At the third ball of the court, the hereditary Prince of Germany took pity on the young Jewess and ordered an officer to invite her to dance.

'By order of his Highness, the Crown Prince,' said the latter to Miss Rothschild, 'I have to ask you for the next quadrille.' The daughter of the banker who taxed France five billions in 1871 accepted with pleasure such an invitation.

The incense burned before these Jews in a measure explains how races degrade themselves. Rome saw a similar degeneration. Juvenal [ca. 100 AD] relates how the patricians, whose ancestors had conquered the world, begged for a place at the table of the sons of slaves who had enriched themselves.

To enter the house of Rothschild is, in the estimation of some, the equivalent of being presented at court, although the Jews receive those who visit them with contempt. Count Vasili, in his Recollections of the Society in Berlin says of Bleichroeder: "True, he will oblige his fellowman, but the banker experiences a devilish pleasure in making the recipient feel the weight of his favor. He takes special pleasure in humiliating him with his vulgar familiarity."

Baron Alphonse is only 57 years old, but he looks like a man of 70. He is a small man, with whitish side whiskers, and with a few scattered hairs upon his head. He personifies the premature decrepitude of his race. What is striking in his physiognomy is the blankness of look, the continual blinking of his eyes. A foreign diplomat once said: "It would seem that the metallic reflection of the gold that that man has contemplated through life has ruined his sight, as it often happens with workmen who weave cloth of a particularly fine tissue." Alphonse, who is very haughty in manner, has, nevertheless, what may be termed popular instincts. He likes to go about Paris incognito, and passes himself off for a photographer with the shop-girls and flower-girls, in whose society he finds a peculiar charm.

His brother Edmund is the real type of the Jew shopkeeper. He has a reddish beard, and is given to ogling the fair sex with an impertinent and vulgar air. He looks like a man who is constantly occupied in searching for something he cannot find.

The other brother, Gustave, with his chestnut beard and tall stature, would present comparatively a distinguished appearance, if he knew how to enter a room and how to leave it. He affects a still more reserved demeanor than the rest of the family. His wife is arrogant beyond description.

Every member of the family is disagreeable and crotchety. Some of them suffer from an affection of the spinal column; this is especially true of Edmund. Others, like Nathaniel, lose their sight at an early age. He is wheeled about in a little carriage through those magnificent apartments, the luxury of which for him no longer exists. Like all Jews, the Rothschilds are ill-bred, morose, aggressive, and in the midst of their opulence they have the misery that comes from satiety. They have nothing to stimulate them, no motive for action. They have aimed to enslave society, and after having attained their object, they feel that society is dying from the effects of their deleterious breath, and that they have only a dead body in their hands.

Alphonse indulges in a sort of bitter humor and of cutting irony in his intercourse with society, which he thoroughly despises, and now and then his contempt becomes apparent in the disobliging and vulgar allusions that he flings at those present.

Let us now describe how, in reality, the interior of the house of these modern kings of the Jews looks. The houses are built like theaters or strongholds, and are securely barricaded inside. *The World*, of London, published a few years ago interesting details respecting one of the Rothschild's mansions, in St. Florentin Street: "Baron Alphonse de Rothschild has just finished the improvements in his house on Florentin Street, and it now looks like a veritable fortress. There are a number of strong iron cases built into the walls, and at the mere touch of a button the rich bric-a-brac, and other ornaments hanging upon the walls, drop into these cases. Each, picture is in a Morocco case, so that in an emergency all can be packed within an hour." But would they have the time to pack?

Their mansion at Versailles was built under the supervision of the English architect, Paxton, but as the great French architect, Delorme, has pointed out, Paxton utterly failed to erect a building that harmonizes externally with the climate, the sky, and the habits of the French people, and the result of his work is one of those queer-looking castles so often seen in England. The Versailles mansion seems expatriated.

The interior is more interesting. After traversing a large vestibule, the ceiling of which is gorgeously ornamented, one enters a small room where there are a few fine paintings by Philippe Rousseau. Then one passes into the large dining-room, which presents a pleasing appearance with its commodious armchairs upholstered with red velvet.

The surprises, however, begin when one enters into the magnificent parlor, called the parlor of Louis XVI. One sees ranged before one's eyes all the wonders of genius that agents throughout the world could collect. There one sees masterpieces of art, carved furniture and tables by the most renowned makers. Artistic bronzes of the finest pattern and workmanship adorn this charming room, over which is a ceiling decorated by Henry Levy. In the middle stands, as a prophet, the incomparable harpsichord that once belonged to Marie Antoinette, an object that one regrets to see in the hands of these Jews. A little dark side room now attracts one's attention. It is the oratory, a room devoted to prayer. It is a very simple room, having for ornament only the rolls of Thora and a candelabrum of seven branches. Next comes the family parlor, which is also called the Parlor of the Leathers of Cordova. It owes its name to the superb hangings of embossed leather, representing the triumph of Mardochee. These leathers, which are perfectly preserved, came originally from Flanders. They were bought, no doubt, from some Spanish lord. They are very curious specimens of the embossed, gilded leathers of which Cervantes so often speaks. There is in the room also a magnificent table cover worked with silver thread, a most interesting and costly article.

One's attention is now attracted to a few books in an ebony case, at the top of which is a wonderfully carved elephant. Desirous to ascertain who are the friends, the literary acquaintances of these people, one goes to the library. One finds there Paul de Kock, Soulie, Pigault-Lebrun, Eugene Sue and Jacob's *History of France*. What an insight these books give one into the tastes of these people and of those who visit them!

Let us now pass into the *perron*. To the right and the left are two elegant vases which cost fifty thousand francs. The outlook is beautiful, especially in summer, as one has opposite him the fountain, and at a distance beyond the park, and farther on a view of the open country.

Let us reenter the apartments. We are in the parlor called the Parlor of Hangings, which contains a few panels by Desportes. On the walls hang tapestries, woven in silk, of a freshness without equal. It was in this room, full of smiling figures and teasing shepherdesses, it was amidst these frivolous scenes that the famous interview took place between Bismarck and Jules Favre, in the war of 1870.

The Venetian room contains nothing particularly attractive. "At the hunting season," said Rothschild, "we have to put some princes in it." The decorations of the smoking-room are by Eugene Lamy, who has reproduced there with remarkable exactness several episodes of the Carnival of Venice.

The hall alone, however, well repays a visit to this house. In the evening this hall, with its eleven hundred jets of gas, which shed their rich light upon the ceiling, the brilliant toilets, diamonds, and flowers, presents a veritable fairy-like scene. It is the most enchanting part of the whole house. Everything there speaks of triumphs. Around the immense gallery that crowns the hall are superb tapestries representing nothing but triumphs: the triumph of Alexander, the triumph of Neptune, the triumph of Peace, etc., etc. One sees there—what does not one see in this prodigious bazaar! Behold! first to the left the picture of Baron James Rothschild, by Flanderin, and of the Baroness, by Ingres. On the walls there is a picture of a man, by Rembrandt, also pictures of the Countess Della Rocca, and of Don Luis de Haro, by Velasquez, and of Diana, the huntress nymph, by Rubens; David and Goliath, by Guide; of Princess Henrietta of England, by Reynolds; Diogenes in Search of an Honest Man, by Van Mol, and The Message, by Bordone.

Everywhere there can be seen Italian cabinets filled with little masterpieces, ivories, emeralds, boxes, a historic mirror of Madame de Pompadour, etc. The monumental mantelpiece is decorated with Italian medallions, and is mounted with a bust of Minerva. An album bound in Morocco leather, that is left ostentatiously upon the table, awakens many a thought. On the first page we read, "Souvenir of the charming day of the 16th of December, 1862. Napoleon"; a little below, "Souvenir of friendship for the charming hospitality of Baron and Baroness James de Rothschild, 20 November 1866. Mathilde."

Charms, charmed, charmers—everything is charming, but abruptly on the following page appears a name written in heavy, bold characters. "Wilhelm, September 21, 1870." The names of Bismarck and Moltke are signed below those of the Emperor. Following the names of the conquerors, we find the signatures of the most illustrious representatives of the nobility of France. The Germans whose names figure in this registry signed there by the right of force. They occupied the house by the right of war, and demanded to be served, not as persons invited, but as conquerors. They toasted not the charms of the Baroness, but their brave Emperor, after God their only master.

But France's nobles went there as persons subsisting on alms. They went there with downcast heads, happy in being admitted to the presence of these Jews.

The impression this house leaves upon one is more that of fatigue than of admiration. It is an incredible warehouse of bric-a-brac. All these objects collected from all the corners of the Earth seem to growl at one another, for these spoils of the universe do not harmonize. One might easily fancy that these products of so many civilizations are looking in defiance at one another. In the words of Goncourt, "There are collections of art that show neither passion, love, nor intelligence; nothing excepting the brutal victory of money."

The love of bric-a-brac, of all odds and ends, or rather the Jews' passion for possession, is often carried to childishness. A small stone pot, not worth more than six francs, serves for a vis-a-vis to an exquisite little figure of artistic design.

The park, vast as it is, presents nothing particularly inviting. There are not, in all this immense park, more than half a dozen statues, and these are so commonplace that they are hardly fit to be placed in a beer garden. The finest spot in all this immense park is the place allotted to the greenhouses and the aviaries. The greenhouses are a delight, filled with plants which are in bloom all the season, collected from every part of the world.

In the immense aviaries, hundreds of birds of rare plumage and of great variety of color seem to reflect the skies of their respective countries. There are partridges from China, red pheasants and pheasants of all known species; toucans, which, with their ugly black bills, attack the pheasants as the Jews attack the Gentiles; flamingos of Egypt, perched upon basins filled with fish; blue magpies of China; doves caught in the Philippine Islands; in a word, the birds of Europe, the birds of Africa, the birds of Asia, the birds of America, the birds of Australia—all are to be found there. They flap their wings in picturesque confusion. In concert they cry, now shrieking, now plaintive. The whole seems like a vision of some corner of a terrestrial paradise. These birds are the life of this somber domain, a domain upon which neither heroism nor genius have put their resplendent seal. Contrast this Jew's palace with the simple house of Wellington, which from top to bottom was adorned only with the flags and trophies captured at Waterloo.

The greatest joy of the Rothschilds is to read a newspaper that contains articles published about them, when either a feast or a marriage enlivens their domain. They pass the newspaper from hand to hand, and, strange though it may seem, every member reads the article aloud. Every member feels a special pride as he peruses these articles written with an inconceivable exaggeration of adjectives.

Upon the loss of a member of the Rothschild family, the salaried minions of the Rothschilds tear their hair and roll upon the ground in despair, if one can believe the accounts published. As a well-known author has said, the very frontiers of hyperbole recede before their expressions of sorrow.

The following newspapers are in the pay of the Rothschilds: *Journal de Paris, La France, Le Constitutionnel, La Liberte, Le Petit Journal, La Patrie, Le Journal des Debats, L'Opinion Nationale, Le Temps, Le Figaro, L'Epoque, L'Evenement, Le Moniteur du Soir, La Correspondance Generale des Dapartments, Le Sport, Le Memorial Diplomatique, La Semaine Financiere.* Astonishing letters are sent to them: "You will pardon me if I disturb you in the midst of your sorrows... My sole excuse please attribute to the interest I take." Behold how the Prince de Joinville, in whose veins runs the blood of Louis XIV, wrote to this manipulator of money, this man of fraudulent antecedents.

Ever since 1868, the spirit of servility has been constantly on the increase. The descriptions published apropos of a Rothschild marriage are bewildering. The toilet of the bride is described in its minutest details of headgear, body-gear, and footgear, all of which gears are said to have been furnished by...so and so...so and so, Purveyors to the Baron. Naturally no names are omitted. We find there Prince Murat, the Duke de Broglie, the Duke de Montmorency, in a word, all the nobility of France present to worship this golden calf, and to proclaim to the world that wealth is the supreme royalty. The entire police force is on duty to secure the streets for the exclusive use of the marriage guests.

To go into ecstasy over these Jews, who have nothing to recommend them but the wealth that has been acquired by questionable means, is a folly almost beyond comprehension.

People often go into raptures over what is termed the inexhaustible charity of the Rothschilds. "Oh, the noble Baroness, the mother of the poor!" exclaims the Jew Wolff. Now, the charity of the Rothschilds is a myth. In proportion to their fortune, the Rothschilds are not so generous as the laboring man who gives a cent a week to the poor. The fact is, the Rothschilds are niggardly. They have founded hospitals, for whom? Their co-religionists. They establish in business those of their race who promise to succeed. In a word, everything they give is given to the Jews, because by strengthening their people they strengthen themselves. They have at their command that admirable secret police which has not its equal in the world. They discharge an obligation—they do not bestow a charity. From their action they derive abundant returns. What is true of the Rothschilds is true of all Jews, who make a display of charity solely to get the applause of the rabble. It is astonishing how successful the Jews are in finding means by which they make a reputation for philanthropy, while really they make the Gentiles alleviate the misery of others.

The catastrophes that have occurred in the course of the last few years have, with very few exceptions, mowed down the ranks of the Jews. Szeged was nearly all occupied by Jews.[1] At the burning of the theatre in Vienna, they furnished most of the victims. The Island of Chios, where more than 11,000 persons perished from earthquake, was inhabited chiefly by Jews, and the victims of the fires in the theatres of London and Paris were mostly Jews.

The fairs given in the name of charity are one of the features of modern life. They have greatly multiplied of late years, and it belongs to the historian, or rather to the moralist, to describe their results. But they offer a double advantage to the Jew. They attest the power of Israel, which puts a city in a ferment as soon as a Jew needs assistance, and permits the obscure Jew to mix with society.

One of the latest and most noted of these charities that demands our notice was the one organized by the Jews for the survivors of the earthquake in Chios [Turkey]. The Jews announced that the fair was to assist the survivors without distinction of race. Accordingly a Kirmess was organized opposite the Tuileries, which Kirmess the Jews called "a market of pleasure." This market of pleasure was closed on Saturdays, and when the Gentiles asked the reason, the Jews responded: "There is a time for everything. Today it is Saturday. We shall open tomorrow. Sunday is the better day for us."

Sunday the place presented an animated spectacle. Circuses, shows, lotteries, flower-stands, everything presented the well-known life of Paris. Joyful exclamations were heard on all sides. But how the funds were distributed nobody has been able to ascertain.

We must not forget to mention that no charity was organized to assist the families of the 30,000 Gentiles murdered in Tonkin.

---

[1] This city in Hungary was ravaged by a great flood in 1879.

One invariably sees in these charity fairs what we may term the old brigade of society, composed always of the same persons, and always described with the same adjectives in the newspapers. Who does not recall, when looking at these dowagers, the old women spoken of in Aristophanes, the sweethearts of death?

The old Greek writer comes to our mind as we stand before these superannuated beauties, who are so obstinate in displaying faces that seem already to have the immobility of mortuary things. This old battalion is really one of the sights peculiar to our epoch. Formerly, when, to use the expression of the poet, "the course of life was half over," people resigned themselves, perhaps not without a deeply drawn sigh, to pass into what is called a retreat. They quitted with dignity the scenes of life where, during the happy hours of youth, they had acted a part at times brilliant. Today, however, the old brigade refuses to disappear, although these figures of society produce the effect of skeletons of the Middle Ages, clothed in silk, covered with jewels, replete with ornaments, but with wrinkled faces, dry lips and toothless mouths.

When we asked how the money arising from the Chios Kirmess was distributed, we were referred by the Jews to their committee, who minced matters, and never gave us a satisfactory answer. Apropos of committees composed of Jews, we recall "The Committee Dupont, which was composed of Dupont, was presided over by Dupont, and reelected Dupont."

Speaking of charity fairs, we are reminded of a singular "Ball of Animals," organized in the month of May, 1885, in Paris, by the Princess de Sagan. At this nameless ball, all the high life, all the true nobility of Europe, was present. This ball took place solely in order that the names of those present might appear in the society paper, *Le Gaulois*, edited by the Jew Arthur Meyer. Meyer is a type of the Jew journalist of the present day. To describe him would be to describe in general the journalists of the Jewish race.

Meyer is a leader in Parisian society, an arbitrator of elegance, an organizer of society affairs. Never before have the Jews produced a type so successful as this Meyer. The son of a dealer in braids, Meyer came to Paris about 20 years ago, as secretary to a certain demi-mondaine. Meanwhile he occupied his spare time in the capacity of a reporter. He buttonholed everybody, in order to obtain a bit of startling news, and more than once he was heard at society festivals to ask those present, "Pray, what is the name of this lady? What is the name of this gentleman? Can you tell me something of

their antecedents?" and so on. He wrote the names given to him with feverish anxiety on his cuffs. He signed the pseudonym of Jean de Paris.

In 1869 a book appeared entitled *Paris that Plays and Paris that
Cheats*. The following faithful account of Arthur Meyer, alias Jean de Paris,
was given under the name of Duke Jean: "Clothes to sell! Old clothes, old
braids, old hats!"

It was, and still is, the device of the Duke Jean family. At the age of fifteen, tired of his apprenticeship to traffic, Arthur Meyer, afterward known as
Duke Jean, the present proprietor of the *Gaulois*, moved heaven and earth to
go to Paris—the only field in France for a nature as industrious as that of
Duke Jean. In Paris, the Duke did a little of everything. He tried commerce,
which, however, did not prove successful, and he then engaged in the business of counterfeiting trademarks. Later on, Duke Jean saw how profitable it
would be to flatter the vanity of some and to extol the coquetry of others.
The first year, however, was a hard one for him. He went to Trouville-sur-
Mer (the Newport of France), where, during his short sojourn, it was discovered that he had more than four aces at his command. He was expelled from
the Casino.

He, however, succeeded in attaching himself to a certain person well
known through his productions depicting a certain grade of Parisian society.
Owing to this friendship, Duke Jean again entered society—but false society,
frequented by young bloods and a certain class of reporters. In this society,
he soon achieved a prominence, which, however, did not satisfy his ambition, for he never ceased to cast longing eyes toward the better circles.

This was Meyer's first start. He quickly made his way, owing to the influence of the Jews, which reached its zenith soon after the Franco-Prussian
War. Today, Duke Jean, after numberless acts of blackguardism and blackmail, is the owner of a newspaper, of a house, and of a carriage. He does not
excite either scorn or envy, but he is looked upon with amazement.

With his sallow complexion, bald head, and glossy beard, he gives the
impression of a Semitic mummy walking about the streets by the aid of a
secret spring. This fantastical being, this blackleg, is a leader in fashionable
society. It is he who put into circulation the words "*pshutt* and *v'lan*," which
French society repeats with an idiotic grimace.

This fellow has been mixed in everything that is low and disgraceful in
the annals of the world. Lately he figured prominently in the Meissonier ver-
sus Madame Mackay affair. He persuaded Madame Mackay to pay the

amount claimed by the artist, which amount Meyer took to Meissonier and paid over to him. Madame Mackay was justified in her dissatisfaction with her picture, and Meissonier disgraced himself with his greediness, by exacting 70,000 francs for a painting to which he devoted only a very few sittings.

"Paris is getting to be a lair of thieves," cry the tourists. This is not true. Paris still has its full share of honest people. If, instead of allowing herself to be surrounded by the thieves who wait for the arrival of tourists at the railroad stations; if, instead of permitting herself to be surrounded by Jews, Madame Mackay, who is certainly a most estimable woman, had selected her associates more wisely, she would have learned that often as fictitious a price is put upon works of art as upon railroad shares. She would have found in Paris many artists that paint as good a portrait as Meissonier. She would have found an artist who would have treated her honorably, and thus she would have escaped the scurrilous attacks made by the public press.

This Meyer is a type of the wriggling, insinuating, low flatterer, the very type of the Jew who puts the patricians to sleep with his flattery. He organizes society fairs with the assistance of titled ladies. At a recent feast, it was announced that he would open the ball with Countess Aimery de La Rochefoucauld. When the time came, the poor Countess was so ashamed to be seen dancing with this low Jew that she took only a turn round the room, followed by this little Jew, who looked like a page holding the train of an Empress.

Clearly to understand what takes place in the sanctums of Jew papers, we refer our readers to *Le Druide*, a novel written by the Countess de Martel, who says concerning the *Gaulois*: "They have special editors for pander and blackmail. They employ an old variety actress, who edits the fashion column, and who claims to teach the latest society manners."

Nothing is more upright, more conscientious, more disinterested than the journalism of Christian newspapers. The true journalist wields a powerful arm with which he wounds the vanity of people, when this vanity has assumed almost morbid proportions; or again he lavishes praise on those to whom praise is due, without a thought ever crossing his mind of deriving any benefit whatever from the praises he bestows. With the Jew, however, the newspaper is only an instrument of blackmail. It is the Jew who says to our judges, "If you do this, you will command the services of an experienced journalist."

In the annals of blackmail, the Jew journalist figures to an astonishing degree. To cite a few examples: Fiorentino, the only critic of a French paper ever convicted of blackmail, was a Jew. At the time of the debut of a poor actress, who had begged of him to wait a little for the money he demanded of her for an article written by him, he wrote: "Miss is a *promising* actress, but whether she will make good her *promises* remains to be seen." David, a well-known financial editor, was also convicted of blackmail, and he too was a Jew. Mr. Albert Christopher, director of the *Crédit Foncier*, declared before the Chamber the manner in which the Jew, Eugene Mayer, obtained the money that enabled him to establish his paper *La Lanterne*.

Mayer commenced by writing some articles *in La Réforme Financiere* detrimental to the *Credit Foncier*, but his articles were ignored. "Accordingly," said Mr. Albert Christopher, "all these articles were collected into one volume, which quite naturally disturbed the directors of the above financial institution. Mayer had the book exposed in the windows of the book-stores throughout Paris." Acting upon the advice of the directors, Mr. Albert Christopher bought the entire edition from Mayer for 30,000 francs, and both the plates and the books were destroyed, with the exception of one copy, which the president of the institution kept. Christopher continued:

> Now, gentlemen, who were the authors of this publication? Who were the makers of this libelous book? Who were those who put it on sale? In fine, who were those who made the shameful traffic that I stand here to denounce? They are those who took the money, those who have used the money to vivify and to enable the newspaper *La Lanterne* to succeed. These are the facts in this case, which I leave to your appreciation, without adding thereto any commentary. These are the facts which, without exaggeration, I stigmatize as an act of financial blackmail.

On 14 July 1883, the Jewish paper *La Lanterne* published a scurrilous article against the Colonel of the 22nd Regiment of Artillery. On the day following, the offices of the paper were full of officers. What were those gentlemen there for? To demand reparation from Mayer? No; they went there, the paper announced in italics, "to offer testimony favorable to their colonel."

"Is it not humiliating" asks Drumont, "for psychologic history to see these heroes, these soldiers of great battles, these Frenchmen occupied in pleading the cause of their colonel before a rascally Jew of Cologne, half blackmailer and half spy?" It is impossible to make either an Englishman, an American, or a German understand such a proceeding. The German officers, those disciples of Hegel, in uniform, who wish to explain everything by philosophical theories, embarrass you with their everlasting questions. "Now," they say, "your officers are very brave. We saw them under fire; they are almost unequalled in attack. How is it that they permit themselves to be so treated?" The absence of moral courage is the only explanation that can be offered.

To demonstrate this absence of moral courage, let the reader read the account of the 37 gendarmes who were hostages of the Commune. These men in the very flower of their age, these men of incontestable courage, which they proved by their death, allowed themselves to be conducted to the slaughter by an escort of 35 German Jews, who would have run away the moment these 37 heroes had shown any fight. During their march to the place of execution, the masses were favorable to them and encouraged them to escape. At the top of Rue de La Roquette, a woman cried out: "For God's sake, run away." "But they marched to the end," says Maxime du Camp, "quietly keeping step as if they were going to military maneuvers."

The events that have occurred during the last ten years prove that the atmosphere of France has become so thoroughly impregnated with Jewish fetidness that there is no more moral courage or strength of character in a French colonel than there is in a simple municipal guard.

Eugene Mayer, however, possesses in the highest degree moral courage and strength of character. One of the uncles of this Mayer, owing to the influence of the Jew Wolff, who is connected with the *Figaro*, was given the position of military contractor during the Crimean and Mexican wars, in which position he made an enormous fortune, which he lost in speculation. Later on, he engaged in a fraudulent speculation in the United States, but, fearing arrest, he fled to Brussels.

Another of his uncles was, in 1860, Director of the Cologne Loan Bank—a sort of pawnshop on a large scale. Having committed numerous embezzlements, he sought refuge first in France, and then in England. He was, in his absence, condemned to prison at hard labor for life. While in

London, he married a notorious procuress established in Piccadilly, who has since moved to the more productive soil of Paris.

As for the father of Mayer, he was incarcerated for a few days in prison, but was shortly afterwards pardoned, thanks to the influence of the marshal. Being implicated, however, a few years ago, in another affair, and finding himself face to face with ruin, he hanged himself in his shop.

How can a people thrive that is a prey to men like Mayer, who are always busy intriguing or scheming, or engaged in some scandal or swindle? Let the Jews have their way for 20 years, and not only Paris and France, but all Europe would be ruined; not even America would escape.[2]

If we could be left with those only already among us! Alas! There are millions of them in the world who come down upon us, one after the other, more famished, more grasping, more zealous in their anarchical doctrines than their predecessors. God speed the anti-anarchical society, the plan of which was recently published in the New York *Evening Post*.

Mayer, however, is more endurable than his contemporary, Albert Wolff, of *Le Figaro*, the most barefaced and shameless blackmailer the Semitic or any other race has thus far produced. He spoke the truth when he called himself "The epoch's great phenomenon." The modern Jew is incarnated in his entirety in this mongrel and singular being.

One day the Queen of Romania asked the Jew Blowitz, who went to that country to introduce the lightning express, to what country he belonged. "Your Majesty," responded the Jew, "I do not myself know. I was born in Bohemia, and I live in France, where I write in the English language." But, as a type of the cosmopolitan Jew, Wolff is still more complete. He has neither country, religion, nor sex. This neutral being, in fact, is a unique product that does not enter into any existing classification.

Bastien-Lepage, the painter, has drawn this anthropomorphous figure in his true colors. This bizarre creature is a common figure in the Boulevards of Paris, a being which recalls those fat women now and then to be seen wearing upon their deformed heads bonnets with an abundance of flowers, with bosoms swinging in dirty camisoles, and with a demeanor of a truly comical solemnity. Wolff has the peculiar leer of these strange matrons. We

---

[2] One can make a good case that America had sold out to the Jews by 1911, when they forced the president to abrogate a longstanding US-Russia treaty. See T. Dalton, *The Jewish Hand in the World Wars* (2025), pp. 20-26 for details. As such, Timayenis was largely correct.

must try to do with the pen what Bastien-Lepage has done with the brush. We have, fortunately, as a guide, a characteristic production by a young literary Jew, entitled *Albert Wolff, a History of a Parisian Chronicler,* by Gustave Totidouze.

Like many other Jew journalists, Wolff was born in Cologne, and it was not till 1857 that this German journalist came to France to eat her bread while instigating the German invasion. Kugelmann made him enter *Le Figaro* office, where he shone brilliantly. What is called by people "Parisian wit" is a frothy creation of the Jews, who speak it best, as it is natural those should do who fabricate the slang.

At the time when Wolff came to Paris, he was not a high-priced man. In return for a loan of five louis, he would lavish upon anyone a thousand compliments. But if ever he was reminded of the loan, he covered the lender with his filthy invectives.

Thanks to *Le Figaro*, Wolff exercises over the art world the influence that Mayer exercises over the social and political. "We saw," says Drumont, "artists of talent tremble in their boots, when that hideous Jew passed before their pictures, a few days before the opening of the Salon."

Were a Gentile to do one-quarter only of what this arch blackmailer has done, the Gentiles would not find sufficient anathemas to hurl at his head. The Jews, on the contrary, sustain and defend their co-religionist. Whatever a man would ordinarily avoid even to hint at is sufficient to prompt Wolff to go into full details.

The coffin of the unfortunate actress, Gabrielle, was not yet closed when Wolff related in its full details the private life of the actress, and published what nobody had ever asked of him, revealing that this woman, now dead, was formerly the mistress of a Jew, a frequenter of the greenroom, named Ernest Blum. Blum profited from the opportunity to advertise himself at the expense of his dead companion. He published scurrilous allusions in the Jewish paper, *Le Rappel.*

But it is Sarah Bernhardt who inspires Wolff. The chronicler of *Le Figaro* blesses this "child," blesses her husband, blesses her children, and compares Sarah to an *angel* who has spread her wings over art, and slighting nothing in his description of the interior of her home.

The fact that people allow these nauseating articles to occupy the front page of *Le Figaro* day after day, without offering the slightest protest, is evidence of the degeneration of moral courage among the masses. Thanks to the

Jews, both the theatre and society threaten to fall into the lowest degradation. Society has become an immense theatre, where each one tries, indeed, to attract to himself the attention of others.[3]

The theatre itself is fast assuming an anomalous importance, which is explained by the invasion of the Jews. The profession of actor is well calculated to tempt the Jews. It promises great returns, satisfies a certain vanity, and does not require in the average actor any extraordinary talent. All the theatres in Paris are in the hands of Jews. Speculators in vaudeville and concerts, like Strakosch, are also Jews. The greater part of the artists are also of the family of Jacob. Stolz, Patti, Sass, Kidds, Devries, Rosine, Bloch, Heilbronn, Bernhardt, Mlle. Isaac, Judie, Madame Israel Reichemberg, Mlle. Milly Meyer, are all Jews. Worms is the son of a Jew butcher whose shop is situated in Vieille-du-Temple Street.

Managers of low variety shows, managers who speculate in the business; managers who, without capital, engage companies and trust to luck, are all Jews. If you speak with an American manager, he will tell you that ever since the Jews entered the business, the theatrical profession has been on the decline.

As soon as it is a question of praising a daughter of Zion, the terms heretofore employed by the entire Christian world in honor of those Gentiles that have ennobled the stage are not sufficiently strong to please the Jews. We have already alluded to the Jewish habit of aggrandizing everything that they touch upon, or, rather, to aggrandize everything that touches them. They see everything through a magnifying glass, and heap up the adjectives, a habit common to the people of the Orient. For them, the poorest artist, if he is only a Jew, becomes something grand.

This apotheosis began with Rachel Felix, who had the force peculiar to the Jews—a force that has already captured the ducats of the entire world, and in course of time will capture everything that remains. The true picture of Rachel was traced by Philarète Chasles, who said: "That lascivious Jewess had the instincts of a tigress, but was withal of a sublime intelligence, for she succeeded in captivating all her contemporaries. It is said that archbishops blessed her, and that France wept for her." It is superfluous to say that the Jews have not ceased their praises, until at last they have made the Gentiles almost believe that Rachel was the noblest and purest of women.

---

[3] Yet another remarkable anticipation of current-day events.

The ordinary conditions of morality, such as are understood by the Gentiles, are completely changed when they affect a Jew or a Jewess. In 1883, a suit was instituted against Sarah Bernhardt, in which her illegitimate children were mixed up in the case. The Jewish newspaper, *Le Gaulois*, immediately, in an article of three columns, sought to convince its readers that these children were the issue of faithful and devoted love; that they were children such as mortals no longer' produce; children such as the world has not seen since the days of Rachel. The article ends with an incomparable apotheosis of the whole race.

Good heartedness and good fellowship among artists of Gentile extraction is a noble trait of the profession. It is related of poor John McCullough that he would often get up from a sick bed to assist or take part in any benefit given for an impoverished actor. Never, however, has a star among the Jews been known to render the slightest aid to a brother artist of Christian extraction, unless by way of shrewd advertisement.

In whatever quarter the Jews may establish themselves, one is certain to find in the neighboring streets in great numbers gambling dens and houses of prostitution. Now and then, we are informed in the morning press of raids made in certain well-known streets. If the police of New York were to pay closer attention to certain uptown streets close upon Lexington Avenue, for instance, of which avenue the Jews have taken almost complete possession, they would find many of the gilded palaces of the metropolis.

The same is true of the Jewish quarters in Paris. The streets where the Jews live abound with what the French call *souteneurs*—supporters of bad women.

If anyone wishes to form a true idea of the condition and habits of the Jews in Paris for the last few years, he should read the book of Jean Macé, entitled, *Le Service de La Sureté par son Ancien Chef.* In its open brutality, in its matter of fact, dry and cold language, this work surpasses everything that has been written about Paris. It discloses the social wounds more cruelly than the most eloquent pens have heretofore done. Naturalism has never produced a more powerful exposure. The chapter on *Souteneurs* is truly sinister. The constantly increasing immorality, owing to the materialistic doctrines openly advocated by the Jewish press, as well as the difficulty of obtaining work, have created certain classes heretofore unknown to civilization. Mace distinctly affirms that married men live from the dishonor of their wives, and that it is the husbands who watch over the debauchery of their better halves. It is needless to say that the Aryan cannot conceive such depravity. The men who commit these acts of unheard-of wickedness are exclusively of the Semitic race.

The army of malefactors is recruited from the *souteneurs*. They rob the houses in the environs of Paris, and do not hesitate to fire upon the officers of the police. Those of the police who do not sympathize with the malefactors are obliged to engage in desperate fights. The *souteneurs* assassinate in full midday; they assassinate near the bridges and the garden of the Tuileries. They recently lassoed a man before the well-known Hill Hotel in Paris, and robbed him. They stop carriages in the streets, as was the custom formerly in the highways. In the month of January 1885, a lady returning from Bordeaux engaged a cab at a railroad station in Paris, and at Contrescarpe Street, three malefactors seized the bridle of the horse, and the lady was obliged to give up all she possessed.

Travelers are killed in wagons, girls in their beds, and merchants in their offices. The police fold their arms before these crimes, utterly powerless to cope with them, although there are today 16,000 policemen in Paris, while under the Empire, the total number was 9,322. The well-known assassin of a young girl is to be seen every day tranquilly walking the streets. Why is he not arrested? His brother Solomon is a member of the police.

The French papers of a single week in January, 1886, mentioned nine murders and five attempts at murder.

The beer saloons kept by women are the plague of this great city. Once there, every son of an honest family is forever lost. He is made to drink, he is made to play, and then he is robbed of all he possesses. Never before did human nature degrade itself to lower depths than it has among these unfortunate women, who depend upon intoxication for their livelihood, and who are called "lazy" whenever their stomachs rebel. There are women who empty as many as fifty glasses of beer a day.

Albert Delpit says concerning these saloons:

> All the Latin Quarter [home to many students] is infested by these beer saloons kept by women. The students go there, abandoning their classes and their examinations, leaving everything in order to run after these women of the ground floor. ... I entered successfully into half a dozen of these beer saloons, and everywhere I saw the same repugnant spectacle:

women decoying and caressing students who, although not more than fifteen to eighteen years old, were pale and withered beings with an old look upon their faces.

The spirit of the pander has invaded all classes of society. The proprietor who rents to a common woman a lodging at three times its worth; the saloon keeper who invites her to his shop in order to draw customers; the coal merchant who sells her coal at false weight, the grocer, the fruiterer, the costume vender, the dressmaker who sell to her goods at a greater price than to others; even the washerwoman who overcharges—all these pilferers of various appellations are in reality so many panders. They all urge her to debauchery, because her debauchery is profitable to them.

Mr. Mace addressed reports upon reports, demands upon demands, to the Chief of Police, asking authority to cleanse Paris of this filth. He met with a formal refusal, which he plainly indicates in his book. "The majority," he says, "of the Tonseil Municipal'" (which we may designate as the *Honorable Body of Aldermen*) "are in friendly relations with these exploiters of vice."

In the month of April 1883, a few students, less degenerate than the majority of their comrades, sought to accomplish the task the police refused to do. In a single night, they would have freed the quarter of the Jewish element which infests it—an element totally addicted to pander and to the business of *souteneurs*. What did the Commissary of the Police, Schnerb, the German Jew, brother to the pornographer Schnerb, do? He marched at the head of a band of panders and *souteneurs*, followed by the police, and rushed upon the students who, attacked with clubs, were obliged to retreat. What did the people do? They rewarded the Jew Schnerb by presenting him with a baton.

The Industrial Crisis

While the Jew is always ready to derive benefit from everything, he despises manual labor. He admires exclusively the broker, the banker, the speculator. "When the church," said Blanc de Saint-Bonnet, "warned the Gentile against the Jew, the Gentile refused to heed. Result—scarcity of useful things, abundance of superfluous things, penury and ruin among the masses, in other words, pauperism."

Christian civilization has ennobled, extolled, poetized, as it were, labor. Jewish civilization exploits it through the Jew capitalist, and disgraces it through the Jew revolutionary. The Jewish press and the anarchical doctrines propagated by the Jews, especially in Europe, embitter the workingman by calling him a convict.

As the working men gravitate into large cities in search of work which they do not find, the drinking saloons in those cities increase. In 1869 there were 366,507 drinking places in Paris; in 1884 there were more than 500,000. People pour beverages into their stomachs in order to experience a sensation that moves, stimulates, and excites the human organization. Women who are weak and sickly prick their arms to inject morphine into the body; the working men drink alcohol: both experience a passing relief, an exhilaration of the nervous system. The liquor trade is exclusively in the hands of the Jews, many of whom, although they do not appear as the real proprietors, still are silent partners. The real backers of liquor dealers in New York, as well as in Paris, are the Jews, who hold in an absolute vassalage all establishments, both high and low, that retail liquor. The retail merchant is little better than an employee. He directs the establishment, which does not belong to him, and the rent of which is usually paid by those who supply him with liquors. A retailer may have five or six different persons who furnish him with liquors, but one can never find at his saloon a brand of liquor different from those manufactured by the men who supply him with the stuffs.

The liquor business, as it is carried on today, has become a business of chemical products, a business of coloring materials and ingredients of all kinds such as are used in. the manufacture of liquors. As soon as a Jew has entered any business, he at once demoralizes it with his spurious concoctions. It is easily understood how disastrous an influence this peculiar chemistry exerts upon private health.

What are called natural or pure wines contain certain healthful principles, and even when taken immoderately produce only a passing inconvenience. In Bourgogne, one may see vine dressers whose full faces are rubicund with the healthy hue of the autumnal vine. Beverages, on the contrary, composed of essences, do not assimilate, but produce the effect of virulent poisons, bring on attacks of delirium tremens, fits of frenzy, and acts of ferocity for which the unfortunate victim is not responsible.

The hatred of the Jew for the poor—a hatred unparalleled in the history of the world—has assumed, of late, various forms. Now it is manifested in the adulteration of liquors; now it is manifested by the rich. Jew, the member of aristocratic clubs, who associates with the vilest of Shylocks, with those who fleece the poor by advances made upon pawn tickets. This peculiar business, this new kind of usury, this business of advancing a contemptible sum of money, in return for which pawn tickets are redeemed, is exclusively in the hands of the German Jews.

A German Jew called Neuburger gave, a few years ago, a considerable impetus to this commerce. He established in Paris several branches called *Neuburgennes*. But, unfortunately for Neuburger, there still existed at this time a shadow of justice, and when the authorities looked into his books, he was condemned to prison for ten months. Today, however, the *Neuburgennes* are in full blast, not only in Paris, but also here in New York.

A Parisian newspaper called *The Battle*, in its number of 25 January 1884, gave a few details respecting the operations of these agencies, all of which are bound together by the close ties of a syndicate. The association has offices in many of the principal streets. Gilded signs make known the fact that pawn tickets are both bought and sold. This business is also carried on in filthy shops, in dens of receivers of stolen goods, in shop windows furnished with goods coming from dealers in second-hand goods. The following narrative, cited in *The Battle*, maybe taken as a faithful picture of the manner usually employed by the Jews in carrying on this nefarious business:

> A citizen who has been victimized by these Jews, came to us yesterday and lodged a complaint. He entered into one of these agencies near Rue de Lafayette. The street does not improve the character of the business. Theft is always theft. Two francs were given to him for a pawn ticket, and also a piece of yellow pasteboard, which we hold for the inspection of anyone who may be curious to examine it. This pasteboard is really a bill of sale, and the loan is thus disguised. At the end of a month, the citizen returned and paid another month's interest, which was 20 per cent, making 240 per cent a year. When two weeks later he went to redeem his pawn ticket, he was told to come again, and finally, after having called seven times, he was told that his ticket had been lost.
>
> Armed with his little yellow pasteboard, the victim summoned the lender before the court. The Jew thereupon put his

hand upon his heart and swore that he had bought the ticket. To prove it, he showed the word, 'paid' upon the bit of pasteboard, and the following notice written in small letters: 'To avoid all misunderstanding, it is hereby understood that this transaction is a sale and not a loan.' Owing to this perfidiousline, the Jews make dupes of their clients.

It is impossible to realize how much poor men often value certain objects, mute but eloquent witnesses of their domestic life, such as the rattle, the cup of the child, or the marriage ring bought during more prosperous days. Some will agree to pay twice the interest asked on condition that a longer time be allowed them to redeem these sacred pledges.

It will astonish our readers, but nevertheless it is a fact to learn that the wealthy, the aristocratic Jew bankers furnish the capital for this nefarious business. To them, from time to time, is rendered an account of the profits that have accrued. "It is not rare," says Mace, "to see before the shops of these cutthroats the equipage of a rich man, dressed in the latest fashion. It is the Jew financier who is there to examine the accounts." In New York, however, it is the Shylock, the cutthroat, who goes to see the rich Jew in his office, where, in "private," these accounts are settled. The smaller scoundrel brings books and vouchers, all of which are carefully examined by his bigger confederate.

The furniture stores that sell on credit, at 300 per cent profit, present another form of Jewish usury. The following incident came recently to our notice. A workingman went to a furniture store, on Eighth Avenue, that sells "yoost zame, cretid or cash" and selected certain furniture; the whole bill amounted to $75. He paid $12 on account. An hour or two later, he decided to change a few of the articles selected, but was told that this could not be done, and that he must either take all the goods he had selected, or lose the $12 he had paid on account.

Advances on furniture constitute another form of Jewish usury. The usual amount varies from $10 to $50, "without removal," which the Jew vulture advances on the furniture. In return, a bill of sale on the property is given, but the amount advanced is raised $10 or $15 "for dhe druble of drawing bapers," and then besides, the legal interest is added. If the money is not promptly paid, the furniture is seized, sold, and bought by a Jew confederate.

How will all this end? Surely in revolution. It has already begun in Russia, whence a great many Jews have been expelled and a part of their ill-gotten possessions taken from them, while the tolerated Jews have been put under special police regulations.

In a society like that of our time, in which sentiments of right are rare, where people suffer from the usuries of the Jew, where selfishness reigns triumphant and men for the most part pursue whatever they think conducive to their own pleasure or interest, the final catastrophe, I repeat it, is only a question of time. There is not a thoughtful man that does not foresee the coming insurrection. Talk with the minister of the church, who watches at a distance the storm that threatens, or with the man about town, who takes little thought of the morrow, and you will find that both have the same forebodings.

"Someday that perhaps is not far distant," writes Aurelien Schroll, "the boiler will explode. Great financial institutions will collapse like over-inflated balloons. There will be only ruin among us, recalling Ischia after the earthquake." It will not be the end of the world, but it will be the end of the world we have described.

For one, I shall not regret it.

CHAPTER 5

THE JEWS' HATRED OF HUMANITY

A Hatred of Children

Servility, which often drives man to espouse the cause of the stronger, as-sumes among the Jews a peculiar character of bitterness that manifests itself in religious persecution. Nothing has undergone change among the Jews. They hate Christ in 1887 precisely as they hated him in the time of Augus-tus. To lash the crucifix on Good Friday, to profane the consecrated wafers, to contaminate the holy images, was the great joy of the Jews during the Middle Ages, and the same is their joy today. Formerly they satisfied their venom by killing Christian children; today they assail them with their atheis-tic teachings. Formerly they bled them; today they poison them. Which of the two is the more criminal?

While affirming the persistency of hatred among the Jews, it may not be amiss to speak somewhat fully of their bloody sacrifices, accusations a thousand times proven, and against which the Jews always defend them-selves with the impudence that characterizes them.

"Has this custom truly existed among them?" Renan, apropos of the af-fair of Tisza Elzlar, gave to the Jews a certificate of good character. "Among the calumnies," he says, "engendered by hate and fanaticism, there is certainly none more absurd than that which affirms that the Jews shed blood at their religious feasts. To believe such stories is nothing less than a monstrous folly."

Unfortunately, numberless facts contradict Renan's suspicious assertion.

In 1071, at Blois, France, a child was crucified by the Jews, and then cast into the river. In 1114, in Norwich, England, a child twelve years old was coaxed into a Jewish house, and was frightfully tortured. In 1179, a child that the Catholic Church venerates under the name of St. Richard, and whose feast occurs the 25th of March, was assassinated by the Jews on Easter Sun-day. In 1236, near Haguenau, three children were sacrificed by the Jews.

In 1244, a Christian child was made to suffer martyrdom. In 1255, a child in Lincoln, England, was concealed until Easter, and then the Jews collected from all parts of England and crucified it. In 1257 and in 1261, the same crimes were committed by the Jews at Welsenbourg. In 1261, at Pforzheim, Germany, a little girl seven years old was strangled by the Jews. In 1283, at Mayence, a child was sold by her nurse to the Jews, who killed it. In 1285, at Munich, a child was bled to death. In 1286, a child fourteen years old, named Uthernher, was made to suffer martyrdom, three days being consumed in putting it to death. In 1287, at Berne, a little boy, Rudolph by name, was killed during Easter. In 1292, 1293, and 1295 the same crimes were committed at Berne.

In 1303, a little boy, Conrad by name, the son of a soldier, was killed by the Jews. In 1345, Henry, who has been canonized by the Catholic Church, was strangled by the Jews. In 1401, at Dussenlofen, in Wurtemburg, a child four years old suffered, death at the hands of the Jews in the same way. In 1407, the Jews were expelled from that country in consequence of these crimes. In 1429, at Rovensbourg, Louis Von Bruck was killed by the Jews at Easter. In 1454, in Castile, a child was cut to pieces by the Jews, and his heart was thrown to the dogs. In 1462, a child called Andrea was crucified. In 1475, Simon, who has also been canonized by the Catholic Church, was killed by the Jews at Trente. In 1480, a repetition of the same crimes occurred in Venice. In 1486, at Ratisbonne, six children were killed by the Jews.

In 1520, at Biring, two children were bled to death by the Jews. In 1541, a child four years old, Michael by name, was tortured for three days and then put to death. In 1547, at Rave, a child was strangled by the Jew Jacques de Leozyka. The same year, a little girl seven years old was assassinated by the Jew Joachim Smieilavicz. In 1597, the Jews strangled a child in order to sprinkle with its blood their new synagogue. In 1550, at Ladaen, a child five years old, Matthews by name, was assassinated. In 1670, the Jew, Raphael Levy, was cast into the flames for having bled to death a child. Similar crimes to this day are committed in the Orient.

All the above-named crimes are attested by numerous historians, whose testimony, were it produced, would prolong this book beyond its prescribed limits. Mr. Louis Rupert, in his *History of the Synagogue*, has cited a few of the most striking facts.

There is not a historian of the Middle Ages that does not mention these murders by the Jews. It is stated that the Jews of Norwich captured a Christian child before Easter, tortured it exactly in the same manner as our Lord was tortured by the Jews, and on Good Friday they hanged it and then burned it.

Chaucer is, however, the most interesting writer that can be consulted upon the subject. His remains lie at Westminster, and he was the true painter of the customs of his times. *The Canterbury Tales* are a sort of *Decameron*. In "The Prioress's Tale" we are introduced to a horrible crime committed by "the cursed Jew," who seized a small boy "young and tender was of age, held him fast, cut his throat, and threw him into a pit." These proofs, we repeat, can be multiplied at pleasure.

La Civilta Cattolica, in its number of 1 April 1882, has reproduced all the legal documents relating to the trial held at Trent, in 1475, which documents are preserved among the Vatican Archives. There is nothing more absorbing than the facts connected with this trial—incontestable facts—and nothing more cynical can be thought of than the confession of the accused themselves. A whole phase of a past epoch suddenly appears before us. A Jew, 80 years old, called "Old Moses," made use of Christian blood during his whole lifetime. There existed dealers in Christian blood, like Isaac of Cologne and Richard of Brescia, who supplied all demands. Ours, of Saxony, was the drummer, the commercial representative of these murderous wretches. This Ours went from city to city, from ghetto to ghetto, offering his frightful merchandise, armed with a letter of recommendation from Rabbi Spring. Another of the accused, Vitale, alias Levita, was initiated into the mysteries of this business by his uncle Solomon, who lived at Monza. The blood of the Gentiles was mixed into cakes in the form of a triangle, which were distributed in the synagogues.

The Two Levys

In later years, the trial of Raphael Levy, which took place in 1670, may also be cited to show the abominations practiced by the Jews. This crime was committed in France, and all the documents to this day can be examined by anyone interested. We have an excellent guide in the account given by a conscientious historian, Amelot de la Houssaye, in his work entitled, *An Abridgment of the Trial made against the Jews of Metz*:

> Wednesday, the 23rd of September, 1669, about one o'clock in the afternoon, one Mangeotte Willemin, wife to Gilles le Moine, went to a fount distant about two hundred paces from where she lived to wash clothes. She was followed by her

child, three years old, who wore a red hat and had blond curly hair. At a distance of about 25 steps from the fountain, the child slipped and fell, and as the mother turned to pick him up, the child said he would himself rise, whereat the mother continued on her way, believing that the child was following.

About a quarter of an hour afterward, the mother, not seeing her child, ran back to the spot where she had left him, and not finding him, returned to her house where she asked her husband, her father-in-law, and her mother-in-law whether they had seen the child anywhere. Upon receiving a negative answer, they all supposed that the child had lost its way, and under this apprehension they vainly searched for it in the village. They then returned to the fountain, accompanied by the burgomaster of the place, examined carefully the bushes, called the child by name, shouted and searched, but all to no purpose. The child could not be found.

The mother, thereupon, in company with her father-in-law; went upon the highway leading to Metz, and there they found traces of the child, which they followed until they were lost among the tracks of the wagons and the horses. She then returned to her husband, told him of her discovery, and he forthwith started for the same path, where he met a horseman belonging to the escort of Count de Vaudemont, and asked him whether he had seen a child. The horseman replied that a short time before he had met a Jew, mounted upon a white horse, going toward Metz, having a child with him that appeared to be from three to four years old. The Jew, upon meeting him, turned out of the road and passed by at a distance of about a pistol shot.

The father, who saw by the description that the Jew had probably stolen his child, went in pursuit. Upon reaching the gates of the city, he asked of those present whether they had seen a Jew pass the gates. One, called Thibault Regnault, told him that he saw a Jew enter, but this information was of little avail, because Regnault could not tell where the Jew had gone, nor where he had taken the child. However, the father having learned almost at the same time that the Jew was Raphael

Levy of Boulay, and that on that same day he had been seen upon the pathway carrying something before him which he anxiously covered with his mantle, and furthermore that when in Metz, he lived at the house of one Garmon, a Jew and a relative of his, went forthwith to the house of the said Jew to ask for his child. Upon reaching the house, he was told that they knew nothing, and that the master of the house was not in, whereupon the father made up his mind to wait, and having noticed while in the house a woman, he told her that he was searching for his child.

Soon afterwards, a young Jewess entered, returning from the city, and she cautioned the woman in German to say not a word in regard to the child. Upon hearing the words of the young girl, the father, who knew German, no longer entertained any doubts as to the fate of his son, and thereafter he was possessed of one thought only—to avenge himself upon Raphael Levy.

Raphael Levy was a man 56 years old, of medium size, with curly hair and with a black, bushy beard. He was a very zealous Israelite, had travelled through the Orient, and also in Italy, Germany, and Holland, and was trusted with many a matter respecting the welfare of the Jewish religion.

The trial was a repetition of all trials instituted against the Jews. All the Israelites of the country were aroused, and brought forward false witnesses, but, unfortunately for them, they produced also a certain correspondence which it was supposed would be of benefit to the accused, but which proved the strongest possible evidence of his guilt. In one of these letters, the accused wrote to the chiefs of the synagogue in Metz:

DEAR DIRECTORS: The servant of the turnkey informed me that the Jew who brings food to me, told her that the child is in safety. Ah, write to me that I may know how matters stand and who are the witnesses. Write to me any way, that I may receive some consolation. The Haman [Raphael Levy gave the name of Haman (Aman) to the chief attorney, in remembrance of Aman, whose name has to this day remained odious among the Jews] was now in prison... Keep an eye upon the Parliament. I pray that I may be assisted, and that I may be freed of this misery. ... I will suffer death as a true son of Israel. ... I only ask that my wife and children may not be left in want. I brought upon myself this misery for the sake of the community.

Another letter is curious, owing to the details it furnishes respecting the Jewish customs. They sent to the accused a bit of straw, with instructions to put it under his tongue at the time of his cross-examination, in order to render his judges favorable to him. They also advised him to pronounce, as a sort of incantation, five Hebrew words.

In the meantime, the Jews held repeated councils at the house of one of the most zealous of their co-religionists, Gideon Levy, and they sought recourse to a stratagem, analogous to the story of the children of Jacob, who, after having sold their brother, told their father that a wild beast had devoured him. They announced that the missing child had been devoured by wolves, and exposed the clothes of the child in a distant wood. They stretched his shirt upon a thicket, and scattered about a few of the articles belonging to the child. Then they advised several persons of the neighborhood to search in the woods, telling them that if they could but find some remnant of the child, they would be rewarded with large sums of money.

A woman living near the wood deposed before the court that three Jews of Metz, whose names were not known to her, sought to find out from her what the people said about the stolen child. The Jews, furthermore, told her that the child was devoured by wolves, whereupon she told them that they ought to search the woods, for some remnant of the child would doubtless be found.

In fact, a few days later, 26 September 1669, four pig-drivers found the head of a child, and stretched upon some bushes two little dresses, a woolen stocking and a red hat, the whole without being torn and without any marks of blood.

When these facts had been communicated to the father of the child, as well as to the prosecuting attorney, the court sent an officer to the wood to examine the condition in which the above-named articles had been found, and also to examine the ground. The pig-drivers testified that owing to the condition in which the clothes had been found, it was not possible that the child could have been devoured by wild beasts, for besides the fact that the clothes were not in the least torn or bloody, it was well known that ferocious beasts first of all devour the head of any domestic animal attacked by them.

In this case, the head had been found a few steps from where the articles belonging to the child were discovered.

This maneuver, the only one that could succeed, and one which had previously succeeded in Austria, where the Jews have always been powerful, had little chance of success in a country like France, in the 17th century, where the court was absolutely unbiased, and judged according to the facts without in the least being influenced by outside considerations.

The neighbors deposed that they had seen Gideon Levy, carrying a basket, enter and leave the wood shortly before the clothes and the head of the child were found. Another witness asserted that the said Gideon told him to search for the remains, and had pointed out to him the spot in the wood where probably the said remains could be found.

Gideon was thrown into prison and the trial ordered to proceed. The crime was now proved. Convicted by overwhelming testimony, Raphael Levy was condemned to be burned alive, and the sentence of the court was carried out on 17 January 1670.

The death of the man was truly heroic. He bade farewell to a few of his co-religionists, begged them to protect and care for his wife and children; and not content with their promise to do so, he made them swear it. He refused to drink the wine they brought him, because it was not *kosher*, cast away the taper that was given him to hold, and gave a vigorous blow with his elbow to the priest who sought to exhort him, declaring in a loud voice that he was a Jew, and wished to die a Jew. "His soul," the Jews declared, "flew one Saturday with holiness and purity into the bosom of God."

The Jews at large did not look upon the murder of the child as a crime, but as the accomplishment of an act imposed upon them by their religion. They venerated the man who, as he himself declared, *had sacrificed himself for the community*. In a word, Raphael Levy was a martyr. Although he had been illiterate, after his death he was proclaimed a rabbi. When his name is pronounced by the Jews, he is alluded to as *Kadosch*, the Saint, and *Chasid*, the Pious. The *Archives Israelites* proposed a few years ago to erect a statue to his memory.

Gideon Levy was banished. The facts brought out by this crime made still more manifest the habit constant among the Jews of outraging the faith of others, and of ridiculing the ceremonies of the Christian religion. On Good Friday of each year, the Jews assembled at the house of one Schaub, where they ridiculed the passion of Christ, and lashed the crucifix.

Father Thomas of Damascus

In connection with the affair of Raphael Levy, which does not leave the slightest doubt that blood was used by the Jews in their ceremonies, we will mention the murder of Father Thomas in Damascus, in 1840, the details of which are well known, and the evidence of which crime it is impossible to deny, since it took place in our day. Father Thomas, a Capuchin, was loved by all in Damascus. He practiced medicine at the same time that he acted as missionary. He saved the soul and took care of the body.

Christians, Turks, and Jews were unanimous in praise of his talents and his inexhaustible charity. All called him the sainted missionary. He had the confidence of all classes of society. But it was especially towards the Jews that Father Thomas had shown himself kind, owing to his zeal in winning their souls to God.

One day when he was menaced with death by a native whose marriage he refused to bless, he extended to him his neck, saying, "I am ready to die, but will not fail in my duty." While the plague ravaged Damascus, he shut himself in with the pest-stricken and lavished upon them his attentions. He never hesitated at any sacrifice where good could be done to his fellow-man. Scheriff Pasha, the Turkish governor, honored him with his friendship, and orders were given to his servants to admit the father to his presence at any hour that he might call.

There were found, however, miserable fanatics who murdered that good man. As he was passing one evening, on 5 February 1840, before the house of a Jew called David Harari, he was asked by the latter to step in. Father Thomas accepted the invitation, for David Harari was considered the most pious Jew in Damascus. No sooner was the door closed upon the father, than David Harari, his two brothers, his uncle and two other Jews fell upon the poor missionary, knocked him down and tightly bound him.

Then the Rabbi Chakam and Soliman, the Jew barber, were asked to come to the house. The latter was ordered to cut the throat of the victim, and as he lacked courage, David Harari, the good and faithful friend of the father, seized the knife. But his hand, too, trembled, whereas his brother Aaron came to his aid, while Soliman held the head of the father by the beard.

The blood was collected, put into a bottle, and was sent to the Grand Rabbi. The body, despoiled of its clothes, was cut into small pieces and thrown into a sink. The miserable Jews thought thus to cause to disappear forever every trace of their victim.

When night came, Ibrahim Amoran, the father's servant, uneasy at not seeing the priest return, and knowing him to be in the Jewish Quarter, went to look for him. He there met the same fate as his master. Like him, he was seized and assassinated by the Jews, to have, as the *l'Union d'Alsace-Lorraine* asserted, Christian blood to put into the sweetbreads used for the feast of the Purim.

But these disappearances were soon noticed. The truth was suspected. The French Consul energetically entered into the matter and demanded an inquiry. It became known that Soliman, the Jew barber, had been called during the night to the house of David Harari. He was arrested, questioned, and upon his confession, the remains of the father were found, and the authors of the crime were apprehended.

Out of sixteen persons arrested, two died during the trial, four were pardoned, among whom was Soliman, on account of the evidence he gave, and ten were condemned to death.

The Jews again gave, during this trial, a new example of their admirable solidarity. All Europe was put in motion. Cremieux and Montefiore hastened to Damascus. They were unable, however, to prevent the condemnation, since the facts were proved. But they renewed their efforts, spent money without stint, and finally succeeded in obtaining from the Viceroy the pardon of the ten who were condemned. They did not justify nor excuse the guilty ones. They simply purchased their pardon.

The *Moniteur de Rome*, in its issue of 15 June 1883, cites many crimes committed by the Jews:

> A few years ago in Smyrna, a little child belonging to one of the first Greek families of the city was stolen about the time of the Jewish Easter. Four days later, at the seashore, his body was found, pricked with a thousand pins. The mother, crazed with grief, loudly accused the Jews of this murder. The Christian population rose in a body and hastened to the Jewish quarter, where a frightful massacre took place. More than a thousand Jews were butchered.
>
> Last year (1882) at Balata, the Jewish Quarter of Constantinople, a child was coaxed into a Jew's house. More than 20

witnesses saw him enter. The following day, his body was found in the Golden Horn. The result was again an uprising of the Gentiles that cost the Jews the lives of more than a hundred of their co-religionists!

At Galata the same thing took place. Lawyer Serouios, the most prominent lawyer of the Greek community, addressed a petition to the representatives of the Powers, demanding justice. But the Jews bribed the Turkish police, which hushed up matters, and caused the witnesses to disappear. The Jews agreed to give a large sum of money to the parents of the murdered child.

In the beginning of 1883, two children of Maltese families were stolen by a Jew. The newspaper *Stamboul*, upon information furnished by the father of one of the stolen children, called the attention of the police to the crime, and demanded the punishment of the guilty parties. The affair created great excitement in the city, and almost caused a revolution. The chief of the Pera police, Vahri Pasha, and the Commissary of the Police at Galata, who had charge of the affair, refused, in the face of overwhelming facts, to interrogate the father and the mother of the child. A thousand francs a month were offered to the editor of the *Stamboul* to stop making any further mention of the matter. It was indignantly refused. What did the Jews do? They bribed the police and obtained the suppression of the newspaper, and thus the matter was hushed up.

Even in Europe, crimes of this kind are only too common. In 1881, at Lutcza, a small village in Austrian Galicia, a young girl called Francesca Mnish was stolen by the Jews. Three of these—Moses Bitter, his wife, and Stochtinski—were accused, tried, found guilty, and condemned to death.

Unable to deny these facts, the Jews have always claimed that these acts were inspired by individual animosity, and were not the outcome of religious precept. There again German science has convicted them of lying. Dr. Justus, in his *Judens Spiegel*, says:

The theological books of the Jews are divided into two categories, to wit: *Peschath* and *Kabala*. To the first category belong the *Talmud* and the *Schulchan*. According to the *Schulchan Aruch*, it is not a crime if a Jew kills a Christian (Laws 50 and

81).[1] In the *Talmud*, published in Amsterdam in 1646, the Jews are ordered to exterminate the disciples of Nazarem.

"It is astonishing," says the Doctor, "that the blood of the *Klipoth*, that is to say, of girls not Jewesses, is claimed to be a sacrifice agreeable to Heaven. Still the sacred books of the Jews expressly state, to shed the blood of a young girl, not a Jewess, is a sacrifice as sacred as that of the most precious perfumes, and a means to reconcile oneself with God and to draw down his blessing."

This fact, at any rate, has been completely demonstrated in a very interesting work entitled *Refutation of the Religion of the Jews and of their Rites, Demonstrated by the Old and the New Testament*. The author is a Jew rabbi [Pablo Christiani], converted to Christianity, and who later became a Greek monk. Nothing is more singular than the fate of this book, even for those who know with how great care the Israelites cause everything to disappear that is calculated to enlighten public opinion about them. It was first published in 1803, in the Moldavian tongue, from which it was translated into the Greek language, and from the latter into the Arabic. Afterward it was printed at intervals in Bou mania, Constantinople, and in many cities in the Orient, but strangely enough it was next to impossible to obtain a copy. "This is owing," said a historian, "to the fact that the Jews are ever ready to spend money to obliterate the memory of this work." An edition printed in the Greek language was published in 1834. It is now well-nigh impossible to obtain a copy in Greek, but in 1883 a translation of the work from Greek into Italian made its appearance. The zeal that the Jews display in obliterating every trace of the Italian edition may well be imagined, and the *Archives Israelites* gave vent to savage outbursts of rage upon the appearance of the work.

An entire phase of the life of the Middle Ages is depicted in this interesting book. A thousand hitherto secret matters are brought to light, and hitherto impenetrable mysteries are made clear. We are introduced into the den of the Jew alchemist, where we find him occupied in concocting strange mixtures demanding Christian blood, which blood he claimed was necessary in the discovery of the philosopher's stone, but in reality was used to celebrate the monstrous rites, the abominable mysteries of Ashtoreth. The miserable dupes who believed in the possibility of discovering the philosopher's

---

[1] In the section of the *Shulchan Aruch* called "Yoreh De'ah" (158,2), we read that heretics who do not believe in the Torah should be killed. See E. Bischoff, *The Book of the Shulchan Aruch* (2023), p. 81.

stone were used as the instruments of crimes that cost the lives of hundreds of Gentiles.

What is worshipped in a Ghetto is not the God of Moses; it is the frightful Semitic Moloch, who claims children and virgins as victims. What else has the existence of ancient Israel been but a perpetual struggle between Molochism and Jehovism? Moloch, whose symbol was a Carthaginian bronze bull, which bull, filled with human victims, at stated intervals was heated red hot, was above all a Semitic divinity. It is towards him and towards Baal, whose symbol was a donkey, that the Jews are constantly drawn, being attracted by race. It is he whom Manasse and the other lying kings installed in the Moloch temple. It is to him that frightful sacrifices were offered on lofty places. It is against him that the prophets opposed themselves unceasingly with an energy in their indignation and a violence in their language that still sounds through centuries. They defied death in order to fight idolatry, and announced future punishment for the idolater. In their intrepid zeal, they did not hesitate to demolish the false Semitic gods, the shameful and barbarous images. There is many a page in the Bible that mentions the efforts of the prophets to defend the idea of the true God against the corrupting influences of the neighboring people.

The *Talmud* itself warns the Jews against their habit of drinking warm blood, either during the chase or before the Temple: "Only be firm. Do not give way; resist the inclination to drink blood. No, you must not drink it; pour it upon the soil like water." The regulations relative to meat, still observed by the Jews of the present day, serve as remembrances of these precautions against the love of blood peculiar to the Semitic race, a taste altogether unknown among the Aryans.

The German writers have thoroughly elucidated these facts. The book of Frederick Daumer, *The Worship of Moloch among the Hebrews of Antiquity*, and that of T. W. Ghillany, entitled *Human Sacrifices among the Jews of Old*, have both arrived at the same conclusions. Both these books show the close relationship existing between the customs of the Israelites and the bloody holocausts of the Middle Ages.

An old engraving by Sadler represents a table of stone that was used for the murder of six children. The following text accompanies the engraving: "The mutilated bodies of the six children have been discovered through the efforts of the Governor of Ratisbonne. The sacrifices had in their strange sanctuary a large stone, mounted upon a pedestal. It was the altar upon

which the victims were sacrificed. Back of this sanctuary there was a labora-
tory devoted to the manufacture of spurious coins." Another engraving by
Sadler represents the murder of a child by the Jews of Munich, which murder gave rise to the persecution of the Jews in 1285. The victim was bound
upon a table in the synagogue, and was pierced with implements having
sharp points. Its eyes were plucked out. The blood was gathered by Jewish
children. The Gentiles became almost frenzied, savagely attacked the Jews,
and the full authority of the bishop was called into requisition before the
people could be stopped. These two engravings were reproduced in the beautiful scientific publication entitled *Cosmos*, 30 May 1885.

Owing to a phenomenal retrogradation, the Jews of the Middle Ages
returned to their primitive errors, and yielding to the first impulse of their
race, plunged once more into sacrifices.

To these reminiscences of Phoenician abominations there was added a
strange, but excusable, sentiment. The Jew was troubled by that atmosphere
of ardent faith that reigned around him during the first centuries of Christianity, and was awed by the miracles performed by the saints. In vain did he try
to oppose himself to the truth. He had moments of terrible anxiety. He was
moved by the clear sense of certain prophecies, and he believed that if Christ
was the Messiah, a drop of a Christian's blood absorbed by one who was
circumcised was sufficient for his salvation.

The book we have mentioned above, entitled *Refutation of the Religion
of the Jews*, written by a converted rabbi, contains full directions for the use
of human blood in the various ceremonies of the Jews for their funerals, as
well as the Purim, etc.

Oral tradition, which transmits itself from father to son, renders the
Jews strong by the habit of keeping in common a terrible secret, and of pre-
serving the mysteries of Judaism. To communicate the secrets of Israel, the
father was wont to choose among his sons the one who seemed to him most
worthy of confidence. This communication was made at a time when the
Jews place upon the head of the child what is called 'the crown of courage.'
The father initiated his son and made him swear, in the most solemn manner,
never to reveal anything, to his brothers, sisters, mother, or any living creature, and above all to no woman:

> 'My son,' the converted rabbi who transmits to us the details
> reports the father to have said, 'may the earth refuse burial to

your body, may she repulse you from her bosom after death, if over, no matter in what persecution you may find yourself, you make known what I impart to you. Be silent, even if you should become a Christian for your own interest or any motive whatsoever.'

Is it only the Jews in the Orient, and other distant semi-civilized countries, where bloody sacrifices are still common, that still adhere to these practices? We are not far from believing that certain isolated cases—that, from time to time, increase the number of undiscovered crimes, as for instance the disappearance of children, or any other enigmatic disappearance upon which no possible light can be thrown—could be traced, if careful investigation were made in this direction.

A Hereditary Hatred

Human sacrifices that proceed from the aversion of the Jews for the Gentile, and are encouraged by their religious books, have certainly nothing in common with the law of Moses. These sacrifices represent a crisis, one of the phases in the eventful career of this strange people—a phase, for instance, that may be termed the warlike or patriotic phase, which was manifested in their defense against the Romans; the conspirator's phase, manifested during the thirteenth and fourteenth centuries in their conspiracy against the Crusaders; the dark and bloody phase displayed after their failure in that conspiracy; the phase of seclusion and meditation manifested during the sixteenth and seventeenth centuries, and finally the socialistic, financial, and cosmopolitan phase so manifest today. Still to this day, their hatred of Christ, of the Gentiles, has remained as keen as ever.

The psychological study of the Jew would be no less interesting than the historical, of which we have just spoken, if the learned, for good reasons, did not abstain from touching upon this question. Were the Jew analyzed psychologically, the resemblance of the civilized Jew to the real Jew of the Orient would be striking in the extreme.

The cause of this hatred felt by the Jew, even against inanimate objects, enters into the category of those phenomena at once moral and psychological, which Ribot has so thoroughly described in his book *On Heredity*. In view of this almost inexorable character of heredity, we must not forget the curious remark of a German doctor, who stated that many Jews are born circumcised.

Accordingly, the hatred of the Jew, which thus manifests itself from generation to generation, can be explained. The vulgar invectives against Christ, the Church, and the clergy, which at times we find among the Gentiles, do not emanate from any real sentiment of this sort among the masses of Aryan origin. It is absolutely artificial; it is cultivated and spread by the Jews, with that ability which they exercise in promoting a financial affair. That the masses of Aryan origin really hold to the traditions of their faith, and that any movement on their part against the same is only artificial, can be seen every day. Shortly after the Commune, 20,000 people followed the coffin of Father Philip, and the less religious among the working men spoke with affection and respect of the good father who had elevated them and made them honest people.

This and other examples that could be adduced tend to show that the people, even those who have become indifferent to their faith, still cling to the religion of their ancestors by the ties of remembrance. Long after the appearance of Christ, the Romans still remained attached to their Penates, and to the genius of the place, which was associated with the very existence of family. Baptism, the first communion, the religious marriage, are still revered and are dear to the majority of Parisians, even among those whose faith seems to have ceased to animate their conscience.

Among the illiterate Jews, this hatred of the Christian emanates from that form of brutal movement known as "irresistible impulse," so common among the alienated. As an illustration, we give the following examples of occurrences which take place nearly every day in various countries in Europe and Asia.

On 2 February 1881, it was a Jew who disturbed a funeral ceremony. "A deplorable incident took place the day before yesterday in the St. Eustache Church. The two poor girls who perished in the fire of the Deux-Ecus Street were being buried. A large crowd was present during this sorrowful ceremony, when suddenly a clamor arose. A drunkard entered and found it amusing to cry at the top of his voice. The janitor endeavored to put the man out, but a number of his companions entered, and stopped the janitor from doing so. When the police arrived and took the ruffian to the station, he gave his name as Eugene David."

The *Gaulois*, of 24 October 1882, related the following:

A man about forty years old entered the Church of St. Bona-
venture with his hat on his head. He advanced toward the altar,
struck the priest, and seizing the communion cup dashed it
upon the ground... All this was done in the twinkling of an
eye. When the people recovered from their stupor and arrested
the man, he declared before the magistrate that he was a Jew.

In the month of December 1885, *La France* related how another Jew, called
Weber, entered a church with his hat on, smoking a cigar, swearing at the top
of his voice at the clergy and those present. The police had to be summoned
to drive away the intruder.

On 1 March 1882, a number of Jews organized at Roubaix an impious
masquerade. "It is an incredible fact," stated the *Journal* of that locality,
"that no active steps have been taken against the scoundrels who organized
the outrageous masquerade aimed against the clergy." Upon a cart, a confessional was placed; on the top of the confessional was a strong iron box. A
person clothed in ecclesiastical garments sat inside the confessional, while a
number of Jewesses, dressed in the costume of Sisters of Charity, were
kneeling in turn before the priest, and pretending to confess to him, after
which they gave him a piece of money, kissed him, and then retired making
the sign of the cross. "The outraged public sought to put an end to this loathsome spectacle, but a number of Jew policemen in front of the cart protected
it against any hostile demonstration."

Everywhere where attacks of this sort are organized, if the facts were to
be looked into it would become known that the said attacks were conceived
by some low, vulgar German Jew.

The law laid down by Maxime du Camp is absolutely true, in a physical as well as in a moral point of view: "The closer men are united through
religion to Judaism, the dirtier they are. The more they are removed from
Judaism, the cleaner they are."

Many an example could be cited to show how this sentiment of heredity, of irresistible impulse, is common among the Jews of all classes. Herold,
who in 1869 sought to obtain a political position in France, in vain protested
against public opinion which affirmed his Jewish origin. He time and again
protested that he was not a Jew. His appearance, however, belied his words.
No doubt he may have belonged to the class of Jew interlopers, who claim
not to be of any religion. Still it suffices to examine the type in order to as-

certain the truth. The grandfather of Herold was an obscure professor of music, while his son employed his time in composing music. He was powerfully assisted by the Jews, who declared that the world never saw anything more remarkable than the author of *Zampa*. The grandson, who obtained the position of chief magistrate, declared that he was a Protestant, although he was never known to have been converted to Protestantism.

When, however, occasion was favorable, hereditary hatred, irresistible impulse, the venom of the German Jew manifested itself. The grandson of the humble music composer became the well-known, frantic, bloodthirsty animal, the moving spirit in carrying out the law that the Jews in France passed against the clergy. He was the man who, at the head of a crowd of Jews, piled up in ash-carts every cross they could seize—a number of which were torn from the burial grounds. He could be seen stamping his feet with joy at every act of infamy; but finally, when he died, he inspired even men of the lowest instincts with disgust.

This phenomenal hatred is nothing less than atavism, the disease that manifests itself in a subsequent generation after an intermission of a generation or two. The author of *Zampa* appears in his portraits a little melancholy, but not wicked. The lower part of his face is as viperine as that of his son, the magistrate, but otherwise he looks very much like one of the old Frankfort usurers. At the same time an impression of revery and of sadness tempers the repulsiveness of his countenance, and even lends a charm to his deceitful eyes.

On the other hand, those who saw the picture of Herold know how repulsive he was with his bleared, watery eyes, his enormous maxillary bones, and his mouth contracted as if by a frightful grimace. Immediately after the musician whom Parisian atmosphere rendered, so to speak, supple and civilized, nature brought forth a Jew of former times, one of those Jews that one sees in old pictures, always uneasy, always trembling lest he be caught and hanged, and always looking for some child to strangle during one of the sacrilegious ceremonies of his race. There are, in a word, men who, besides the sin of our first parents, carry the weight of one of those inheritances that a writer has called "a second original sin."

Jewish Influence in Schools

Hatred of the clergy is a veritable monomania among the Jews. In the month of February, 1885, Camille Dreyfus gave rise to a grotesque debate before the Council. He sought to proscribe the books of Victor Hugo from the schools because the name of God was found in the works of the poet. The municipal council actually discussed this absurd proposal of the Jew!

Again in the month of March, 1885, it was the Jew Lyon Allemand who denounced before the council a professor, Pellissier, an estimable man. What was the crime committed by the learned professor? He had simply used his right as an individual, his freedom of thought, a sacred liberty, to publish under the title *Lessons of Ancient Christianity* a book replete with noble teachings and eloquent observations, a book that has been since crowned with praise by the French Academy. In this book the author affirmed and demonstrated the moral and fruitful influence of Christianity. But the German Jew, Lyon Allemand, was indignant at the audacity of the unhappy professor, who was brutally discharged after 25 years of service.

Higher education in France will, in a few years, be entirely in the hands of the Jews. In the schools of "higher studies" we already find the following Jews: Philosophy, Henry Weil; comparative grammar, Michael Breal; Zend language, James Darmesteter; Semitic language, Joseph Derenbourg; Arabian language, Hartwig Derenbourg; Ethiopian language, Joseph Halevy; philology and Assyrian antiquities, Jules Oppert.

Let not the reader be impressed by the learning of the Jew on account of the above imposing array. The teaching of languages demands original research and patient investigation. It is a well-known fact that the Jew is not original. All his learning is derived from the investigations of others, which he, with effrontery, parades as his own. These positions are held by the Jews, not because the Jews merit them, but because they have been pushed into them by influence."

How many thoughts, how many recollections does the word influence awake in our mind! No matter where our thoughts may turn, we are confronted by that remorseless monster, influence. In our present social organization, it is seldom that merit, talent, or education ensures success. It is influence.

John D. Rockefeller, for instance, the President of the Standard Oil Company, the man of thirty millions, illiterate though he may be, would have no difficulty in appointing the man of his choice to occupy the pulpit of his church. His influence outweighs all other considerations. Influence bestows the degree of Doctor of Divinity upon men of no scholarship, and the influence of the Church is often prostituted to further the interests of its favorites.

Among the Jews who direct the work of education abroad, a place apart must be reserved for the German Jew, Michael Breal. This contemptible Jew has discouraged the study of national French literature in the schools of France, and has introduced new systems of instruction calculated to degrade the mind, and to fill it with absurd ideas. As examples of his methods, we may mention the two most loudly-advertised systems in America, "the Natural Method of teaching languages," and "the Meisterschaft system," the latter introduced here by the Jew, Rosenthal. People are expected to spend three years of apprenticeship before they become proficient in a trade, yet in a circular now before us we read that there exists a certain School of Languages in New York, directed by a Jew, where one can acquire a thorough knowledge of the German language in about 40 lessons. Shades of Goethe defend us! These systems, advertised with so much effrontery, are not calculated to flatter the intelligence of native Americans, for it would seem that dupes are not wanting who suffer themselves to be gulled by these empty promises. Owing to the peculiar methods of teaching advocated by the Jew, Michael Breal, the brains of children, confused by a thousand heterogeneous notions, become incapable of serious effort.

Eminent men of the old school bitterly complain of this lamentable decadence. A man who best of all understands the question of teaching, Mr. Albert Duruy, published upon this subject a remarkable work, showing the harm accomplished by trying to impart to the youth an education contrary to national genius and to methods heretofore adopted. "In this struggle," he remarks, "it is no longer simply a question of ancient or modern literature, but it is the fact that national genius is getting tarnished. It is our children whose talents are stifled, it is our stricken country which they seek to ruin by foolish methods of foreign culture, methods propagated and encouraged by the Jews. To all their other faults, they add that of being antipathetic to our race. They are not born in our land. They have been conceived beyond the Rhine."

It is the Jew, Camille See, who seeks in schools for girls to exclude all religious teaching. It is the Jew who discourages trade schools, where women formerly were taught an honest trade that enabled them to earn their living. Frenchmen who are little zealous in their faith say to these Jews:

> You intend to give to these young girls what you call a refined
> education, an education superior to their position in the world.
> You seek to teach them music, painting, etc. Still, you know

how difficult it is for them to gain a living with an education of this sort. Placed between dishonor and poverty, which will be harder for them to bear than for others of less education, these girls, who belong mostly to the middle classes, who are the girls of old soldiers, will be surrounded by many temptations. Why not give them a practical education, imbue their hearts with a belief that will sustain them in life, a belief which consoles, elevates, and which often saves?

But the Jew smiles with a meaning smile. He often, after a convivial dinner, lets his private thoughts escape. To the rich Jew banker, to the parvenu of yesterday, to the Jew who has simply a light coat of civilization, there is need of young girls. There is need of "*Klipoth*"—girls not Jewesses—to console, to amuse these beings attacked with neurosis and hypochondria, just as David appeased with his harp the melancholy of Saul. In the newspaper, *L'Echo*, of Paris, an old soldier wrote an article stating that out of 50,000 girls who presented themselves at the teacher's examination with a view of obtaining a situation to teach, only 3,000 were accepted. He traced the following brutal, but alas too true picture of these unfortunate girls:

> Like famished wolves upon a stray traveler, these women rush to the assault of promised places. Last year 3,000 places were filled. Perhaps the reader may say that this is a large number, but the demand was for 50,000. What will the 47,000 teachers do who are without employment and without hope of obtaining any? Where will they be found?

We know that it is useless to look for them in the workshop or in the store. They will not stoop to this, but if we search well, we shall find them in the society of young journalists without a journal, of lawyers without a case—in fact, in the society of men who try to live by their wits. It is also in the smoke of beer saloons that we shall find their ironical and scoffing silhouettes. Amid the noise of beer glasses and glasses of absinthe, we shall hear these useless products of normal schools railing against society.

Paris is thoroughly poisoned by these women. We meet these young Bohemians in petticoats at every step, wearing short hair, a masculine collar, and withal the unmistakable air of a dissatisfied "schoolmarm." They often correct the letters in which working women beg for the money that is due them from their heartless Jewish employers, or write love letters for their grossly ignorant associates, the girls of the Boulevards.

To establish their superiority, they have certain ways of their own, different from these of the everyday *grisette*, and by which ways they contribute to the propagation and the development of that lesbian worship before whose altars we see such vast numbers kneeling.

We may find them also in those spacious establishments, the restaurants, especially those kept in Paris, by Duval, which someone defined "The Soup Houses of Love."

To pervert the young is the one essential point, the main point to which the Jew's efforts are directed. It is a Jew who published at the publishing house of the Jew, Leopold Cerf, a book entitled *Practical Manual of School Law*. He finds the question exceedingly promising to the Jews. He explains the duties of this question with complacency and threatens those who would hesitate to obey. "Public schools," he writes, "being amenable to *our* law, in fact, public schools being absolutely secular, it follows that in schools, no religious emblem whatsoever ought to figure."

A religious newspaper once called attention to the pitiful condition of public schools in France, the pupils of which are brought up with atheistic tendencies, as no religious instruction is encouraged, and no notions of the Deity are instilled into the young minds. The mere mention of the word 'God,' by any of the teachers, is a sufficient ground for his immediate discharge. Gentile teachers find it difficult to secure employment, while a Jew is given preference, even if deficient in scholarship.

The Jewish newspaper *La Lanterne*, in an article so filthy that we abstain from reproducing it here, lost no time in denouncing the editor of the religious paper as a blackleg, a bandit, etc.

It is the part of Jew editors to willfully degrade the profession of journalism. They give way knowingly to the lowest instincts of animal life. They are reckless of private character, and are promoters of private scandal. They neither regard truth, nor respect public opinion.[2]

If Anthony Comstock, instead of making himself ridiculous by his interference in Mr. Knoedler's business, instead of treading upon the sacred domains of art, of which he is entirely ignorant, would try to bring to justice

---

[2] Another remarkable anticipation of the present-day Jewish role in media.

the Jew editors that disgrace public morals by their filthy articles, he would be applauded by the entire Christian community, and would win public esteem instead of censure and ridicule.

Jewish Blood, Aryan Blood

Everywhere, we repeat it, the Jew is untiring in his work of infamy, in his incessant attacks against the Christian religion and its ministers. Take, for instance, the episode of the second expulsion of the Benedictine priests, an expulsion which was of a character particularly revolting. These poor priests, after they had been expelled from their places, little by little sought to return to them. They were known to have no resources whatsoever. They would not live outside of their monastery, where they had passed their lives, where their library was, and where they had acquired those habits of industrious labor, which, as everybody knows, have been so fruitful in results.

Among the most violent radicals, the majority knowing the facts kept silent, saying that the representative men of this order were those who had saved civilization during the Middle Ages by collecting in their cells the masterpieces of the human mind. But the Jewish newspaper, *Le Paris*, instituted a veritable campaign of blackmail against these monks, who joined science to faith, the love of God to the love of letters. The Aryan is incapable of acts of this nature.

Were the Jews again banished from Europe, and were the Aryans to know that the rabbis would again unite, in order to *myauder*, the Aryan would not denounce them. *Myauder* means to unite, in order to study the Talmud doctrine, called *Kulacca*. According to the Talmud, God, after quitting the Temple, reserved in Heaven a certain place where he *Myaude* a part of the day. In *Yeschuot* we are told:

> The day has twelve hours. During the first three God *myaude*; during the second quarter, God is seated and judges the world. But seeing that the entire world is guilty, he rises from his seat of justice and sits upon the seat of pity. During the third quarter of the day, God is seated and nourishes the entire world from the rhinoceros to the bugs. During the fourth quarter, God is seated and plays with Leviathan. As it is also said in

the Psalms [104:26], 'Leviathan, whom Thou hast created in order to play with him.'

This transmission through heredity of religious hatred, of irresistible impulse, of fatality and of antisocial instincts, is one of the most striking spectacles of our epoch. Without attributing to heredity the fatal character that modern science attributes to it, it must be admitted that it plays an important part in the constitution of man. We meet, in fact, veritable diabolical predestinations.

As we write the above, we involuntarily recall the account of the old Byzantine writer given in the early pages of this book, and many a prominent figure in our financial affairs is brought to our mind. Has ever a man of observation asked himself the question: "Is there any Jewish blood in the veins of John D. Rockefeller?" We do not hesitate to affirm from an intimate knowledge of the man, that if Rockefeller is not actually a Jew, he has many Jewish traits. True, he is a prominent member of the Baptist Church, but in the actual pursuits of ambition, of interest, of pleasure, and even in the common occupations and intercourse of ordinary life, scriptural precepts appear in his case to be left for Sunday.

We confess that we feel powerless to adequately describe the mysterious, secret, insinuating air that he possesses. When he walks, his step is as light as that of a cat. He glides along as if he were afraid to look his fellow man in the face. He casts mysterious side glances, as if in dread of some lurking enemy. He is about 50 years old, rather tall, but owing to his habit of constantly looking upon the ground, and of casting side glances, his form is prematurely stooping. He looks as if he were a victim to dyspepsia. Neither his head, forehead, eyes, nor any feature of his indicates peculiar talent, or even a higher degree of intelligence than is possessed by the ordinary mortal. His face seldom lights up with a kindly sentiment. He never loses his temper. He seems to be afraid of the sound of his own voice. When compelled to speak, he articulates his words slowly, one by one, as if loath to part with them.

He has an elongated face, which, owing to the shape of his mouth, his prominent nose, and sensual lips, resembles strikingly the pictures of the old interlopers, those Jews who in years past established themselves in Bordeaux under the name of *new Christians*. If, however, the face of John Rockefeller seldom lights up with a human feeling, still we must make an exception in the case of his eyes, in which jealousy, obduracy, anxiety are by turns manifested.

Like men of little or no education, like the parvenu of yesterday, Rockefeller is fond of vulgar ostentation. Before he bought the house on 54th Street, New York, he lived for years in the Buckingham Hotel. His family consists of three daughters and one son, the latter also called John, after his father, whom he strikingly resembles.

Rockefeller is abstemious. In this he differs from his brother William, who has a box at the opera, entertains, and who, when a guest at dinner, does not turn his wineglass upside down, in order to make a parade of his abstemiousness. John has not a box at the opera, never goes to the theatre, nor does he allow any member of his family to do so. We doubt whether any one of his children ever saw the inside of a place of amusement, unless perhaps it was a church fair or festival.

Here we have one who only a few years ago was, comparatively speaking, a poor man, for he started in life by borrowing a few hundred dollars; a man who within the recollection of many who know him, was engaged in the modest business of a dealer in coal and wood, gaining within a short time a fortune counted by the millions. Has "heredity" anything to do with it? If not, how has he come to this wealth? It is well known that he does not possess extraordinary ability. On the other hand, the spirit of the Standard Oil Company is simply the spirit of monopoly, of cruelty, of annihilation of all competitors, a spirit in fact such as manifests itself in the scandalous enterprises of the Jews.

Speaking of the character and wealth of such a man as Rockefeller, the reader may ask, do the same remarks apply to the other millionaires, such as the Vanderbilts and Jay Gould?

The Vanderbilts are no more to be compared with John D. Rockefeller than is the generous, open, unsuspecting nature of the average American to be compared to the close, calculating nature of the average Jew. The Vanderbilts are, above all, Aryans—Aryans in every sense of the word—with an Aryan's faults, perhaps, but still they are Aryans. They have generous impulses, they have acquired their wealth honestly, they have never been known to wrong any man, and they are esteemed in the community in which they dwell. In the Vanderbilt household, we find the true Christian development exemplified in a high degree. From the time of the sturdy old Commodore to the present day, we have the true succession of that Christian gradation that is so common in our American history. The Vanderbilts spend their wealth lavishly—not ostentatiously. They are patrons of art; they are generous and patriotic. They have the true spirit of Americans, and were this country ever to become involved in serious wars, they would not hesitate to spend their last dollar in its defense. In brief, they are not Jews.

Jay Gould cannot be included in any existing human category. He is neither a Jew nor an Aryan. He is the special phenomenon of the nineteenth century. The different elements that the observer meets in describing Gould are many and complex in the extreme. Gould possesses the apathy of a Turk, the cruelty of a Zulu, the cunning of a Greek, the changeableness of a Frenchman, the stability of a German, the insincerity of an Armenian, the deceitfulness of a Jew, the treachery of an Indian, the greed of an Englishman, the enterprise and smartness of an American.

Much more might be said in regard to the Jewish traits of prominent men of the present day who are not recognized Jews. Is it, however, so certain that in the long line of their descent some stream of Hebrew taint has not, perhaps in the remote past, defiled what would otherwise be a pure Aryan type? The tree must be judged by its fruit. It is an interesting question, but the scope of our book does not permit us to discuss it further.

To return then to the subject of "heredity." In 1790, the Marquis of Rochefort, after losing his property, became a Revolutionist, and planted in the yard of his chateau the first tree of liberty ever seen in Bourgogne. The tree was blessed by the priest Pyat. The Marquis was the grandfather of Henri Rochefort, the editor of the *Intrensigent*, known throughout the world for his Communistic doctrines and hatred of aristocracy. As for the priest Pyat, he married a sister of charity, by whom he had two sons, the younger of whom was Felix. It is certainly strange to find the names of Pyat and Rochefort so prominent during the last Commune.

Can the son of a convict be a saint? The Church says yes, but the sociologist, while accepting this affirmation, is obliged to acknowledge that in order to remain in the path of virtue, greater efforts must be put forth by him than by others. If the son of a convict receives an education, we generally find him shielding his wicked designs against society behind certain highsounding phrases in which progress, emancipation, and liberty are prominent. He will lean upon a collectivity, composed of the ignorant among the masses, but withal he will remain the son of a convict. Parents have children who, while outwardly they may not resemble them, still bear the resemblance in the depths of their hearts.

Take, for instance, the Jew Challemal-Lacour, an ex-magistrate of France. His life is a human document of considerable importance. One of his ancestors, Armand Fiddle Lacour, a grocer, was declared, on 12 May 1838, by the Court, a fraudulent bankrupt, and the Court ordered a watch to be kept upon him. The grandfather and the grand uncle of the ex-magistrate were condemned for forgery, the first to twenty years, and the latter to six years, imprisonment at hard labor. The great-grandfather was, in like manner condemned to prison for fraudulent acts, and the son of the grandfather was imprisoned for committing acts of a criminal nature. If the ex-magistrate had received no education, he would, no doubt, have been engaged in acts of the same nature. But his education acted simply as a light coat of varnish, for it did not succeed in changing his original perverted temperament. His culture only enabled him to do evil to the great majority, while apparently honestly occupied in furthering the interests of his dupes.

Jews and Pornography

To these means of warfare, to these means of attack against the Church and the clergy, the Jew has called to his assistance not only his blackmailing press, but also obscene publications—in a word, pornography.

According to the Talmud, it is a good omen to dream of filth.[3] Nearly all obscene publications are the work of the Jews. In all matters pertaining to corruption and pollution, in matters that defile moral character, the Jew stands unequalled.

The hog is the emblem of the Jew—of the Jew who is not ashamed to wallow in corruption, baseness, ignominy, and usury in order to increase his capital, and who does not find any speculation too infamous when there is a profit to be derived from it.

Heredity appears also among the Jews in a somewhat imperious and peculiar character. That foul place called the Ghetto, that proverbial place of filth, where the Jew has lived for centuries, has impregnated his whole system. The Jew manifests that form of disease called *pica*, which makes the patient crave what is unfit for food, as is evident from the incredible torrent

---

[3] Berakhot 57a,14: "One who defecates in a dream, it is a good omen for him, as it is stated: 'The oppressed will soon be set free; they will not die in the dungeon, nor will they be without food' (Isaiah 51:14). The Gemara notes that this only applies where he does not wipe and get his hands dirty."

of scurrilous publications that have inundated the world during the last ten years. The Jews have established in France the indecencies formerly practiced in the orgies of Bacchus, without, however, the artistic side that was prominent at Rome and Athens. They exhibit their phallic publications throughout Paris. Croissant Street is a veritable Jewish sink, the market of pornographic newspapers, where the Israelite shops in close array fight among themselves as to which shall exhibit the most loathsome pictures.

The historian of the future who shall attempt to describe the catalogue of the filthy publications issued by the Jews during the last ten years will scarcely believe the evidence of his own eyes. Scenes of gross debauchery, representing drunken monks in the society of girls, priests lashing nude women, filthy groups, and other outrageous pictures, are displayed on all sides, with Jewish effrontery, in the windows and stores. Formerly, fathers of families, men of the people, would have made life burdensome for those who tolerate and encourage such turpitudes. Today, however, we see in the populous quarters fathers, mothers, little girls and boys gazing upon these obscene publications. To this condition have the Jews reduced France.

The Jews have a great advantage on their side. It is the honesty of their adversaries, which prevents them from paying them back in their own coin. Suppose that a Gentile should take it into his head to publish some unpleasant reflection on a well-known Jewish society belle. Imagine how severely the Christian clergy would reprimand an action of this kind, and how the writer would be despised by his friends and associates. The last of the Aryans would say to him, "Don't do that; don't degrade a woman; don't attack the weaker sex." The editors of *La Lanterne* have not these scruples. They published tranquilly that a sister of charity, the Sister St. Charles, was delivered of a child in the train of Aix. They did not mind the fine of a few hundred francs which they were condemned to pay. Incredible though it may seem, the presiding judge opposed any payment of personal damages, and this is the logic of that representative of public morality: "It is useless to grant personal damages. There has been, no doubt, defamation of character, but Sister St. Charles is a respectable person and well known to be so. Hence the prejudice is so much the less, as the person suffering thereby is more respected and better known."

According to this logic, the court made little account of the reputation of Madame Hugues, who, in 1885, was granted, as personal damages, two thousand francs, while the same court condemned the editors of *La Lanterne* to five hundred francs in the case of Sister St. Charles. One can see in all this only the servility of the magistrates to the Jews. In the same manner, one who would discuss the morality of Johann Most would be more guilty than he who would drag St. Vincent de Paul into the mire.

What has been said of Sister St. Charles may be applied to all similar slanders fabricated by the Jews. Suppose that a Jew is unfortunate in his domestic life. Feeling himself about to die, he takes from the woman who has deceived him the care of his son, and begs his own mother, whom he venerates, to raise the child in the path of virtue. A rabbi goes to console the man and to bring to him the hope of a better life. Do you suppose that any respectable Catholic or Protestant sheet would discuss this private drama, attack the grandmother, or insult the rabbi? No. See, on the contrary, what the Jewish press *Le Paris*, of the Jew Beil Picard; *La Lanterne*, of the Jew Mayer; *Le Voltaire*, of the Jews Lafitte and Strauss, make out of any scandal, true or false, out of every murmur affecting the fair name of a respectable Aryan family. They drag it into the mire where they themselves wallow; they feel happy to see somebody else stained with their filth.

It is not our intention to enumerate all the vile utterances of the Jewish press, to recall all the wanton insults they heap upon the Gentile. If you read the European Jewish press, you will find that the most beautiful, the most touching ceremonies of Christian worship, are occasions of blasphemy. Christian processions are called clerical masquerades, etc. These are the pariahs, the slaves, the outcasts of a few centuries ago who today so arrogantly parade their triumph.

What is most remarkable in all this is the total absence of originality. Take the Jewish newspapers, and you will fail to find there a new idea, an unpublished infamy. It is the Talmud poured into the press. It is Hebraic blasphemy translated into slang. There again the poverty of Jewish imagination makes itself manifest; for, for the Jewish press, as well as for the Talmud, preaching is barking, *Nabuab*; the saints are libertines, *Kedeschim*; the women saints are prostitutes, *Kedeschot*; the churches are places of prostitution, *Betmoschab* or *Betkyce*; the crosses are abominations, *Toeba*; holy water is dirty water, *Mayim temeim*; blessing is malediction, *Kelala*; sacrament is an impure sacrifice, *Zabut temi*. To all these forms of attack we must add the terrible persecution that takes place from the highest to the lowest step of the social ladder, now that the Jews have driven honest people from all important positions.

Hebrew Lawyers

Where does all this persecution begin, and where does it end? It is impossible to say. It is of everyday occurrence. It has been proclaimed in a thousand different manners. This persecution assumes all disguises, it denounces, calumniates, lays traps, organizes scandals, and casts a stigma upon the names of those against whom a sufficient number of witnesses cannot be bribed to bear false testimony. This persecution drives some to madness, others to suicide, and as soon as one tries to smother it, to seize it, it slips, it vanishes, it eludes one's grasp.

Throughout the world, those who disgrace the profession of law—those who are ready to espouse any side for pay, those who have monopolized the lowest and dirtiest practice of the lawyer's profession, and who have acquired that narrow and confined mode of thinking that a liberal mind would so greatly despise as to be unable to acquire it—are all Jews. Lawyers of infamous character, blasted with imputations of the most atrocious kinds, in the walks of private and domestic life, are Jews.

There is no order in the community more contemptible than that of those Jew practitioners of the law, who, without one liberal principle of justice or of equity, possess skill in little else than quibbles, and are strong in those points only by which villainy is taught to proceed with impunity, cunning enabled to elude legal enactments, and truth perplexed, obscured, and lost in the mazes of chicanery.

Should such men preside as judges where life and death, liberty and property are at stake? What justice, for instance, can a Gentile obtain if he has a case against a Jew, and the case is tried before a Jew judge! See the Talmud. "If a Christian and an Israelite come before you to decide any difference whatsoever, see that the Israelite wins the case... If you cannot openly do so, have the Israelite win the case in any way, through craft and deceit."

What security, we repeat, can a person have if judicial positions fall into the hands of Jews? Our country would be thrust into a darkness as dark as Rome's in her decadence.

A Plea to the Working Man

Workingmen, never cease, with your votes and your influence, to oppose the Jew—the Jew who has no character, who is steeped in libertinism, in infidelity, in every kind of profligacy which tends to harden the heart and to deaden the feelings of humanity—no less than to stifle the sentiments of true honor. Do not listen to them, workingmen, when they preach to you the German doctrines of socialism, which are those of the German Jew, Karl Marx. The Jew was not, is not, and never will be your friend. Do not let him deceive you. The strike is a system of warfare that belongs to the Jew. The labor strike is the outcome of the preaching of Karl Marx; it is an idea peculiarly Jewish, an idea of death. It is the death of work under pretext of a struggle against the capitalist. We repeat it to you, workingmen, the strike comes of the teachings of the German Jew, a thing fostered by anarchists, by violators of law, by men who seek to use you as instruments of their private designs; in a word, by the Jews.

Workingmen, if you suffer evils, enlighten yourselves with regard to the nature and the origin of these evils before you surrender yourselves, body and soul, to socialism. Trust not the foreigner who whispers in your ears un-American doctrines, and, above all, do not trust the Jew. It is he who has invented, in order to seduce you, aggressive and insolent liberalism.

One cannot compass anything by this course, unless it be to provoke disorders and mutual resistance, evils which stop production, kill the industries of the country, and ruin its prosperity.

Workingmen, as soon as you study the maneuvers of the Jew, you will declare him a criminal. His work among you is revolution and disorder. His pretended love for you is the love of the fox for the geese. He is like the swimmer who makes a great ado in the water, but makes no headway. The Jew is a false brother. He is constantly occupied in concealing his designs, the designs of the socialist and the enemy of good order. The hatred of the Jew for the Gentile is a historic fact which the Jew writers themselves are unable to deny. Formerly they bought Gentile prisoners from the Romans solely to torment them and to put them to death. Do not be deceived by smiles, for the smiles of the fiend are dangerous.

Workingmen, you, like us, come from generations that have lived in this country. Our ancestors fashioned our heritage, successively improved it, aggrandized it in honor and dignity. They have given us a history in accordance with our character, our hopes, our ambitions. These ancestors are our own, our dead, just as the fallen leaves of autumn are the ancestors, so to speak, of the leaves of the following spring. The Jew can have no love for this country of yours, for it is not his.

To preserve the honor and dignity of this country, workingmen, to keep its reputation untarnished, is a duty which you must discharge with the same watchful care as that with which you would protect the lives and the honor of your wives and daughters. No one of you would allow his daughter or wife to associate with libertines, with men of low and bad character. How much more earnest and watchful you ought to be of your country! This country cannot tolerate the Jew. She sees him sowing poison everywhere, and she implores you to defend her against the Jew before it is too late.

The men who made both France and Spain so great in the past were neither malefactors nor imbeciles. The measures they adopted against the Jews were not the whims of tyrants, but were forced upon them by existing perils. The workingmen of old refused to endure the oppression of the Semite, refused to listen to his anarchical doctrines, and were unanimous in boycotting everything sold by a Jew. They knew that the furniture, for instance, the Jew sold was of poor workmanship; they knew that the provisions he sold were of bad quality and that he gave false weight. They knew that to secure their own advancement, it was necessary to transact no business with the Jews. An association of individuals thinking alike, a community representing certain sentiments, beliefs, aspirations, aptitudes and traditions, defended itself properly against a race that represented sentiments, beliefs, aspirations, aptitudes, and traditions absolutely hostile to its own.

The faith of Abraham definitely puts the Jew beyond our law, because the law that the Jews obey in their homes is the negation of ours. The Jew has never done anything that entitles him to be called "the chosen." If our space permitted us to analyze the characters of many of their most prominent men, we should have no difficulty in showing that the best among them were imitators and arrant plagiarists. The strength of the Jew is the strength of the weak—deceitfulness. In the past he was a sorcerer, because as a sorcerer he had no difficulty in deceiving the people. Some people claim that the destiny of the Jew is sad and humiliating, and that consequently he is entitled to our sympathy. Sympathy bestowed upon a Jew is misplaced sympathy.

One does not pity the criminal who does not wish to be pitied. If the Jew is without the pale of law, it is his own fault. He does not change his course. He asserts that he wishes to follow our laws, yet he adheres to his own. Can he ever conform to our usages and really obey our laws? He does not work, he does not produce, he lives by exploitation and dishonest transactions. He proclaims himself a cosmopolitan, a layman, and employs against us violence and exaction, which are the essence of his law—a religious law. He seeks to share the advantages and comforts of our homes, while he aims to deprive us of them. He says he is hungry; we give him free access to our tables, while he moves Heaven and Earth to deprive us of our daily bread. He is cold, and asks an asylum in our house; he enters, and it is not long before the house is his. He proposes to engage in commercial affairs with us, so that he may sell us trash or stolen goods.

The Jew reminds us of the words of Mirabeau: "There are only two kinds of men, those who work and those who do not work; those who earn their living and those who steal." The Jew does not earn his living; he does not produce. He thrives only through usury and exploitation. His life is a continued plot; he is a thief. In a word, hypocrisy and lying are the salient features in the Jew.

Attacking the Poor

If the Jew is not engaged in blackmailing the rich, the aristocrat, he plots to keep down the poor. The children of the poor whose lives promise to be the hardest, and who most of all need a hope, an ideal, are deprived of all religious teaching in the public schools. Reared without a God, living without a God, they will die without a God.

The Jews passed a law in France ordering the expulsion of Sisters of Charity from the hospitals. The demand for nursing is one of the demands of civilization. Formerly, when a poor man, a young man, or a stranger in Paris fell sick, he found near his bedside a sister of charity, a being of goodness, who consoled and took care of him. He found a nurse intelligent and full of resources, tender in touch, a kind of mother when the natural mother was not available. But the Jews expelled the sister of charity, the poor man's nurse, from his bedside. The Jews placed there instead the paid nurse—coarse in manners and in touch, ignorant and superstitious, vulgar and intemperate in habits, rough in speech, given often to heavy and perhaps drunken sleep at those critical hours of the night when fever, delirium, and pain do their worst, and the patient needs a watchful friend.

This persecution of the poor man is the crime of crimes among the criminal deeds of the Jews, for by the expulsion of the sisters they have made the hospitals in France a veritable hell, over which may be written the words of Dante, "Abandon ye all hope." The paid nurses who have replaced the sisters of charity in the hospitals claim a gratuity from the poor for the slightest service they render, and extend the hand not to assist, but to receive money. It is no exaggeration to say that the Jew's paid nurses have brought the hospitals abroad into disgrace. The newspaper *Le Francais* published lately the following:

> Yesterday, Friday, the court had before it a case of unparalleled debauchery in which a hospital nurse, one of the new kind that has replaced the sisters of charity, figured. The judge said to her, 'You are a nurse in the hospital of St. Louis, and you pass your nights in beer saloons.' ... The indignation of those present was apparent by their suppressed murmurs.

These paid nurses constantly figure in the tribunals of Paris. What care must the poor patients receive at the hands of women who pass their nights among rum-sellers!

In the month of April, 1884, two paid nurses were condemned to two months' imprisonment for having almost killed a patient who sought to prevent them from stealing wine.

The newspaper *Le Cri du Peuple*, of 5 November 1884, gives a heart-rending account of the scenes enacted in a lunatic asylum at Bicetre where a well-known atheist, a man of many offices—for he is at once a deputy, an editor, and a head doctor—directs the establishment. The nurses consider it a pastime to strike the unfortunate inmates with their fists and with heavy bunches of keys. When in good humor, they garrote the patients, or give them to the bather, who plunges them into a cold bath, and holds their heads under water until the face becomes purple. We mention these facts because it is the Jews who brought about the expulsion of the sisters of charity from the hospitals, and because the greater part of the nurses throughout the charitable institutions of France are of the faith of the Jews.

At the meeting of 28 January 1885, the municipal council discussed the question of reinstating the sisters, whereupon a member offered to read an ignoble and slanderous letter against the sisters. Upon being requested by the assembly to state who was the author of the letter, he at first refused, but was finally obliged to confess that it was written by a Jew named David.

As we have stated, the greater part of these hospital attendants are Jews, who seem to this day do not to forget the advice given to them in the year

1489 by the rabbis of Constantinople: "Make your children physicians and apothecaries in order that they may be enabled to poison and kill the Gentiles without fear of either detection or punishment." On 26 June 1882, a poor lunatic was literally boiled to death in her bath, where a Jewess nurse shut her in, and afterwards claimed to have forgotten her. At the hospital Tenon, a patient, Mlle. Devillers, expired amid excruciating pains through the mistake of a nurse in not giving her the proper medicine. A child was burned alive in this same hospital in June, 1883. At the hospital Allener, another nurse caused the death of a child two months old by giving it the wrong medicine. In the month of July, 1885, two patients of the hospital of St. Louis, named Charles Vandeleyem and Charles Lecouteux, died a frightful death, for instead of two spoonfuls of brandy as ordered by the doctor, two tablespoonfuls of strychnine were administered to them.

These crimes are so common since the Jews caused the law to be passed expelling the sisters from the hospitals, that people no longer pay attention to them. A physician lately published an article in which he expresses his astonishment that his prescriptions are administered in a manner exactly opposed to his orders.

Behold the condition to which the Jews have reduced the hospitals, which have a subsidy of 34,000,000 of francs. Where does this money go to? The Jews have the direction in their hands. Theft is everywhere. One fine morning, it was discovered that the quinine no longer produced any effect, and upon being analyzed it was found that instead of quinine, the Jew director of the hospital had bought a large amount of spurious quinine, manufactured by a Jew establishment in Germany.

The reader may now well understand the horror with which poor men throughout France look upon the hospitals in which formerly they so blindly trusted. During the cholera, the poor dared not confess that they were sick from fear of being surrendered to the tender mercies of these paid hospital nurses, and asked of the physicians as a favor not to betray them. Lately a nurse, who, with the assistance of the police, sought to take away a sick man, was almost killed by the people of the neighborhood. A physician who attended two patients was obliged to report to the authorities that one of his patients, a woman, was suffering from cholera. The poor woman, upon being informed that she was going to be carried to the hospital, begged of her husband not to allow her to be taken there, and both of them, the woman stricken with cholera, and the man almost out of his senses with sorrow, set out in the dead of night and went aimlessly about the streets of Paris, wandering like the beast that seeks a corner to die in. When they were discovered and were taken to the hospital, the woman, as soon as she entered the building, fell dead.

Figures speak more eloquently than words. In April, 1884, a circular was printed proclaiming in the most energetic manner the scandalous waste that rules today in all hospitals where half-intoxicated women have replaced the sisters, and where the ignorant nurses are unable to distinguish one medicine from the other. In the hospitals, there is neither control nor discipline. The newspaper *De National* is obliged to acknowledge that decayed meat is distributed to the patients, and that while formerly the attendants were devoted and humane, today they are cruel and remiss in their duty.

Dr. Chalvan, on 22 December 1884, wrote:

> The evil that has been inflicted upon the hospitals is even greater than I care to say. Order and morality have been banished from our hospitals ever since the sisters were expelled. Recently at one of the hospitals, the women and the men among the attendants exchanged clothes, and in this disguise, they appeared before the patients.
>
> One great difference always exists between the sisters and the paid nurses. The former do not embrace the profession of nurse as a means of subsistence. The reason for their choice is because of a more sublime character. The latter, however, adopt this vocation which often they despise because they are compelled to do so, because they cannot find anything better. ... In *working for an idea*, even if it is false, there is always something nobler than in *working for a living*. In the army, the volunteers are always preferred to the paid substitutes.

Could anything be more revolting, time and place considered, than the masquerade mentioned by the doctor? Imagine these male and female nurses, half dressed, playing hide and seek in hospital wards filled with suffering humanity! The patients suddenly awoke, and sitting up looked at these men dressed like women, and these women dressed like men, and asked themselves whether perchance they were not the victims of a nightmare.

In a few years, owing to the influence of the materialism spread by the Jews, the respect for the dead, once so marked a feature among Frenchmen, will totally disappear. A Frenchman used always reverently to raise his hat when passing a funeral, as if saluting the dead. Recently, at the hospital St. Denis, the dead body of a child was allowed to remain for four days by the side of its mother.

The sisters have protested against their expulsion from the hospitals. They redoubled their heroism and devotion at the time of cholera. True, they were driven away, but they were recalled when it was found necessary to fight death, and they returned saying, as is their custom, "Let Thy will be done."

In Closing

From the beginning to the end of this book, what has the reader seen? Nothing but the hatred of the Jew for the Gentile. In this respect, nothing has changed for the last 1,800 years. It is the same lie, the same hatred, the same people. Let the reader consider the havoc that the Jew has wrought in France, and let him ask himself if he is willing to have the Jew accomplish the same in America. It is the duty of all, irrespective of faith or nationality, of all who live in America, of all who have the good of America at heart, to combine and to resist Jewish encroachment. Let stringent laws be passed, forbidding Jews to enter the country. Let all her voters, irrespective of party, be imbued with one thought: Not to permit a candidate known to have one drop of Jewish blood in his veins to be nominated, much less to be elected to any political office, even the lowest.

Nothing could be more absurd than the opinion one sometimes hears expressed, that the Jews among us are peacefully disposed; that when they quit Europe for America, they leave their prejudices behind, and try to adopt our American ideas. The Jew never rids himself of his venom. A serpent is a serpent, whether in the old world or in the new.

We have in this book pictured the Jew as he is, has been, and always will be.

BIBLIOGRAPHY

Bischoff, E. 2023. *The Book of the Shulchan Aruch.* Clemens & Blair.

Dalton, T. (ed.). 2022. *Classic Essays on the Jewish Question: 1850 to 1945.* Clemens & Blair.

Dalton, T. (ed.). 2023. *Protocols of the Elders of Zion: The Definitive English Edition.* Clemens & Blair.

Dalton, T. (ed.). 2025. *Classic Essays on the Jewish Question: Volume Two.* Clemens & Blair.

Dalton, T. 2025. *The Jewish Hand in the World Wars* (revised 2nd edition). Clemens & Blair.

Dalton, T. 2025. *Eternal Strangers: Critical Views of Jews and Judaism Through the Ages* (revised 2nd edition). Clemens & Blair.

Drumont, E. 1886. *La France Juive* ("Jewish France"): *Essai d'histoire contemporaine.* Paris: Marpon & Flammarion.

Ford, H. 2024. *The International Jew: The Definitive Edition* (2 volumes; T. Dalton, ed.). Clemens & Blair.

Krueger, F. 1938/2026. *Jewry in England.* Clemens & Blair.

Luther, M. 2025. *On the Jews and Their Lies.* Clemens & Blair.

Timayenis, T. 1888. *The Original Mr. Jacobs: A Startling Exposé.* New York: Minerva.

Timayenis, T. 1888. *The American Jew: An Exposé of his Career.* New York: Minerva.

Timayenis, T. 1889. *Judas Iscariot: An Old Type in a New Form.* New York: Minerva.

Toaff, A. 2020. *Passovers of Blood.* Clemens & Blair.

Toussenel, A. 1845. *Les Juifs: Rois de L'Epoque* ("The Jews: Kings of the Epoch"). Paris: Librairie de L'Ecole Societaire.

INDEX

www.ingramcontent.com/pod-product-compliance
Lightning Source LLC
Chambersburg PA
CBHW051150120626
46547CB00012B/1024